Florence Lin's
Chinese
Regional
Cookbook

柠檬

辛亥年琪写

Florence Lin's Chinese Regional Cookbook

A GUIDE TO THE ORIGINS, INGREDIENTS,
AND COOKING METHODS
OF OVER 200 REGIONAL SPECIALTIES
AND NATIONAL FAVORITES

*With special sections on
Chinese eating and cooking utensils;
planning and preparation of menus;
Chinese teas, wines, and spirits*

Florence Lin

*Foreword by Lin Yutang
Decorative and instructive illustrations by Nai Gi*

HAWTHORN BOOKS, INC.
Publishers/New York

To my husband,
without whose encouragement
and Epicurean sensitivity
this book
would not have been possible

Acknowledgment is gratefully made to *The New York Times* for the right to reprint the following recipes: Stir-Fried Egg Yolks and Hot Pepper Oil from "Home Cooking From Peking" by Florence Lin (*The New York Times Magazine,* November 4, 1973); Pork with Szechuan Preserved Vegetable Soup, Steamed Fish with Ginger Sauce, and Plain Boiled Rice from "Filling, Not Fattening" by Florence Lin (*The New York Times Magazine,* January 6, 1974); and Buddha's Delight, Shredded Chicken with Bean Sprouts, Lion's Head, Spicy Dried Beef, Chicken with Peanuts, and Twice-Cooked Pork from "East is Red—and West is Hot" by Florence Lin (*The New York Times Magazine,* May 19, 1974). © 1973/1974 by The New York Times Company. Reprinted by permission.

FLORENCE LIN'S CHINESE REGIONAL COOKBOOK

Library of Congress Catalog Card Number: 73-19382

ISBN: 0-8015-2673-6

1 2 3 4 5 6 7 8 9 10

Foreword

Pung-shia (Florence), my niece, has been teaching cooking classes for years at the China Institute in New York, where she demonstrates the preparation and methods of Chinese cooking. I am delighted to see skills and techniques that she has used now made available in book form. I know that it will become a "must" book for all students of Chinese cooking. I know of no cooking teacher that realizes so well the needs of Americans. I shall always remember the exquisite curry puffs that she makes with much masterly delicacy, both with regard to fluffy blending and stuffing—a delight to all gourmets.

LIN YUTANG
Hong Kong

調和鼎鼐

甲寅孟春琪作

CONTENTS

月色潴潴夜

甲寅初春乃琪作

仁者壽

癸丑秋乃琳作

PART I
BEFORE YOU BEGIN

1 The History and Development of Chinese Regional Cooking

A BRIEF BACKGROUND OF CHINESE COOKING

Chinese culinary art is an intrinsic part of Chinese culture that can be traced back thousands of years. According to traditional Chinese history, it was Huang-Ti, the Yellow Emperor, who led the Chinese people along the Yellow River in North China, where they settled about five thousand years ago, and it was Emperor Fu-Hsi who taught the Chinese how to cultivate their land and cook their food.

Chinese culture started to take form in the Chou Dynasty (1122–249 B.C.), as did Chinese cooking. Confucius (551–479 B.C.), the great teacher of China and an expert in the ancient Chinese rituals of his time, tried to establish an ideal social order that would result in peaceful and harmonious human relationships. Great emphasis was placed on temple rituals, public ceremonies, and social festivities. In addition to rites and music at these occasions, special festival foods were eaten. Accordingly, food and cooking became an increasingly more important part of Chinese culture.

Confucius also set up standards of food to be eaten. It was noted in the *Analects* of Confucius that rice should be polished, vegetables should be fresh and in season, meat should be properly cut and minced, and flavors and tastes should be properly blended. Confucius would not eat unless the dining table was properly set and the food properly cooked and served.

The basic Confucian teaching of a humanistic culture—love and respect for one another, and peace and harmony within an ideal society—had an immense impact on Chinese history. Not only were Confucius' teachings closely followed, but also his love and respect of good food influenced the Chinese way of life. To this day, whether one is literate or illiterate, rich or poor, young or old, the love of good food naturally becomes a part of the Chinese way of life.

3

CHRONOLOGICAL CHART OF MAIN
PERIODS IN CHINESE HISTORY

DYNASTIES	CAPITALS LOCATED AT

	DYNASTIES	CAPITALS LOCATED AT
1200–	SHANG	Anyang
1100– –1122(?)————————————————		
1000–		
900–	CHOU	
800–		
700–		
600–		
B.C.		
500–	Period of Confucius	
400–		
	Period of Warring States	
300–		
200– –221 ————————— CH'IN —————————		Sian
–206 (Unification)		
100–		
0–	HAN	Sian
		Loyang
100–	Confucianism established	
200– –222 ————————————————————		
300–	"SIX DYNASTIES" PERIOD	
400–	Decline of central government	
	Barbarian inroads	
500–	Introduction of Buddhism (No. Wei)	
600– –589 ————————— SUI —————————		
–618		
700–	(Unification of second empire)	
		Ch'ang-an (Sian)
800–	T'ANG	
900– –907 ————————————————————		
A.D.	SUNG	
1000–	No. Sung (Liao in No. China)	Kaifeng
1100– –1127 ———————		

From *The United States and China*, 3rd ed., copyright 1948, 1958, and 1971 by the
President and Fellows of Harvard College.

1200–	So. Sung (Chin in No. China)	Hangchow
1300– −1279 −1368	YUAN (Mongols)	Peking
1400–		
1500–	MING	Nanking Peking
1600–		
1700– −1644		
1800–	CH'ING (Manchus)	Peking
1900– −1912 −1949	REPUBLIC	Nanking
	PEOPLE'S REPUBLIC	Peking

THE DEVELOPMENT OF REGIONAL CHINESE COOKING

Geographically, China is a big subcontinental country, very much like the United States. However, it is quite different in its development due to the difference in topography. As we mentioned earlier, the Chinese first settled in Northern China along the Yellow River, ranging from the Hopei and Shantung provinces along the seacoast in the east to the Honan, Shensi, and Kansu provinces in the west. The earliest capitals were Anyang (in Honan), Sian (in Shensi), and Loyang (in Honan).

From the ancient capitals of Anyang, Sian, and Loyang, the Chinese people moved southwest, further inland into Szechuan, Hunan (not to be confused with Honan), and neighboring provinces. Then the Chinese moved southeast by land, river, and canal into Kiangsu, Chekiang, and eventually, Fukien provinces. Chinese cooking paralleled Chinese history, starting in northern China and gradually developing different styles in the eastern and the western regions along the Yangtze River. The Yangtze Valley forms the underlying structure of China, connecting Szechuan province in the western region with Kiangsu province in the eastern region. There was a great amount of exchanging of goods and cooking styles in the early days, and in this manner the Chuan-Yang group (Chuan for Szechuan and Yang for Yangchow of Kiangsu) of Chinese chefs was formed. However, the cooking of the eastern region and the western region remains quite different today.

Finally, the Chinese moved further southward, reaching Kwangtung and Kwangsi provinces, which are connected by the West River. Kwangtung province became particularly important to China

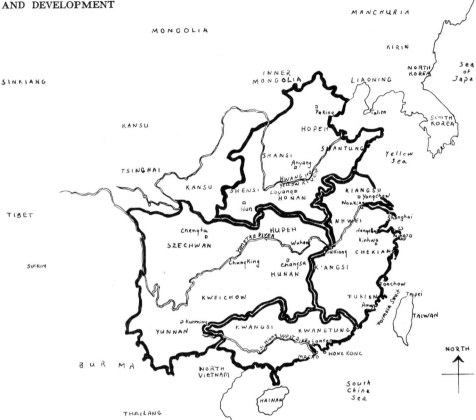

in its early history because it was the gateway to the sea, Southeast Asia, and the rest of the world.

Based on historical developments and geographical distribution of foods within the four major regions, Chinese cooking developed into four different styles.

THE FOUR MAJOR STYLES OF CHINESE REGIONAL COOKING AND THEIR FEATURES

The northern style of cooking developed primarily in Honan, Hopei, and Shantung provinces. According to ancient history, the best cooking was supposed to have been done in the capital city or in the Imperial Palace. Today the center of northern cooking is Peking. As a whole, northern cooking tends to be light and mild. Wine stock, a special feature of northern cooking, is commonly used for its prestigious and delicate flavor. Typical banquet dishes are Bird's Nest Soup, Peking Duck, and Stir-Fried Chicken Velvet (for the recipes of the dishes mentioned here, please refer to the Index).

On the other hand, daily meals in northern China consist of noodle dishes, dumplings, or buns, which are made of wheat flour. Wheat substitutes for rice as the main staple in northern China. As for country cooking, some of the better known dishes include Fish with Sweet-and-Sour Sauce, Mu Shu Pork, and Mongolian Fire Pot, which was introduced to China by Mongolians during the Yuan Dynasty. Northern cooking is actually quite hearty and wholesome. Although garlic and scallions are very commonly used in country cooking, northern cooking is less spicy and less oily than that of the western region of China. Foods are generally cooked medium, neither well done, as in the eastern region, nor underdone (not rare), as in the southern region.

In the western region of China, particularly the provinces of Szechuan and Hunan, another style of cooking predominates. Its most outstanding feature is that it is hot and spicy. This is understandable, since Szechuan is a province surrounded by mountains, and its climate is generally humid throughout the year. Since it is inland, there is not much fish or seafood available, and small freshwater fish are highly treasured.

In this region oil is generally used in combination with hot spices to seal in the taste of the ingredients. Special hot sauces of various kinds usually are served along with the dishes. Also, hot spices are mixed with scallions and garlic to increase the flavor of the food. Chengtu, the capital of Szechuan province, is known for its restaurants and is often called Little Peking. The best known Szechuan dishes are Szechuan Duck (a cousin of Peking Duck), Chicken with Hot Peppers, and Carp with Spicy Sauce. Country dishes include Twice-Cooked Pork, Fish-Flavor Shredded Pork, and Fried Green Beans with Minced Meat.

Hunan and Szechuan cuisines are similar in their general cooking methods and use of spices. The Hunanese eat even hotter dishes than do the Szechuanese, since hot peppers are grown abundantly in that province. In addition to hot dishes, Hunan—the rice province of China—is also known for its hardy preserved pork and bacon.

Another special feature of the cooking in the western region is that more than one cooking method may often be used in the preparation of a dish in order to obtain the ultimate in textures and flavors. While spiciness is the outstanding feature of daily meals, formal dinners or banquets in Szechuan include practically no hot or spicy courses.

The eastern region of China, particularly in Kiangsu and Chekiang provinces, is best known for red cooking—cooking with soy sauce by slow fire. This region also uses salt or sugar or both at the same time to enhance the tastes. Kiangsu and Chekiang cooking centers in Shanghai, spreading out to Soochow, Hangchow, and Ningpo. Ningpo food uses a great deal of salt, and the city is known for its special salty dishes that go with family meals; Soochow cooking always uses extra sugar for a sweet taste in the dishes. Because of the West Lake, Hangchow is especially known for freshwater fish and shellfish, such as fresh carp and live shrimp. Yangchow, near the connecting point of the Grand Canal and Yangtze River, was the business center in the old days, and it is best known for its *tien hsin*, a northern style of pastry (known as *dim sum*, in Cantonese), and for special dishes, such as Yangchow Lion's Head, Yangchow Fried Rice, and Yangchow Noodles in Soup.

Eastern cooking is rich but not as oily as western cooking. The red cooking method is often used for rice dishes in family meals. Since the eastern provinces are coastal regions, seafood and meat dishes are equally available. Eastern cooking is further enhanced by an abundance of vegetables, including fresh bamboo shoots, which are unique for their texture and taste.

Further south within the eastern region lies Fukien province. Fukien, particularly in the city of Amoy, produces the best soy sauce in China, and it greatly influences Chinese cuisines in general, especially the eastern style of cooking.

The northern center of Fukien cuisine is in Foochow, the provincial capital. Here there are many excellent fish dishes. In addition, Fukien cuisine is well-known for its clear and savory dishes. Red wine paste, which is made in Foochow, is another special ingredient that is used in Fukien cooking, primarily in pork, chicken, and duck dishes. The southern center of Fukien cuisine, Amoy, has some well-known specialties, such as Popia, or Amoy Spring Rolls, Pork Liver and Noodles in Soup, and Pigs' Knuckles and Transparent Noodles. They are eaten either on special occasions or as special snacks during the day.

According to a Chinese adage, "If you like to eat good food, go to Canton." Canton, the capital of Kwantung, is the center of southern cooking. A great assortment of food is available, including a variety of meat, poultry, fish, and seafood, as well as many kinds of fresh vegetables. Stir-frying and blanching are the favored cooking methods. Blanching is particularly suited for cooking fresh fish and seafood, since tenderness and natural tastes are preserved. On the other hand, stir-frying can be applied to all kinds of foods and is an especially good method for cooking fresh green vegetables.

The Chinese usually eat three meals a day, and the well-to-do people may have one *tien hsin* (*dim sum*) in the afternoon with tea. But it is not uncommon for the Cantonese to have four, five, and even six meals a day. The quantity of food consumed at each meal may be different, but every meal seems to have endless varieties of foods designed for various appetites. Obviously, the Cantonese love to eat and enjoy good food.

In addition to stir-fried dishes, southern cooking is also well-known for dishes braised in master marinade (sauce) and roasted for ready-to-eat cold or hot plates, such as roast pork, roast duck, or roast chicken. The ready-to-eat and stir-fried dishes compliment each other and are tasty and easy to serve; hence these dishes are often used in restaurants that serve quick meals. Cantonese restaurants are popular all over China and have propagated in big cities around the world, particularly in Chinatowns in America.

In summary, Chinese cooking can be divided into four regional styles. Each region has dishes with features that are characteristic of or special to the region itself. Regional dishes can be identified not only by the ingredients used but also by the condiments that are served with the dishes, as well as by the cooking methods employed. On the other hand, it should be stressed that many dishes exist that are common to every region of China, and they are enjoyed and appreciated by the Chinese at banquet dinners as well as at daily family meals. These "national" dishes are just as important as the regional dishes. For further study of the regional characteristic ingredients and cooking methods, see the individual chapter charts in Part II.

2 Chinese Cooking and Eating Utensils

It is not necessary for the average American home with modern cooking facilities and utensils to have special Chinese utensils in order to cook Chinese food. However, basic equipment and utensils, such as a Chinese wok, steamer, chopsticks, and cleaver, make both preparation and cooking easier and faster. People who learn Chinese cooking methods find these utensils to be indispensable and often begin to rely upon them for other styles of cooking.

CHINESE CLEAVER

A cleaver is the most important cutting tool in a Chinese kitchen. Chinese foods generally must be cut into uniform, bite-size pieces. Also, sizes and shapes can often vary for different cooking methods. The skill of cutting is highly regarded. Only when cooking materials are properly cut can they be properly cooked. Not only does the proper form appeal to the eye of the gourmet but it also influences the cooking, whether it is braising or stir-frying. For stir-fried dishes, the size and the thinness in conjunction with the texture of the food are of great importance. Thus a good chef shows his skill in the cutting of the ingredients for the dishes he prepares, just as an artist shows his talents in the strokes of his painting. Once you learn how to use a cleaver, it becomes easy to manage.

The cleaver can be used as a butcher knife for chopping meat with bones. For other purposes, a pair of Chinese kitchen scissors is very useful. Of course, a boning or carving knife and a small paring knife are helpful too.

Chinese cleavers come in different weights and sizes and are made of different metals, such as carbon steel or stainless steel. Although stainless steel cleavers are easy to take care of, a good cook generally prefers carbon steel cleavers, as they are easier to sharpen to a fine edge. As to weight and size, they are up to the individual's tastes and habits. For most purposes, a heavyweight, medium-size cleaver is usually the best choice, because the weight gives one better control when cutting through large bones and meat. A lightweight cleaver is used for cutting vegetables.

In order to keep a cleaver sharp, one should always clean it and dry it after each use. When a cleaver loses its keenness due to repeated use, sharpening with a honing stone or metal sharpener can be helpful. For cutting and chopping, a chopping board is the natural partner of a good cleaver.

Basic Cutting Method

Stand close to the table and the cutting board so that you can look directly down from the top of the cleaver and see the blade while cutting. With the right hand firmly grasp the handle and part of the blade of the cleaver. With the left hand hold and press in place the item to be cut. Both hands should be diagonal and comfortable in position. The right hand slices while the left hand moves backward, exposing the material to be cut. The first joints of the fingers of the left hand will protect the fingertips, which should be bent under a little. In this way the fingertips will help to hold the item securely. On each cut, the cleaver should be lifted just above the item, with the side of the blade touching the first joints of the fingers of the left hand. After cutting, one can use the flat side of the cleaver as a spatula to lift the cut pieces into a dish.

To Slice

Follow the Basic Cutting Method described above. Use the left hand, which is holding the item, to regulate the size of each slice. The farther the left hand moves backward, the thicker the slice; the less it moves, the thinner the slice.

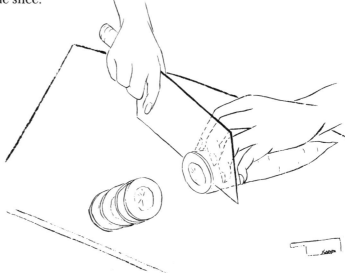

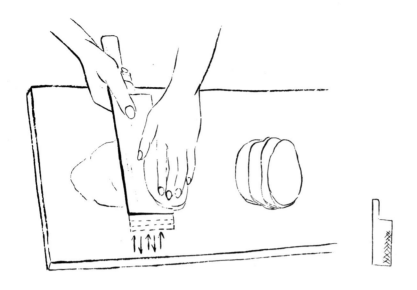

To Slant and Parallel Slice

Use this method to make thin slices from small or flat pieces. Lay the item flat and hold the cleaver at a slant or parallel to the cutting surface. Slice the item carefully between the cutting surface and the left-hand fingers. Do this slowly, feeling the movement of the blade through the item with the tips of the fingers.

To Shred

First cut the item into thin slices. Keep the slices in place, overlapping, and pat them flat. Cut them diagonally at different angles into uniform-size strips about 2 inches long.

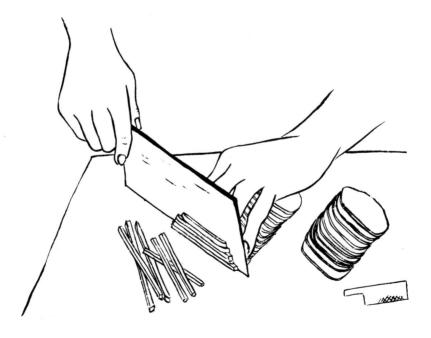

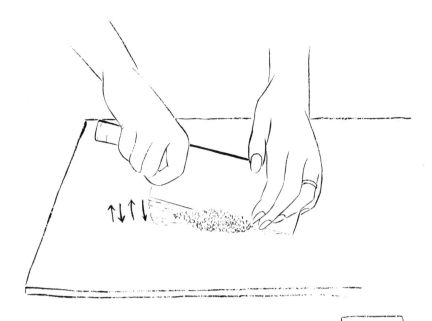

To Mince

Keep the tip of the cleaver on the cutting surface, and rest the left hand on top of the cleaver away from the handle. Pivot the blade on the tip to make different angles while cutting the item continuously with a rocking motion. This method is easy, quiet, and not messy.

Meat grinders are quite useful, but for a small amount of meat there is a simpler way: First cut the meat into small pieces. Then, with a straight up-and-down motion, chop them into tiny pieces. Using the flat side of the cleaver as a spatula, turn the meat over. Continue to chop and turn the meat until it is minced to the desired fineness. To help prevent the meat from sticking to the cleaver, rinse the cleaver occasionally with cold water.

To Crush

Put the item near the edge of the cutting board. Strike the item to be crushed with the flat side of the cleaver.

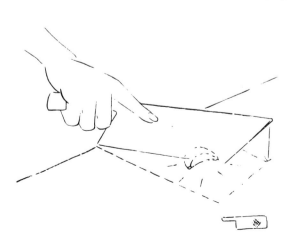

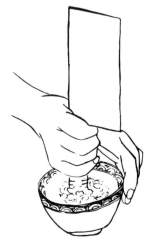

To Chop

There are two weights of cleavers, light and heavy, and many different sizes. I prefer the all-purpose heavyweight, medium size. Both weights can slice vegetables and meat, although only the heavyweight cleaver can easily chop through poultry and meat bones. To chop, use a straight up-and-down motion, holding the handle and blade. Do not wiggle or twist the cleaver from side to side, as this might damage the blade. When chopping, always keep the free hand clear. If the poultry is large and the bone cannot be cleanly cut with one chop, keep the cleaver in place after the first chop; with a potholder to protect the left hand, use the hand as a hammer, or use a rubber mallet and strike the blunt top of the cleaver until the bone breaks.

To Tenderize

Use the blunt edge of the cleaver to pound the meat in crisscross lines. The flat side of the cleaver may also be used to slap the meat.

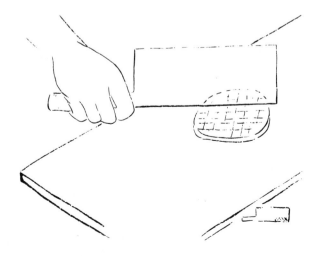

To Roll Cut

This is the Chinese method of cutting long, round items, such as carrots and potatoes, into uniform pieces. Turn the item to be cut with the left hand while the right hand holds the cleaver and cuts the item diagonally. Adjust the angle of the blade for uniform-size pieces. Roll back a quarter turn and cut the side that is up. Make diagonal cuts each time the item is rolled back.

To Chop Chicken or Duck

Use a heavy cleaver, and remove the wings and legs from the chicken body. Cut the chicken lengthwise through the breastbone and backbone. Cut each chicken half lengthwise once more. Chop the backbone with meat crosswise into ¾-inch pieces. Use the

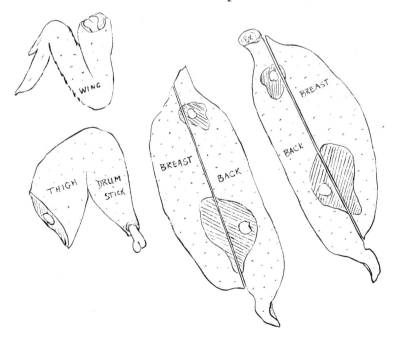

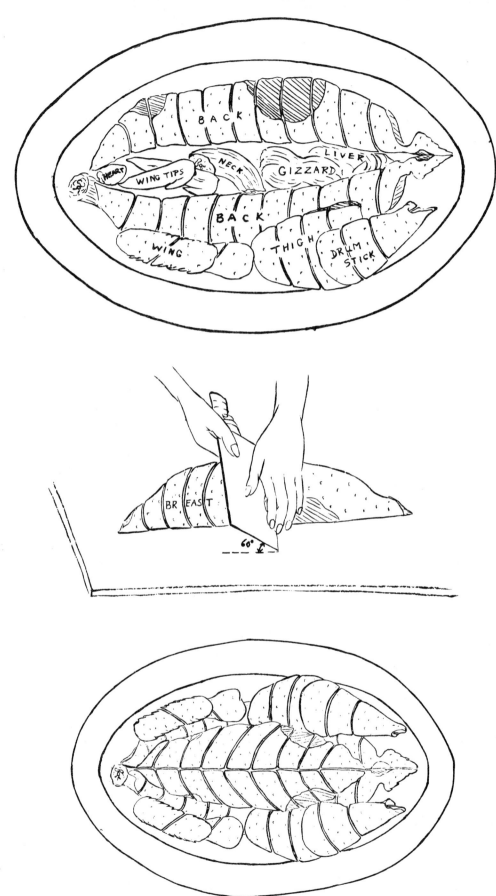

16

cleaver to transfer the chicken pieces to the center of a serving platter. Cut each wing into four pieces and put them at the upper corners of the platter. Cut each leg at the joint, separating the upper leg from the thigh, and remove the bones carefully without disturbing the skin. Cut the leg meat lengthwise into 2 x ¾ -inch pieces and arrange at the lower corners of the platter. Remove the breastbone and cut each breast crosswise at ¾ -inch intervals and place in the center with some pieces overlapping the leg meat. In this manner the original shape of the bird is reconstructed on the platter.

WOK: THE ALL-PURPOSE UTENSIL

The wok is the basic cooking utensil of Chinese cooking and is practically as old as the cuisine itself. It is an all-in-one utensil that is used for stewing, braising, deep frying, stir-frying, and even for steaming, with a cover and a rack.

Since the wok originally was designed for the Chinese stove and does not quite fit the modern range, one can buy a metal ring for the round-bottomed wok to sit upon on the range. However, it should be pointed out that these rings must have plenty of holes for ventilation, especially when the high heat of a gas range is used for wok cooking. I would suggest cutting the ring with metal cutters to make sure that there is enough oxygen for gas-range cooking with the wok. If a wok sits well on a burner, it is not necessary to have the metal ring.

A Chinese iron wok is recommended over woks made of other metals, such as stainless steel, copper, or aluminum, because it distributes heat evenly and heats and cools quickly. In contrast to American iron pots and pans, the Chinese iron wok is lightweight. For practical purposes, a 14-inch-diameter wok is commonly chosen for its large capacity and easy manipulation of food. However, a 12-inch diameter is sufficient for a smaller-size range.

When an iron wok is first purchased, it should be seasoned by heating over low heat. Then brush the inside surface of the wok with vegetable oil and leave it for a minute or so. Next, wipe the wok with paper towels. Repeat the oiling process one or two more times. The wok is now seasoned and ready to use.

Woks should be kept dry and clean to prevent rusting. After cooking, while the wok is still warm, use a scrub brush to clean it with hot water. If the wok is very greasy, use some soap. After washing and rinsing, heating the wok is highly recommended in order to get it really dry.

OTHER COOKING UTENSILS

Chinese chefs usually use one long-handled spatula and one long-handled ladle for stir-frying, and one perforated scoop or strainer for deep frying. For family cooking, an ordinary Chinese spatula and an ordinary Chinese strainer are good enough. Bamboo chopsticks are often used during preparatory processes for stirring and beating. Chopsticks are also used to pick up chunks and to assist in cooking.

CHINESE STEAMERS AND FIREPOTS

In China steaming is one of the major cooking methods. Steamers are used in all regions of China for cooking all kinds of food, be it fish or other seafoods, meat or poultry, rice or vegetables. The importance of the steamer in Chinese cooking is comparable only to that of the oven in western cooking. Steamers are considered an important utensil, second only to woks.

Traditionally, the Chinese have used bamboo steamers. Bamboo steamers are still the best kind available because they have their own ventilation system, unlike metal steamers. Metal steamers are easier to take care of but accumulate more water in the dish.

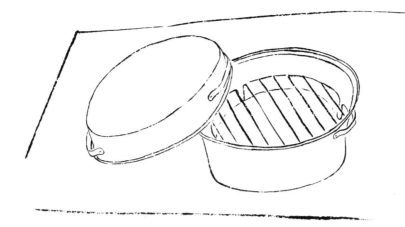

A steamer usually rests upon a wok and should be 2 inches smaller in diameter than the wok. The rimmed food dish used inside the steamer should be at least one inch smaller. In other words, for a 14-inch wok one should buy a 12-inch steamer and use an 11-inch or smaller dish. To improvise, one can use a clam steamer or a big pot like a wok with a rack in it. It is important that there is plenty of room for steam to circulate while cooking. For this purpose, a domed cover should be used with a wok.

The Chinese firepot is a unique cooking and serving utensil. Although it is seldom used at banquets, it is popular in homes and in restaurants. In northern China a firepot, sometimes called a Mongolian firepot, is used primarily for cooking lamb. The pleasure of cooking it yourself extends to all parts of China, particularly when it is cold outside.

Ever since firepots were first brought to the table for cooking and serving, they have been created with many artistic and elegant designs. They are made of metal, usually copper or brass. Beside the pot for cooking, there is a base for charcoal for heating, and there is a big fat chimney to give more fire power. Today electric firepots are available, and one can also substitute electric Dutch ovens and fondue pots.

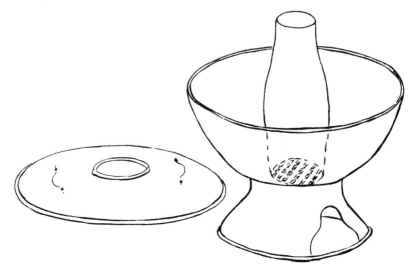

EATING UTENSILS AND HOW TO USE CHOPSTICKS

Among the Chinese eating utensils, chopsticks and rice bowls are of the most importance. As mentioned before, rice is the main staple for the Chinese. A rice bowl also connotes one's livelihood, and when a rice bowl is broken, it is a bad omen. Thus it should always be held carefully.

The Chinese use chopsticks and rice bowls as Westerners use knives, forks, and plates. The use of chopsticks intead of fingers is a sign of cultural improvement. Since Chinese food is either cut into bite-size pieces or cooked until tender, it can easily be eaten without the necessity of using a knife to cut it. To the Chinese, any knife can be used as a weapon and should not be brought out and used at the dining table if it can be helped.

Chopsticks are made of silver, ivory, lacquer (wood), plastic, or bamboo. While the first two are used for formal parties and among well-to-do people, the latter three are for general use. For practical purposes, bamboo chopsticks are the best because they can stand hot and cold temperatures and are not slippery. As a matter of fact, bamboo chopsticks are used as cooking utensils, especially for family cooking.

How to Use Chopsticks

Chopsticks should be properly handled in order to show proper manners, as does the proper handling of knife and fork. The proper way to handle them is to first place one chopstick in your right hand, holding it about two thirds of the way from the narrow end. Place it in the crook of the thumb, with the longer end resting on the ring finger (Fig. 1). Then place the second chopstick between the index finger and the thumb, with the longer end resting between the index and the third fingers, holding it as one would a pencil. Move the second chopstick down to grasp the food (Fig. 2). Always keep the tops of the chopsticks even. Practice a few times before using them. They become easier to handle as one relaxes.

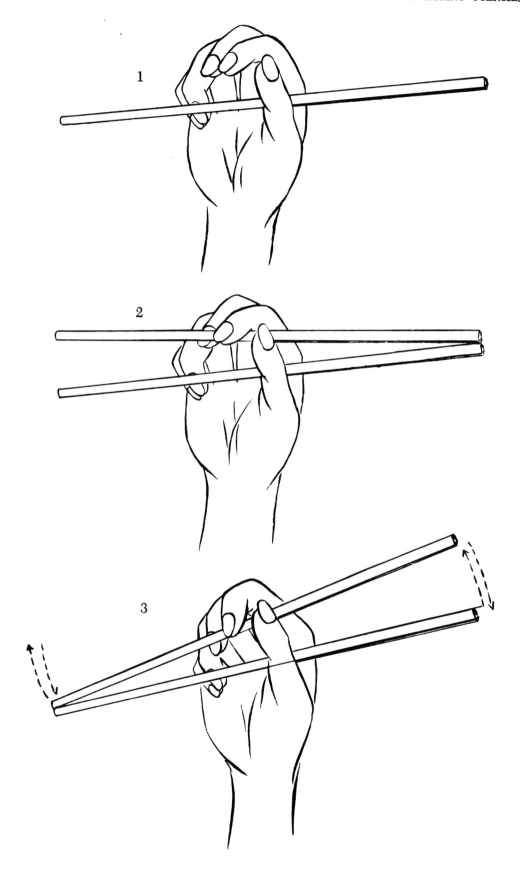

3 Chinese Cooking Methods

As we used to say in China, the Chinese eat anything that is edible. This covers such a wide variety of food that the Chinese have developed all kinds of cooking methods to meet the demand. Furthermore, there are endless techniques connected with each cooking method to meet special requirements. This is particularly true in Chinese regional cooking.

In order to make the various Chinese cooking methods easier to understand, they are generally divided into the following five major categories: 1) cooking in oil: Deep Frying; Shallow Frying; and Stir-Frying; 2) cooking in Liquid: in Water, Stock, or Soy Sauce and Seasonings; 3) steaming; 4) cooking directly over fire: Broiling; Roasting; and Barbecuing; 5) smoking and other cooking methods: Cold Mixing; Salting or Pickling; Drying.

It should be mentioned here that some dishes have to go through more than one method of cooking, but that does not mean it is more difficult. Sometimes two small steps are easier to carry out than one big step in attaining well-prepared food.

COOKING IN OIL

Deep Frying; Shallow Frying and Stir-frying

In general, frying in oil can be done with high heat, (375° and up), moderate heat (around 350°), and low heat (250° to 300°). Without a thermometer, one can test the temperature of the oil with a piece of scallion or a green vegetable leaf. If the scallion does not sizzle when placed in the oil, it is low heat; if it sizzles but remains green for a while, it is moderate heat; and if it burns immediately, it is high heat.

A basic requirement before cooking in oil is that the wok or pan always be heated to the smoking point. Only then is the oil added and heated to the desired degree, depending on whether you are preparing meat, seafood, or vegetables; the pan's size; and the amount of food involved. This is mainly to prevent sticking and to seal in the juices.

Since high-temperature deep frying is well known in Western cooking, it is easy to understand and to apply. In China deep frying is a popular cooking method, particularly in the eastern and the western regions. In high-temperature deep frying the main purpose is to have a crispy outside and tenderly cooked inside. To accomplish this, the oil should be heated to above 375°.

In Chinese cooking there is an alternate method of deep frying, low-temperature deep frying, in which the wok is kept hot but the oil is maintained at a low heat, between 250° and 300°. Food should be quickly stirred in the oil for tenderness inside and smoothness outside. Low-temperature deep frying is used quite often in restaurant cooking and for banquet dishes. Food precooked in this manner is tastier but usually a little too oily for family cooking or for daily consumption.

Shallow frying is a simple method that usually uses low heat and longer cooking so that a brown crust forms. This method is commonly used in all of the regions of China.

Stir-frying is a uniquely Chinese cooking method called *Ch'ao*. After the wok is heated to the smoking point, the oil is added and also heated to the desired degree, usually on the high side, 375° and up. Then the ingredients are added and stir-fried quickly until cooked. While stir-frying, one should always watch the food and not be afraid to adjust the heat if it seems either too high or too low for the ingredients. This will insure that the food is stir-fried to the proper degree, so that it offers its best natural flavors.

After the food is stir-fried, it is quite common to add 1 part of cornstarch mixed with 3 parts of cold water to thicken the liquid. The cornstarch should be thoroughly mixed with the water and then slowly poured into the boiling liquid in the wok. Continue to stir while pouring and keep on stirring until the liquid comes to a boil again. The sauce will become a clear glaze. Continue to stir the sauce with the food until all of the food is evenly coated. This is a quick process and should be done carefully so that the sauce is neither too thick nor too thin. An experienced cook usually prepares a little extra cornstarch mixed with cold water so that the sauce may be adjusted if necessary. Then the desired degrees of smoothness and thickness may be obtained.

If one is not familiar with stir-fry cooking, the cooking methods in each recipe should be closely followed. More important, however, are actual experience and constant practice, which always improve one's skills.

Stir-fry cooking is widely used in all of the regions of China and is applied to practically all varieties of food. However, it is most popular in southern cooking and is highly regarded by the chefs themselves.

Since stir-frying requires quick cooking over high heat, it is better to limit the amount of food in the wok to one pound. Actually, the smaller the quantity the better because it is easier to stir-fry thoroughly. Furthermore, a family range usually is not powerful enough to provide and maintain the high heat required for stir-frying larger quantities.

It should also be noted that in combination dishes the vegetables and meat should first be stir-fried separately and then combined and stir-fried together for the final presentation. In this way one allows for the differences in cooking times for different kinds of foods.

In order to get the best out of stir-fried dishes, they should be served immediately after cooking. The simple reason is that tastes change when the food cools off. As the Chinese put it, you should be ready and waiting for the food to come; good food and good cooking cannot wait for you.

Since it requires quick action at the last moment, beginners should limit stir-fry cooking to one dish at a time. Be sure you have all the ingredients and seasonings well organized and arranged, ready for stir-frying.

In stir-frying, it is not unusual to add an extra touch to the dish by splashing a little wine or special seasonings onto the food and stir-frying for a few seconds longer. Splashing usually adds a little extra flavor.

In northern China stir-frying is further extended into *pao*, or stir-frying over very high heat so that the oil or special sauce quickly forms a coating over the food. Another method is *liu*, a special method of cooking a sauce with an oil base and then adding precooked seafood, meat, or vegetables and cooking them with the sauce. In *liu* there should be plenty of sauce to go with the food, and the sauce is smooth and light in nature instead of thick and heavy as in the case of *pao*.

There is another Chinese method of cooking, called *hui* ("meeting"), in which most of the foods are precooked—whether deep fried, shallow fried, stir-fried, or parboiled—and then combined at the last moment of cooking with oil and clear stock.

COOKING IN LIQUID: IN WATER, STOCK, OR SOY SAUCE AND SEASONINGS

Boiling in Stock or Water:
Blanching, Poaching, Dipping and Rinsing

Although boiling water cannot be counted as a cooking method, cooking in boiling water is another matter. Blanching and poaching are well known in Western cooking, but dipping and rinsing with boiling water, particularly for seafood, requires special know-how and good timing. Cooking white-cut chicken in boiling water and letting it "cook" while cooling off without fire is another specialty.

For some dishes, boiling stock is used instead of boiling water. This is necessary for food that has good texture for eating pleasure but not much taste. And of course, good stock always plays an important role in good cooking.

Stewing

This is a very common process of cooking by simmering which softens the tissues of the ingredients. To the Chinese, there are three ways of stewing:

Plain stewing is usually accompanied by seasonings such as ginger, scallions, salt, pepper, and other spices. In some dishes there is a small amount of gravy, while in others more liquid is used, as in soups.

Red cooking, or stewing with soy sauce, is a Chinese specialty because of the soy sauce. The food cooked by red cooking is usually accompanied by a heavy sauce and always goes well with plain rice. A red-cooked dish should be served accompanied by mild dishes to balance tastes and provide variety. Red-cooked dishes are usually served hot but can be served cold too; they keep well in the refrigerator and can easily be reheated and served again at any time. In the latter case, new vegetables may be added for extra flavor and taste.

Lu, or stewing in master marinade, involves a master marinade made of extracts of pork and chicken, along with spices, herbs, and other seasonings. Once it is prepared, it is reusable. However, lamb and game, which have strong flavors, should be cooked in individual master marinades. In China there is usually a special earthenware pot containing the master marinade. Foods prepared this way are considered a special group. They are usually served cold and are particularly suited as appetizers with drinks, as cold plates, or as sandwiches.

There are two types of master marinades: One is a brown marinade made of soy sauce; the other is a white marinade made of salt. Because of the addition of spices and herbs, foods cooked in a master marinade have a special flavor and fragrance. Basically, food cooked in a master marinade is lighter than that prepared by red cooking and it is neither greasy nor oily. Food is also easy to cook in this manner once the master marinade is made and set up.

Braising

This consists of searing food in oil and then simmering it in a covered pot or wok. In China there are two kinds of braising: plain braising in natural sauce and braising in a brown sauce made of soy sauce. Because of less moisture and slow cooking over a period of time, the sauce is heavier and richer than in red cooking. The browning and the concentrated sauce add to the extra taste of the food.

STEAMING

Steaming, a major and typical Chinese cooking method, is as important as baking in Western cooking. When food is steamed, it usually presents the best of its natural flavors. There is no need for oil in the cooking or for any extra sauce, so the food is neither oily nor greasy. If steaming is done by putting the food in a deep dish, the original tasty juice is collected.

Steaming can be done either over high heat or over low heat. The food can either be placed above the water or can be partly submerged in it. In the latter case, the container can be covered or uncovered, depending on the desired effect of the steaming.

COOKING DIRECTLY OVER FIRE: BROILING, ROASTING, AND BARBECUING

Since the Chinese stove was originally built for cooking with a wok, barbecuing and roasting were usually done outside of the family kitchen and more often carried out by restaurants or special food stores. Today, with modern cooking facilities, broiling, roasting, or barbecuing can easily be done at home if the preparation directions are carefully followed. Hence it is good to know the Chinese method of roasting, especially for pork and poultry.

SMOKING AND OTHER COOKING METHODS

Smoking is a popular Chinese cooking method that adds extra flavor to foods. In Chinese cooking smoking is mostly applied to fish or poultry. Chinese use tea, rice, and brown sugar for smoking, but it is better and easier to use hickory chips instead of brown sugar, and the chips are readily accessible.

Other Chinese cooking methods include:

Cold Mixing

Cold mixing consists of combining cold, cut-up food with a dressing and then serving, as you would prepare a cold salad. Chinese vegetables are sometimes parboiled first. The special mixing of the sauce, or dressing, which may consist of soy sauce, sugar, sesame oil, etc., is also a key factor in the success of cold mixing. Typical Chinese dishes that utilize this method include Agar-Agar Salad and Cucumber Salad.

Salting or Pickling

These are common processes widely used for preserving fish, meat, or vegetables. In China it is not uncommon to salt fish or meat over a period of an hour, a day, or longer. The length of the salting period depends upon the desired texture and flavor. The longer a food is preserved, the firmer its texture and the stronger its taste will become.

Salted or pickled vegetables are very common in China. They are not only used as substitutes for fresh vegetables, but in many cases have also become important separate items of food. This is mainly because they taste quite different from their fresh counterparts. They are available in all seasons and are usually quite reasonable in price.

Drying

In addition to salting and pickling, drying also preserves food for eating and cooking. There are two types of drying: sun drying and air drying (or wind drying). This process sometimes makes food edible without cooking, such as dried shrimp, which can be cooked or eaten raw. Usually, however, seafood and meat require redeveloping before being actually cooked. The variety of Chinese preserved foods is practically as large as that of fresh foods. By offering different textures and tastes, preserved foods broaden the horizon of food to the fullest extent.

4 Planning and Preparation

Historically, Chinese society was founded on a big family system. Thus it is easy to understand how important family cooking has been all these years. Even in a small family of four to six people a family meal usually consists of four to six dishes and a soup. These dishes are all served at the same time for everyone to share. Normally an average meal consists of four dishes—one meat or poultry dish, one fish or other seafood dish, and two vegetable dishes—as well as rice or buns. Since the Chinese consider rice to be an important part of a daily meal, there is usually one dish that is a little saltier and more savory to stimulate the palate to go with plain rice. Traditionally, the Chinese eat rice along with other foods. When a meal is well-balanced, at the end of eating one should feel comfortable and satisfied; there is no need or desire for desserts.

Home-cooked meals are quite different from restaurant banquets. In Chinese home cooking more vegetables and bean products are used. For the majority of Chinese people, a daily meal consists of something to go with a bowl of rice rather than a few tablespoons of rice along with a big slab of fish or meat. Often a Chinese vegetable dish is flavored with a few strips of meat or dried shrimp. Like the southern Italians, who prefer to eat a large plate of spaghetti along with a few tablespoons of good meat sauce, the Chinese favor a large bowl of rice served with *some* well-seasoned, salty vegetables and a relatively small amount of meat. These dishes are sometimes called rice-sending dishes.

Balance of Diet Through Variety of Food

Fresh food is provided by nature, and preserved food is created by human ingenuity. The Chinese eat a wide variety of food. Even for simple meals, one should always keep in mind the basic concept of four dishes: meat or poultry, seafood, soybean products, and vegetables. Although fresh food is necessary for good cooking, Chinese preserved foods, which are less well-known to the Western world, create another dimension in Chinese cooking and eating.

The Harmony of Flavor and Taste and the Importance of Texture

In order to make food more interesting to eat, it should appeal not only to the palate but also to the eyes and nose. Aroma, shape, and color play important roles in the presentation of good cooking. For greatest satisfaction, taste and texture play equally important parts. It is up to a good cook to be aware of all these factors when serving food. For instance, a highly seasoned or spicy dish should be accompanied by a mild, subtle one. If one dish is dry, such as deep-fried chicken or dried stir-fried beef, there should be one dish that has some sauce to balance it. Some foods should be cooked to as soft a state as possible, while others should remain firm and crisp. On the other hand, a good dish may stand out by itself and be well-balanced because of its variety of ingredients and seasonings.

Use of Different Cooking Methods for Cooking Convenience

Since the Chinese have a great variety of dishes and many cooking methods, a good cook can plan his menu and cook many dishes ahead of time. In simple stewing or red cooking, foods are usually reheatable, as are deep-fried dishes. One may also use cold mixing or cold dishes for a change of pace. There are also many Chinese dishes that can be precooked and only need a final touch at the last minute. Oven-ready or steamed dishes are also easy to serve. However, one or two stir-fried dishes are about all one can handle at one meal. One should serve a variety of food cooked by different cooking methods. The planning of a menu is very important. One should choose some dishes that can be cooked ahead of time and then reheated. Finally, some dishes can be precooked in parts and then cooked together. The preparation and cooking of a meal should be so organized as to avoid last-minute chaos.

Simplified Family Meals and Dinner Parties at Home

People are often too busy to cook elaborately. In this case, a simplified family meal might consist of two dishes—one meat or fish and one vegetable. However, it is important that these dishes have more than one major ingredient. For example, one could serve fish with bean curd or stir-fried meat with vegetables. The latter could even be served as a one-dish meal for a simple dinner or a quick luncheon.

On the other hand, in order to serve a small party of four to six, one could add one or two dishes or simply increase the portions of the food that is served. Also, it is a Chinese custom to upgrade the dishes by using more expensive, exotic ingredients. The same principle applies to bigger parties, but the host and hostess should keep in mind the nature of the occasion as well as the tastes of their honored guests.

Although the Chinese usually have banquets in restaurants, it is also possible to arrange banquets at home. A simple Chinese banquet usually consists of three parts:

Four cold dishes. Cold dishes, which can be prepared ahead of time, go well with drinks. They can be quite simple or quite elaborate; the important thing is to serve a variety in order to stimulate the appetites of guests. Cold dishes may consist of seafood, such as smoked fish or jellyfish; poultry such as wine chicken or glazed duck; meat, such as Star Anise Beef; and vegetables, such as Agar-Agar Salad.

Two to four hot fried dishes. These dishes can be deep fried or stir-fried and are eaten like hot appetizers. Usually they consist of fresh ingredients. Typical dishes include stir-fried shrimp and fillet of sole, deep-fried shrimp balls, and butterfly shrimp. In addition, one can serve stir-fried diced or shredded chicken or meat mixed with vegetables or preserved foods, such as chicken with walnuts and chicken velvet with ham and snow pea pods.

Four main courses. The main-course dishes usually consist of fish or seafood, whole chicken or duck, meat, exotic foods, and vegetables. The latter can be hearts of vegetables with meat, seafood, mushrooms, or bamboo shoots. One or two courses of soup can be served before or after main courses. The banquets usually end up with one or two courses of dessert.

SHOPPING FOR CHINESE COOKING

Shopping for good ingredients is a part of the pleasure of cooking. The Chinese always prefer to buy fresh ingredients whenever they are available, simply because they taste better. Also, it is important to buy fresh food in season: It is not only better in quality but also more economical.

Although many major food items are available all year round in American food markets, it is not surprising to find Chinese house-wives shopping in Chinese food stores or ordering food by mail, since some Chinese ingredients and condiments are not carried by American food stores. In order to cook authentic Chinese dishes, one has to have these special things.

Chinese condiments. Seasoning sauces and condiments are an important part of Chinese cooking. These can be divided into three major groups:

Group A
1. Soy sauce—light and dark
2. Oyster sauce
3. Fish sauce
4. Sesame oil

Group B
1. Hoisin sauce
2. Brown bean sauce—plain and hot
3. Salted black beans
4. Sesame seed paste
5. Fermented bean curd—white and red

Group C
1. Ginger, scallions, garlic, and coriander leaves
2. Five-spice powder, star anise, dried tangerine peel, cinnamon bark, and fennel seeds
3. White and black peppers, hot pepper (whole and crushed), and Szechuan peppercorns

Chinese fresh vegetables. The Chinese eat a wide variety of fresh vegetables, some of which are not available in American markets. Hence it is necessary to shop in Chinese marketplaces from time to time. Fresh vegetables are generally divided into the following groups:

Group A
Leafy vegetables, such as Chinese cabbage or *bok choy*, celery cabbage, and mustard greens

Group B
Peas, beans, and bean products, such as snow pea pods, bean sprouts, and bean curd

Group C
Fresh hot peppers, water chestnuts, and items from the turnip and squash families

Chinese preserved food. Chinese preserved food is an important group by itself. It is not just a substitute for fresh food because it offers entirely different flavors, textures, and tastes. Many exotic delicacies are preserved and require careful development, or a developing process to restore the food back to a state in which they may be cooked and eaten. Furthermore, since many preserved foods are salted or have strong flavors, only small amounts are used; consequently, they are economical, too. Chinese preserved foods can be divided into the following groups:

Group A
Dried beans, bean products, and wheat gluten: There are a lot of varieties of dried beans, but soybeans, mung beans, and red beans are considered the most important in Chinese cooking. Soybeans and mung beans can be germinated into sprouts and made into different bean products; red beans are often used to make bean paste, a filling for sweet pastries. A simple list of beans and bean products would be:
1. Mung beans, mung bean sheets, and cellophane noodles
2. Red beans and red bean paste
3. Soybeans and soybean products: bean curd, bean milk, and different kinds of bean milk skin
4. Wheat gluten: fried, dried, and canned

Group B
Chinese preserved vegetables: These are usually dried or salted. However, some salted vegetables are really very special, even for the Chinese, such as:
1. Pickled cabbage or red-in-snow
2. Szechuan and Tientsin preserved vegetables

Other preserved vegetables that are well-known and widely used are:

1. Dried or canned mushrooms: winter or straw mushrooms
2. Dried or canned bamboo shoots: winter or spring bamboo shoots or flat-tip bamboo shoots
3. Canned water chestnuts (fresh water chestnuts are also available, and they are much sweeter in taste)
4. Tiger lily buds
5. Tree ears
6. Dried or canned lotus roots (fresh lotus roots are available, and they are crisp and tasty)

Group C
Dried seeds, nuts, and dates: These are often used in Chinese cooking. Some of the major items, such as chestnuts, walnuts, and almonds, are available in American markets. The following are special Chinese items that are particularly interesting:
1. Lotus seeds
2. Sesame seeds—black and white
3. Gingko nuts
4. Jujubes, or Chinese red dates

Preserved seafood (canned, dried, or salted). This also is a Chinese food specialty, particularly the dried products. Although some are not very unusual, others, such as the following, are considered rare delicacies:

1. Preserved fish—dried or salted
2. Dried shrimp, dried scallops, and dried oysters
3. Abalone and jellyfish
4. Sea cucumber and squid
5. Fish maw and sharks' fins
6. Bird's nests
7. Shrimp eggs and fish roe

Chinese preserved meats and preserved eggs.

1. Chinese cured meat and sausages
2. Pressed duck
3. Salted eggs
4. Thousand-year eggs

SORTING, STORING, AND READYING FOR COOKING

Sorting and Storing

Despite all the modern conveniences, shopping in neighborhood food stores or making a special trip to Chinatown should be planned ahead of time not only to get the food you want from various stores but also to save time and energy and make shopping pleasant. A shopping list is important, since there are so many distractions that can easily cause one to forget to buy important items.

After the shopping is done, food should be sorted out for immediate cooking or for storing to be used at a later time. To keep Chinese vegetables fresh for as long as possible, they should be stored in a paper bag inside a plastic bag: Vegetables will rot if they are wet and kept in a sealed plastic bag; the paper bag will absorb the droplets of water that condense, keeping the vegetables moist, and the plastic bag will keep them from drying out. Although fresh-salting is used for some regional cooking, fish and seafood should usually be cleaned and cooked on the same day as they are purchased. Many kinds of fish and seafood should be eaten as soon as they are cooked, but others, particularly fish cooked with soy sauce, can be served cold. Very fresh seafood may be stored in a freezer, or if lightly salted, it may be refrigerated for one day. Meat and poultry can easily be stored in the freezer. Since Chinese cooking usually requires only a small portion of meat at a time, it should be cut to order as it will be used and packed flat in half-pound or one-pound quantities. These packages of food can easily be thawed. It is quite common to use a whole chicken or duck in Chinese cooking, so they can be stored whole in the freezer. But it is also very common to use part of a chicken, so keep chicken parts in small packages—say, one package for chicken breasts and another package for chicken wings and legs to be cooked in different ways and served on different days.

In short, sorting and storing foods after shopping are very important for busy cooks in order to facilitate food preparation during the week.

Readying for Cooking

Before the actual cooking, food should be readied. Because the Chinese usually serve food that is cut into bite-size pieces and cooked by different cooking methods, readying is an important process. Various methods are used, depending on the foods involved:

Developing: Since the Chinese use many kinds of dried or salted preserved foods, these foods do require a developing (reconstituting) process. This involves soaking them in water or boiling them in water or a combination of both. The developing process not only makes a food ready for cooking but also affects the texture of the food. This is particularly important for some exotic foods, such as sharks' fins, sea cucumbers, etc. Be sure to follow the directions for the developing process, checking the food from time to time, in order to insure the right texture for the preserved food.

Cutting: Meat or poultry should be defrosted ahead of time so that it can be cut. It is easier to make thin slices and fine shreds when meat is semifrozen. One should follow the recipe and cut the ingredients as suggested.

Coating and marinating: These are important processes in good cooking. A good cook always uses his or her hands in mixing the marinade because this is the only way one can feel the consistency. One should squeeze the meat so that it soaks up the coating and marinade. For chopped meat, the mixing should always be done in one direction so that the meat holds together. The coating and marinating should be timed according to the recipe.

Cleaning and picking: Since the Chinese eat a great quantity of vegetables, cleaning and picking become an important part of preparation. If vegetables are cleaned and picked ahead of time, they should be covered or put in a plastic bag to prevent exposure to the air for too long a period. However, they will be kept fresh and slightly wet, so just before you stir-fry them over high heat, they will be juicier.

Thickening agents: Many Chinese dishes use cornstarch mixed with water to thicken the liquid. Although each recipe in the book calls for a definite proportion of cornstarch and water, one should always use good judgment as to how much thickening ought to be used. A dish with vegetables may sometimes have more, other times less, liquid. It is usually a good idea to have a little more thickening agent prepared, as that way one does not run short at the last moment. Thickening agents should be mixed at the last minute or as close to cooking time as possible; otherwise the cornstarch settles to the bottom of the mixture and packs into a hardened mass.

Precooking: Ingredients should be precooked for many Chinese dishes. This is particularly true in restaurant cooking but can be easily applied at home as well. Precooking usually adds some taste to the food or makes last-minute cooking easier. Precooking can be applied to vegetables, fish, and meats, either by roasting, parboiling, blanching, or deep frying in hot or warm oil.

Personal Notes for Readying

It is very important to organize the procedure one will follow to prepare a meal, be it a simple family meal or a dinner party. Once the menu is set, frozen food should be thawed and dried food should be redeveloped. The best way to thaw is to take the frozen food from the freezer one day ahead of time and let it thaw gradually in the refrigerator. Thawing a whole chicken, duck, or large piece of meat may take a longer time. On the other hand, a small piece of meat taken out of the freezer in the morning will be ready for cutting and cooking in time for the evening meal. As mentioned above, meats are easier to cut, particularly into thin slices, when they are semifrozen. Fresh foods sometimes require salting or marinating; these processes should be attended to ahead of time. In each case one should follow the recipe as much as possible.

It is easiest to work on a counter with the range on one side and the sink on the other. For cleaning, picking, and cutting, place a can, tray, bag, or piece of paper that the food was wrapped in, in front of you so that you can discard anything there. There is no need to reach for the garbage can every time there is trash to be thrown out.

Always work on one dish at a time. Set all ingredients on a large plate with each ingredient at one corner. This is particularly important in stir-frying so that all you have to do is slide the ingredients one by one from the plate into the pan as the recipe calls for them.

Remember to wash, dry, and put away utensils and equipment as you go along. It is easier to clean and dry them immediately than to have them piled up and cluttering the cooking area.

Always follow the recipe closely, and read the recipe through once before you start cooking. It is good to remember that the heat of your range might be different from the heat of a "standard" range or the one used in the recipe. So always use good judgment and adjust the heat of your range to coordinate with the cooking time if necessary. Especially in stir-frying, if the recipe calls for high heat and your ingredients happen to be kind of dry, they will cook in a little less time than the recipe calls for. If the heat is too high for too long, the food will burn.

Most of the recipes in this book are best served with plain rice, no matter whether it is boiled or steamed. So I always set up the rice first—washed, drained, and ready to cook. Then I cut up the meats and vegetables and set them on a large plate. Set the table while the rice is cooking. If there are more than two dishes to be served, heat up the one that was cooked ahead of time. Give yourself a few minutes of no-more-work-to-do before dinner. This will give you a good feeling, and you will have a pleasant, relaxed meal.

5 The Chinese Way of Drinking and Chinese Wines and Spirits

GOOD WINES AND GOOD FOOD GO HAND IN HAND

Chinese wines and Chinese food go hand in hand. For the Chinese, wine—and especially good wine—enhances the interest and appreciation of good food. It should be noted here that the term "Chinese wines," or "*chiew*," in Chinese, includes wines as well as spirits. The Chinese *kaoliang* or *paikan* is stronger than Russian vodka or English gin. On the other hand, Chinese *shaohsing* wine is milder and drier than dry sherry.

In ordinary daily life the Chinese always like to have a good meal, with or without wine. But wine is a must whenever there is a special occasion. At formal dinners or at any celebration a toast with wine is a necessity. Even at a dinner party for social or business entertainment, drinking and eating have become inseparable.

THE TRADITIONAL CHINESE WAY OF DRINKING

Unlike the American way of having a cocktail before dinner, the Chinese traditionally drink at mealtime and with the food. The food can be either hot or cold. The important point is that there must be food accompanying the wine because the Chinese do not like to drink on empty stomachs. This is a good habit because it is better for your stomach and your health as well as for the appreciation of good food. The practice of eating while drinking is carried one step farther in that the Chinese enjoy their spirits as well as their wines throughout their meals, as do the French, instead of stopping with cocktails before dinner.

The Chinese drink their wines or spirits in a special small wine cup. The wine is poured out from a wine pot made of porcelain or pewter. *Shaohsing* wine, the typical Chinese wine, is always served warm or sometimes as hot as is "comfortable" to drink, about 176°F.

If it is too hot, it will spoil the taste of the wine. Chinese pewter is commonly used to maintain the temperature and is thus suitable and convenient for drinking *shaohsing* wine. Warm wines go well with good food and are also good for the stomach and for blood circulation. The Chinese do not drink wine cold, nor do they put ice in their drinks. Furthermore, Chinese wines are drunk straight, not mixed.

In short, the basic differences between the Chinese and Western ways of drinking are as follows: The Chinese always drink their wines straight, not mixed; *shaohsing* wine is served warm or hot, not cold or with ice; and finally, wines are always served with food, not as cocktails before dinner.

THE CHINESE WINE GAME

There would be something missing if one discussed wine and food without mentioning the wine game. It is very common at big parties to see the Chinese playing the wine game, also known as the finger game, and challenging each other from table to table. It is a simple game played by two persons. Each person throws out his fist, extending any number of fingers from none to five. His opponent does the same, and they simultaneously call out their guesses as to the total number of fingers put out by both. Whoever guesses the correct number is the winner, and the loser must take a "punishment" drink. Of course, the loser does not mind drinking, especially if the drink is good and the food is good.

Since this is a simple game, anyone can play for fun, but it is difficult to master. It requires quick thinking and some psychology in judging what the opponent intends to do at a particular moment. When two players are good, neither one can figure out the exact total number, and the game goes on and on. This game can really become very exciting. Losing a bout means drinking one small cup of wine. Each game involves 3 cups of wine, and when the 3 cups have been drunk by either or both players, the game has ended. But there is no limit to the number of games that can be played!

The regular players of the Chinese wine game also call out their figures in prose or poetic verses. These verses include wishes for good luck or good friendship. For example, the phrases following the numbers could run as follows: Instead of simply calling, "One!" one could say, "*Yi-p'in,*" meaning "first-ranking officialdom"; for two, "*Liang hsiang hao*," meaning "good for the friendly two"; for three, "*San yuan*," or "three imperial awards," or "the perfect three scores"; for four, "*Szu hsi*," or "four kinds of happiness or satisfaction" (health, wealth, happiness, and good luck); for five, "*Wu chin kuan*," or "five pieces of gold"; for six, "*Lou lou shun*," or "good luck whenever and wherever"; for seven, "*Ch'i ch'iao*," or "everything clicks"; for eight, "*Pa hsien*," meaning "eight immortals or angels"; for nine, "*Chiu, chiu, chiu*," or "wine, wine, wine (to you)"; and for ten, "*Chuan chia fo*," or "happiness to your whole family."

No doubt the Chinese wine game is a friendly game. The longer it is played, the happier and noisier it gets. Winning or losing does not really matter as long as you are in good company and enjoying good wine and good food. Indeed, the game makes people happy.

REGIONAL CHINESE WINES AND SPIRITS

Chinese wines are made of rice or other grains. In northern China people make *kaoliang* wine out of sorghum. It is very strong and good in the cold weather. Since there is not much flavor in *kaoliang* wine, rose petals and various kinds of fruit are used to enhance the flavor and color. In southern China, where the weather is subtropical, there are half-strength, milder drinks, as well as the stronger double- and triple-distilled drinks. There are also fruit-flavored wines, such as lychee wine, orange wine, and green plum wine. These wines usually use glutinous rice wine as a base.

In the western part of central China, *da-chu*, sometimes called *pai-kan*, of Szechuan province, and *mao-tai*, of Kweichow province, are well-known. The former is distilled from sorghum, wheat, or other local grains, while the latter is distilled from wheat and millet. These spirits are strong in taste and colorless or amber in color. They are drunk in small quantities, little by little, from a small wine cup.

In the eastern part of central China, the Chinese usually drink *shaohsing* wine, generally known as the yellow wine, although amber in color. It is fermented from rice and traditionally should be aged at least seven years to be drinkable and fifteen to be really mature. This is the best Chinese wine for Chinese food and should be served hot from a porcelain or a pewter wine pot.

A Simple List of Chinese
Wines and Spirits by Regions

Northern:

Pai-kan or *kaoliang chiew*	(Spirit)
Rose petal *chiew*	(Spirit)
Chu yoh ching chiew (Shensi)	(Spirit)

Southern:

Liao-pan chiew (half strength)	(Spirit)
Double-distilled *chiew*	(Spirit)
Triple-distilled *chiew*	(Spirit)
Lychee *chiew*	(Wine)
Orange *chiew*	(Wine)
Green Plum *chiew*	(Wine)

Eastern:

Shaohsing chiew	(Wine)
Oo-long and plum *chiew*	(Wine)
Fu chiew	(Wine)
Red-Dew *chiew*	(Wine)

Western:

Da-chu chiew (Luchow, Szechuan)	(Spirit)
Mao-tai chiew (Kweichow)	(Spirit)

The above-mentioned are table wines and spirits mostly served during meals, although drinkers may have their preferences as to how and when to drink them. The following is a list of Chinese herb or medicinal wines. According to Chinese medicine, each kind of herb or medicinal *chiew* has its own value for men and women and for the aged.

Ginseng and deer antler *chiew*	(Spirit)
Tiger bone *chiew*	(Spirit)
Snake *chiew*	(Spirit)
Snake and pheasant *chiew*	(Spirit)
Wu chia pi (pronounced in Cantonese as "*ng ka py*")	(Spirit)
Black bone chicken *chiew*	(Spirit)

The one thing that these medicinal wines have in common is that they all use the spirit *kaoliang chiew* as a base.

6 Chinese Teas

Tea was discovered in China as far back as the beginning of recorded Chinese history and was highly recognized and greatly appreciated in the Tang Dynasty (618–906 A.D.). In China tea is the most common beverage. Practically everybody, from the noblest to the humblest, drinks tea during the day, either to quench the thirst or to take off a little time from the day's activities. Today, although not as much as in the past, people often go to teahouses to chat, to discuss business, and even to settle their disputes over a cup of tea.

The best tea is the purest and most natural kind, with a fragrant aroma impossible to match or duplicate. For the Chinese, tea must be clear and refreshing. It goes well with the Chinese philosophy of Taoism, leading drinkers to quiet contemplation and inner tranquility.

Whenever there is a visitor, whether at home or in a business office, it is a sign of friendliness and a gesture of courtesy to offer a cup of tea. The tea can be ready made, but usually a special cup of freshly made quality tea is offered to a special friend or a special visitor. For a tea connoisseur or a special friend, special tea is offered to celebrate the meeting. This can be quite expensive, as good Chinese teas are sold by the ounce.

Although the Chinese drink tea all day, they usually do not serve tea with meals. At home soup is usually served with the meal, and in restaurants or at special dinners wines are also served. However, Chinese tea has a special place after dinner, for good tea after dinner is like having a liqueur after a meal. It has to be high-quality tea, served as hot as possible. It is good for the digestive system, and it refreshes the spirits of people enjoying good friends as well as a satisfying dinner.

Chinese refer to tea-drinking as sipping. The delicate flavor and the depth in taste of a good cup of tea can only be enjoyed at leisure —with a small amount each time and without haste. In Fukien, as well as in Chaochow in Kwangtung, tea-drinkers go as far as to use very small cups the size of tiny Chinese liquor cups, holding only enough for a few sips.

DIFFERENT KINDS OF CHINESE TEA

Tea is grown in various parts of China, but few places are really known for their teas. The most common classification of tea today is green tea, which is unfermented tea; black tea, which is fully fermented; and oolong, which is partially fermented. This division is based upon the different methods of manufacturing. Most Chinese classify teas into two general categories—red and green—probably from the color of the brew or liquor. In the Western world, they are known as black or green teas, primarily from the color of the dry leaf. Thus, the Chinese usually also refer to oolong as red tea because its liquor is red.

While *hyson*, gunpower (known as pearl tea in China), and *chun mee* are perhaps the best-known green teas in the West, the most sought-after and probably the most expensive green teas among Chinese tea connoisseurs are *loong ching* (translated as "dragon well") and *pi lo chun* (meaning "green conch spring"). The finest of these are seldom found in the Western world, primarily because they should be enjoyed when fresh and also because they fetch unbelievably high prices.

The best-known among the Chinese, inside as well as outside China, is Fukien cliff tea, *teh kuan yin* (sometimes translated as "the iron goddess of mercy") of the oolong family. However, this name has been loosely used by tea merchants in recent years. Of course, in the Western world Formosa oolong and Darjeeling (from India) have both been cherished by tea-tasters all over the world for many decades. Keemun *congou* (*congou* means "time and labor"), the favorite among northern China *congous*, became so popular in England and America that it is known as English breakfast tea. The bouquet of this black tea goes very well with milk and sugar. However, few Chinese drink tea with milk, sugar and milk, or lemon. They drink their tea straight.

Chinese people like the taste of scented teas. Teas are scented with laurel, rose, lotus, *chu-lan*, jasmine, lychee, etc. By far, jasmine is the most popular because its serene fragrance complements the flavor of tea. Unfortunately, many mediocre jasmine teas on the market today are not really scented with jasmine but with *chu-lan*, *huang-chih*, or some other flavors of similar fragrance. The scent is flowery but not serene. The scented Earl Grey tea, allegedly a favorite of the late Earl Grey of England, who learned the secret of scenting from a Mandarin, is quite popular in the West but is not drunk at all by the Chinese. Smoked teas, such as *lapsang souchong*, are more popular in America than in China. People who smoke cigars or pipes seem to prefer the flavors of smoked teas.

HOW TO BREW TEA

In order to make good tea, one has to know the kind of tea used and its quality. As one connoisseur puts it, you have to make tea at the strength that suits your taste, but it has to be within the maximum and the minimum strength of the tea. For those who like their tea weaker, it may be diluted with hot water after it is made.

Tea may be made in a pot or in a cup. The usual rule is to use one level teaspoon of tea leaves for each cup. With good tea, the leaves can be made to last through more than one steeping, and it is quite common to have second or even third servings from the same tea leaves. However, one should always remember to leave the last third of a cup or pot of tea as a residue. With good tea leaves, one may like the second serving even more than the first, probably because by then the tea releases its fragrance and aroma to the fullest extent for maximum enjoyment.

As a rule, one should use porcelain or earthenware teacups or teapots and avoid silver or metal teapots, especially for really good tea. When boiling water, one should start with fresh cold water and bring it to a rolling boil. Otherwise, the tea leaves cannot really open up to give you their full benefits and full strength. One more rule of equal importance in making good tea is to use spring water or fresh water, as fresh as you can get, being sure to release stale water before drawing from the tap. Fresh water is the only other ingredient that is necessary for making good tea. The Chinese know that those who make their tea with fresh water enjoy it a lot more than those who don't.

PART II
CHARTS AND RECIPES

7 Poultry and Eggs

NAME OF DISH	NATURE OF DISH
White-Cut Chicken: Basic Recipe	A basic recipe for many chicken dishes
White-Cut Chicken with Sauce	White-cut chicken served with either a sesame-flavored sauce or ginger-scallion sauce
Chicken with Ham on Green Paradise	A meat and vegetable dish that can be used as a one-dish meal
Drunk Chicken	A chicken marinated in wine that can be cooked ahead of time and kept in the refrigerator
Peng Peng Chicken	A cold chicken salad with peppery sesame paste sauce
Odd-Flavored Chicken	Another white-cut chicken recipe with a wonderful hot sauce
Roasted Stuffed Boneless Chicken Steamed Stuffed Boneless Chicken	A whole boneless chicken stuffed with Chinese sausages, mushrooms, and glutinous rice
Chicken with Walnuts	Peeling the walnuts may take a little time, but it is worthwhile in this dish
Shredded Chicken with Bean Sprouts	With roots and heads removed, the bean sprouts become a luxury ingredient
Chicken with Chestnuts	Sweet and smooth chestnuts make this dish very special
Stir-Fried Chicken Velvet	Pureed chicken cooked in a not-too-hot oil; the result has a velvety, melt-in-your-mouth texture
Braised Chicken Wings	Soy sauce to braise the most delicate part of the chicken with bamboo shoots and mushrooms
Beggar's Chicken	Dough-wrapped stuffed chicken; serve the dough along with the chicken
Chicken in Casserole, Cantonese Style	A one-dish meal with its own juice
Lemon Chicken	Batter-coated deep-fried chicken with fresh lemon flavoring
Steamed Chicken with Sausage	Chicken with skin and bones, steamed with Chinese sausages and mushrooms to produce better flavor
Princess Chicken	Stuffed chicken wings, the most delicate part of the chicken
Chicken with Peanuts	Dried hot chili pepper to give this dish an extra-peppery hot taste

COOKING METHOD	LAST-MINUTE COOKING TIME REQUIRED	REGION OF COOKING BY ORIGIN OR POPULARITY
Simmering in clear stock	20 minutes	Southern—Canton
Frying ginger and scallion in hot oil with peppery flavor	30 minutes	Eastern—Shanghai with soy sauce Southern—Canton with ginger sauce Northern—Peking with garlic
Simmering in clear stock	20 minutes	Southern—Canton
After cooking in clear stock, soak in rice wine marinade	20 minutes	Eastern—Shanghai and Ningpo
Boiling; serving cold	15 minutes	Western—Szechuan
Simmering in clear stock, then topping with hot sauce	10 minutes	Western—Szechuan
Stir-frying and roasting or steaming	45 minutes	Southern—roasted before serving Eastern—steamed before serving
Quick stir-frying	5 minutes	Eastern—Shanghai Southern—Canton
Preliminary deep frying and finally quick stir-frying	5 minutes	Northern—Peking Eastern—Shanghai
Braising with soy sauce	45 minutes	Eastern—Shanghai
Deep frying the puree of chicken first, then quick stir-frying	5 minutes	Northern—Shantung
Braising with soy sauce	35 minutes	Eastern—Shanghai
Baking in the oven	2½ hours	Eastern—Kiangsu
Braising in casserole	35 minutes	Southern—Canton
Deep frying the chicken with batter and stir-frying the sauce	30 minutes	Southern—Canton
Steaming over high heat	30 minutes	Southern—Canton
Braising the chicken wings in a wok	15 minutes	Southern—Canton
Preliminary deep frying and finally quick stir-frying	5 minutes	Western—Szechuan and Hunan

NAME OF DISH	NATURE OF DISH
Fish-Flavored Chicken	A characteristic Szechuan dish, with the sauce usually cooked with fish
Chicken with Bean Sauce	Boneless chicken breast with sweet bean sauce
Peking-Style Fried Chicken	Fried chicken eaten with chopsticks
Smoked Chicken	Marinated, steamed, smoked chicken or duck
Red-Cooked Duck	A good family dish to serve with plain rice
Boneless Duck with Vegetables	One more step of cooking after Red-Cooked Duck; a banquet dish for company
Glazed Duck	An appetizer or buffet dish that can be cooked ahead of time
Pressed Duck	Cooked duck that is pressed, fried, and served with sauce and nut garnish
Szechuan Crispy Duckling	Fragrant, tasty, and crispy skin and bone; usually sandwiched between hot lotus leaf buns
Peking Duck	An easy way to cook Peking Duck for family dinners
Mandarin Pancakes	These pancakes can be made ahead of time and reheated for Peking Duck or Mu Shu Pork
Fried Squab	A delicious delicacy only for those who fully appreciate them
Tea Eggs	A convenient food for all occasions, very easy to prepare
Egg and Pork Rolls	A meat-filled soft egg roll; can be used as appetizer or main course; egg is used to make the skin
Egg Fu Jung	An authentic Chinese omelet with meat and vegetables
Fish-Flavored Egg Patty	A fluffy omelet with hot pepper–meat sauce
Stir-Fried Egg Yolks	A rich, creamy egg dish

COOKING METHOD	LAST-MINUTE COOKING TIME REQUIRED	REGION OF COOKING BY ORIGIN OR POPULARITY
Preliminary deep frying and finally quick stir-frying	5 minutes	Western—Szechuan
Quick stir-frying	5 minutes	Northern—Shantung
Deep frying chicken without batter	20 minutes	Northern—Peking
Steaming, then smoking on hickory chips and tea	1 hour	Northern—Peking Western—Szechuan
Stewing in soy sauce	2½ hours	Eastern—Shanghai
Stewing in soy sauce, then steaming at the last minute	45 minutes	Eastern—Hangchow, West Lake
Stewing with herb and spice bundle	1 hour, 10 minutes	Eastern—Soochow
Steaming and last-minute deep frying in oil	10 minutes	Southern—Canton
Steaming and deep frying	20 minutes	Western—Szechuan
Dipping in a boiling sauce mixture and roasting in the oven	1 hour, 45 minutes	Northern—Peking
Panfrying in a dry frying pan; can be reheated in the steamer	30 minutes	Northern—Peking
Blanching in water, cooking in master marinade, then deep frying	10 minutes	Southern—Canton
Simmering in sauce; can be eaten hot or cold	2 to 3 hours	Eastern—Ningpo
Filling egg pancakes with meat; steaming	20 minutes	Southern—Canton
Scrambling eggs with stir-fried meat and vegetables	5 minutes	Southern—Canton
Making the omelet in a frying pan and stir-frying the meat sauce	10 minutes	Western—Szechuan
Scrambling egg yolks over low heat	5 minutes	Northern—Peking

Pai Ch'ieh Chi

白切雞

WHITE-CUT CHICKEN: BASIC RECIPE

This recipe demonstrates the most basic method of preparing chicken and is the first of a host of delicious dishes that can be served at brunches, at lunches as appetizers, and at dinners. Actually, it is the Chinese version of fricasseed chicken; here, however, the chicken is cooked only 20 minutes instead of the usual 2 hours. A whole chicken is submerged in broth and cooked in a deep, tightly covered pot. After 20 minutes the heat is turned off and the cover is left on the pot until the thicker parts have finished cooking and the chicken is cool enough to handle. Meanwhile, the muscle tissues will absorb the broth and the meat will be exceptionally tender and flavorful. One should use a mature chicken that is 4 pounds or heavier and a stewing pot that is just deep enough so that the chicken is completely submerged in liquid. Many Chinese kitchens have clear chicken stock on hand, but clear canned broth diluted with an equal quantity of water may be used as a substitute.

6 to 8 cups clear chicken stock or canned chicken
        broth diluted with an equal amount of water
1 3- to 5-pound chicken

Heat chicken stock or broth in a heavy pot that is large and deep enough to permit submerging the chicken.

Wash and dry the chicken. Place a metal teaspoon in the chicken's cavity to retain the heat while cooking. Submerge the chicken, breast down, in the boiling stock. If the stock does not cover the chicken, add enough boiling water to cover. Cover the pot and bring the liquid to a boil again. Allow the liquid to boil for 2 to 3 minutes. Remove the scum as it rises to the top. Lower the heat, cover, and allow to simmer for 20 minutes. Turn off heat, leaving the pot covered, and let the chicken cool for at least 2 hours.

Remove the warm chicken from the broth and take out the metal spoon. Save the broth for other uses; you may boil it down to a more concentrated broth for easier storage in a refrigerator or freezer.

Cut the chicken into pieces, shreds, or slices, or carve at the table, depending upon how you wish to serve it. See the recipes for White-Cut Chicken with Sauce (page 51), Chicken with Ham on Green

Paradise (page 52), Peng Peng Chicken (page 54), Odd-Flavored Chicken (page 55), and Drunk Chicken (page 53) for a variety of ways in which to serve White-Cut Chicken.

Variation: Chicken parts can also be cooked successively by this method. For instance, cook chicken legs and thighs in stock over low heat for 10 minutes, leaving them submerged in the hot stock for about 1 hour. Chicken breasts may be cooked in the same manner, but simmer them over low heat for 5 minutes and leave them in the stock for 15 minutes.

Ts'ung Yu Pai Ch'ieh Chi
WHITE-CUT CHICKEN WITH SAUCE

葱油白切雞

Sesame-Flavored Sauce

½ tablespoon sesame oil
2 tablespoons light soy sauce
¼ teaspoon sugar

Combine the sesame oil, soy sauce, and sugar and serve in individual dip dishes or in a saucer. The sauce is concentrated and should be used sparingly.

Optional: For the garlic lover, add 1 teaspoon fresh garlic paste to the above sauce, using a mortar and pestle to mash peeled garlic into a paste.

Ginger-Scallion Sauce

4 scallions, using the white parts only
½ tablespoon finely minced fresh gingerroot
    (a grater can be used)
½ teaspoon sugar
¼ cup peanut or corn oil
1 teaspoon salt
½ teaspoon cayenne pepper

Clean the white parts of the scallions and finely shred them. You should have about ½ cup. Put the minced gingerroot, scallions, and sugar in a heatproof dish.

In a small frying pan heat the peanut oil or corn oil and salt over medium heat until the oil becomes very hot but is not smoking. Add the cayenne pepper. Pour the hot pepper, salt, and oil mixture over the gingerroot and scallions. Cool and serve as a dip.

Assembling White-Cut Chicken with Sauce:
Follow the basic recipe for White-Cut Chicken (page 50). After
the chicken has sat in the stock for 2 hours, remove it (taking out
the metal spoon) and dip the chicken into a pot of cold water for
30 seconds. Drain and dry. Rub sesame oil all over the chicken. Let
it cool.

Cut the cooled chicken, with bone and skin, into ½ x 2-inch pieces
(see instructions for cutting chicken, page 15). Use either one or
both of the above sauces as dips.

Yield: 6 servings or up to 12 when served with other dishes.

Note: The chicken may be served whole and carved at the dining
table.

Yü Lan Chi

CHICKEN WITH HAM ON GREEN PARADISE

  1 *4- to 5-pound roasting chicken (preferably freshly*
     killed)
  2 *teaspoons sesame oil*
½ *pound cooked Smithfield ham, sliced into 1 x 2 x ⅛-*
     inch pieces
  2 *cups Chinese or regular broccoli with stems,*
     cut up into ½ x ½ x 2-inch pieces
  2 *cups clear chicken stock*
Salt

Sauce:
½ *cup clear chicken stock*
½ *teaspoon salt*
  1 *teaspoon cornstarch combined with 2 tablespoons*
     water
  1 *tablespoon chicken fat or peanut oil*

Follow the basic recipe for White-Cut Chicken (page 50). When
the chicken is cooked, remove it from the stock (taking out the
metal spoon) and rub it with sesame oil.

Disjoint the wings; cut off the tips and discard. Lay the wings on
one side of two corners of a large heated platter. Bone the rest of the
chicken and cut the boned chicken with skin into ½ x 2-inch pieces.

Alternately place the chicken and ham on the platter toward the center. Set the leg meat at the lower sides to reconstruct the whole chicken on the platter. Keep warm in the oven.

Parboil the broccoli in the 2 cups chicken stock with a little salt for 2 minutes. Drain. Arrange the broccoli pieces along the side of the chicken platter. (Save the stock for other uses.)

Combine the ½ cup chicken stock with the salt in a small saucepan and bring to a boil. Stir the cornstarch into the water until it is mixed well and add to the sauce, stirring until it thickens. Add the chicken fat, blend, and pour over the chicken, ham, and broccoli. Serve hot.

Yield: 6 to 8 servings or up to 12 when served with other dishes.

Tsui Chi

DRUNK CHICKEN

   1 *3-pound (approximately) broiler or fryer chicken*
   2 *tablespoons plus 1 teaspoon coarse salt*
1½ *cups* shaohsing *wine*
1½ *cups cold canned chicken broth*

Follow the basic recipe for White-Cut Chicken (page 50). When it is done, let it cool. Remove the chicken from the broth and take out the metal spoon. Cut the chicken into 8 large pieces. Then cut the wings into 2 pieces, the legs into 4 pieces, and the breast into 2 pieces. Save the back for another use. Sprinkle 2 tablespoons salt all over the chicken. Pack in a covered container and place overnight in the refrigerator.

Combine the *shaohsing* rice wine with the broth in a large wide-mouth jar. Put the salted chicken pieces into the jar. The wine and broth will cover the chicken. Sprinkle 1 teaspoon salt on top. Cover tightly and keep in the refrigerator for at least 1 day.

When ready to eat, take out as much chicken as desired. Cut into ½ x 2-inch pieces along with bone and skin and spoon some wine sauce on top. Serve cold.

Yield: 8 to 12 servings as an appetizer; 6 servings or up to 12 when served with other dishes.

Note: If a large chicken is used, marinate with more salt. The chicken can be kept in the jar in the refrigerator for as long as a month. The wine and broth can be used for cooking or may be reused for the same dish; just add some more wine.

Peng Peng Chi

棒 棒 雞

PENG PENG CHICKEN

  1 *cucumber*
½ *teaspoon salt*
  1 *large chicken breast or 2 cups cooked chicken*
       (*see White-Cut Chicken, page 50*)
  2 *dried mung bean sheets*

Sauce:
  2 *tablespoons Chinese sesame seed paste diluted with*
       2 tablespoons warm water
½ *teaspoon salt*
  2 *teaspoons sugar*
¼ *teaspoon monosodium glutamate*
¼ *teaspoon ground Roasted Szechuan Peppercorns* (*page 208*)
  2 *tablespoons soy sauce*
  1 *tablespoon wine vinegar*
  1 *tablespoon sesame oil*
  2 *to 4 teaspoons hot chili pepper oil* (*to taste*)

  2 *cloves garlic, finely chopped*
  2 *tablespoons finely chopped scallions*
¼ *cup shredded scallions or coriander leaves*

Peel the cucumber, cut off and discard the two ends, and split lengthwise into two pieces. Remove the seeds and slice thinly to make about 2 cups. Sprinkle with ½ teaspoon salt, toss, and let stand for 20 minutes.

Place the chicken breast in a saucepan. Cover with water and bring to a boil. Cover and let simmer for 5 minutes. Turn off heat and let chicken stand in water with pot covered until cool, about 15 minutes. Use fingers to shred the chicken meat into irregular julienne strips. Set aside.

Soak the dried mung bean sheets in boiling water for 2 minutes. Drain and cover with cold water. Leave in the cold water until cool. Drain and cut into 1 x 2-inch pieces to make about 1 cup. Set in a serving dish. Squeeze the water from the salted cucumber. Mix with mung bean sheet slices in a serving dish. Add the shredded chicken on top.

Mix the sauce ingredients together into a very smooth, thin sauce. Add the finely chopped garlic and scallion. Pour about half of this sauce on top of the chicken dish before serving and serve the rest in a separate sauce bowl. Garnish the chicken with shredded scallions and serve cold.

Yield: 4 servings or up to 8 when served with other dishes.

Note: This entire dish can be prepared ahead of time.

Variations: Peanut butter and salad oil may be used instead of sesame seed paste and sesame oil. Soaked shredded jellyfish or soaked agar-agar can be used in place of mung bean sheets, and blanched fresh bean sprouts or shredded lettuce can be substituted for the cucumber. Also, the chicken and sauce may be served without the vegetables.

Kuai Wei Chi
ODD-FLAVORED CHICKEN

- ½ *cup finely chopped scallions*
- 2 *tablespoons minced fresh gingerroot*
- 1 *clove garlic, finely minced*
- ½ *teaspoon ground Roasted Szechuan Peppercorns* (*page* 208)
- 1 *teaspoon crushed red chili peppers*
- 1 *4-pound* (*approximately*) *pullet or roasting chicken*
- 3 *tablespoons peanut or corn oil*

Sauce:
- 1½ *tablespoons sugar*
- ½ *teaspoon salt*
- ¼ *teaspoon monosodium glutamate*
- 4 *tablespoons light soy sauce*
- 1 *tablespoon sesame oil*

- 6 *large lettuce leaves, washed and drained*
- 1 *large tomato, thinly sliced*

Preparation:
Set the scallions, ginger, and garlic aside with the crushed peppercorns and chili peppers on a large plate.

Follow the basic recipe for White-Cut Chicken (page 50). When the chicken is done, remove from the warm broth. Bone the chicken but leave the wings and drumsticks intact. Remove and discard the wing tips and cut each wing into two pieces. Cut each drumstick into smaller chunks. Put the wing and drumstick pieces at the two ends of a large platter. Cut the boned chicken with the skin into ½ x 2-inch pieces and lay in the center of the platter. Keep warm in the oven.

Cooking:
Heat wok with peanut oil and add the scallions, gingerroot, garlic, peppercorns and chili peppers. Let brown slightly, then add the sauce ingredients. Mix well and bring just to a boil.

Break the lettuce leaves into small pieces. Arrange the lettuce with sliced tomato on a large heated platter. Slide the warm chicken pieces from the platter to the bed of lettuce and tomato. Pour the hot sauce over it. Serve hot or warm.

Yield: 4 servings or up to 10 when served with other dishes.

Ts'ui P'i Pa Pao Chi
ROASTED STUFFED BONELESS CHICKEN　脆皮八寶雞

    1 3- *to 4-pound broiler or fryer chicken*
    2 *teaspoons salt*
    1 *cup raw glutinous rice, soaked in cold water for*
        about 4 hours
    2 *tablespoons soy sauce*
    ½ *teaspoon sugar*
    1 *teaspoon cornstarch*
    2 *tablespoons peanut or corn oil*
    2 *Chinese sausages, diced*
    6 *dried mushrooms, soaked in warm water until soft*
        and then diced
    6 *water chestnuts, diced*
    2 *teaspoons corn syrup*

Preparation:
Remove the carcass from the chicken in the following manner: Wash and dry the chicken. Fold the neck skin as far back as it will go and wiggle each wing to find the joint where it meets the carcass. Using kitchen shears or a sharp knife, cut through the joint to

detach. (Try not to pierce the chicken's skin, and always cut as close to the bones as you can.) With tiny snips or cuts, free the meat around the neck cavity from the carcass. Continue to free the meat from the carcass in the same manner, turning the chicken over and pulling the skin back as you work. Free the meat around each thigh and cut the joint to detach the drumstick from the thigh. Leave the thigh bones on the carcass. Cut the meat away from the rest of the carcass. Cut through the joint where the tailbone is attached to the backbone of the chicken, leaving the tail with the skin and meat. Now free the meat halfway down the length of the drumstick bone, then cut off and remove the exposed half of the bone. Leave the bottom intact.

Carefully remove the breast and thigh meat attached to the skin. Set aside in a bowl. Sprinkle 1 teaspoon salt on the remaining meat (drumsticks and wings). Now turn the skin of the boned chicken right side out, keeping the wings and tips of the drumsticks intact. After the skin has been stuffed and roasted, it will look like a whole chicken.

Drain the soaked glutinous rice. In a steamer tier spread the rice evenly (¼ inch deep) on a piece of cheesecloth. (With a small steamer use two tiers.) Cover and steam on high heat for 30 minutes.

Dice the chicken breast, thigh meat, and giblets into ½-inch cubes. Use your hand to mix the chicken well with the soy sauce, sugar, and cornstarch. Set aside.

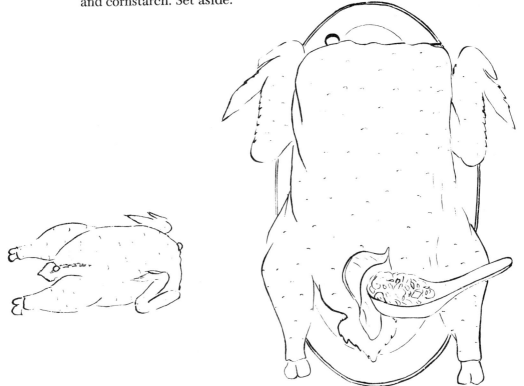

Heat a wok and add the peanut oil. Stir-fry the chicken meat for 2 minutes. Add the cut-up sausages, mushrooms, and water chestnuts. Stir and cook for 2 more minutes. Add 2 cups cooked glutinous rice and the remaining 1 teaspoon salt. (The rice should be warm for easier mixing.) Mix well and let cool to use as a filling.

Close the chicken neck end with a 4-inch skewer. Spoon the stuffing into the chicken from the bottom, then close the bottom end with another skewer.

Cooking:

Oil a sizzling roasting pan or plate. Set the chicken in the pan. Brush the chicken with corn syrup, then with oil. Roast the chicken in a preheated 375° oven for 45 minutes. Pour off the excess oil in the plate, remove the skewers, and serve the chicken hot on the sizzling plate or transfer to a heated serving platter. It is quite elegant for a host or hostess to cut and serve a boneless roast chicken at the dinner table.

Yield: 6 servings or up to 12 when served with other dishes.

Variations: Barley may be used instead of glutinous rice, Smithfield ham may be used instead of sausage, and duck may be used instead of chicken, but leave the duck's skin and meat intact. Use 2 cups raw rice instead of 1 cup, add to the other stuffing ingredients, and adjust seasonings.

Hung Shao Pa Pao Chi
STEAMED STUFFED BONELESS CHICKEN   紅燒八寶雞

In Shanghai, stuffed boneless chicken is steamed rather than roasted, as it is in Canton, southern China. Follow the recipe for Roasted Stuffed Boneless Chicken (page 56) up until the cooking instructions and continue with the cooking procedure below.

Cooking:

Smear 1 tablespoon soy sauce all over the uncooked stuffed boneless chicken. Set breast down in a large, deep dish.

Steam the whole boneless chicken dish in a preheated steamer for 45 minutes. Pour off the liquid from the dish into a saucepan (there will be about ¾ cup) and reserve. (Add chicken broth if there is not enough liquid to make ¾ cup.)

Invert the chicken breast up onto a large heated serving platter with a rim. Keep warm in the oven.

Bring the reserved liquid to a boil in the saucepan. Adjust the seasoning with soy sauce and sugar. Add a mixture of cornstarch and water to thicken the liquid. Pour this brown sauce over the chicken. Cut the whole chicken into serving pieces at the dinner table and serve hot.

Ho T'ao Chi Ting
CHICKEN WITH WALNUTS

核桃雞丁

¾ cup shelled walnuts
 2 whole chicken breasts or 4 legs, skinned and boned

Marinade:
 1 small egg white
½ teaspoon salt
 2 teaspoons cornstarch
 1 tablespoon cold water

¾ cup diced green pepper
 1 cup peanut or corn oil
 1 tablespoon dry sherry
 1 teaspoon sugar
 1 teaspoon salt
 1 teaspoon cornstarch combined with 2 tablespoons
      water

Preparation:
Put walnuts in 2 cups boiling water, let boil for 1 minute, then remove a few at a time and peel off the skins. Set aside.

Cut the chicken into ½-inch cubes to make about 1½ cups. Using your hand, mix thoroughly the chicken with the marinade ingredients. Set in the refrigerator for at least 30 minutes.

Parboil the green pepper for 2 minutes. Rinse in cold water to cool. Drain well.

Cooking:
Heat the peanut oil in a wok, and fry the peeled walnuts for about 2 minutes or until lightly browned. Do not let them get too dark, for walnuts burn quickly. Remove and drain on paper towels.

Pour off (but reserve) all the oil except for 4 tablespoons. Heat the oil over moderate heat and stir-fry the chicken until it separates into cubes or until most of the chicken changes color. Splash the sherry onto the chicken and stir well. Add the sugar and salt and the cooked green pepper. Mix well. Stir the cornstarch and water well and pour over the chicken. Stir until the sauce thickens and coats the chicken with clear glaze. Remove chicken and pepper onto a hot platter. Pour remaining sauce over all the pieces and garnish with the walnuts.

Yield: 3 or 4 servings or up to 8 when served with other dishes.

Sheng Ch'ao Chi Szu
SHREDDED CHICKEN WITH BEAN SPROUTS 生炒雞絲

   1 *whole chicken breast, skinned and boned*
   ½ *egg white*
   1¼ *teaspoons salt*
   2 *teaspoons cornstarch*
   1 *tablespoon cold water*
   2 *cups fresh bean sprouts, with roots and heads*
       removed
   ¼ *cup julienne strips of cooked Smithfield ham*
   2 *tablespoons shredded snow pea pods or green*
       pepper
   1 *cup peanut or corn oil*
   1 *tablespoon dry sherry*
   ½ *teaspoon sugar*
   ⅛ *teaspoon monosodium glutamate*
   1 *teaspoon cornstarch combined with 2 tablespoons*
       water

Preparation:
Slice chicken with the grain to a thickness of ⅛ inch. Cut again into 2-inch-long julienne strips. (For easier slicing, semifreeze the chicken.) Use your hand to mix the chicken with the egg white, ¼ teaspoon salt, cornstarch, and cold water thoroughly. Keep in the refrigerator for at least 30 minutes.

Soak the bean sprouts in cold water. Drain well before cooking.

Set the cooked Smithfield ham aside on a plate with the shredded snow pea pods.

Cooking:

Place a strainer over a pot near the cooking area. Heat a wok to very hot over medium heat. Add the peanut oil and heat to about 280°. Add the chicken and stir quickly; the chicken shreds should separate within a minute. Pour the oil and the chicken into the strainer. As soon as the oil has drained away, transfer the chicken to a dish. Reserve the oil.

Heat the same wok over high heat with 2 tablespoons of the drained oil. Add the bean sprouts and snow pea pods and stir-fry for 1 minute. Add the ham and cooked chicken. Stir and mix, splash on the sherry, then add the remaining 1 teaspoon salt, sugar, and monosodium glutamate. Stir and mix well. Mix the cornstarch and water very well and add to the chicken, stirring over high heat until the liquid thickens and coats the chicken with a clear glaze. Serve hot.

Yield: 2 servings or up to 6 when served with other dishes.

Note: One can use 5 tablespoons of oil to cook the chicken instead of 1 cup. Use a slotted spoon to remove chicken and use the remaining oil in the wok to cook the vegetables.

Li Tzu Chi

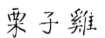

CHICKEN WITH CHESTNUTS

This dish is very popular, particularly in Shanghai and Peking. It uses red cooking by stewing. The chicken can be cooked to chopstick tenderness in 30 minutes and can be reheated. The sweet flavor and smooth texture of the chestnuts make this dish distinctive.

- 1 *3-pound (approximately) broiler chicken*
- 1 *pound fresh chestnuts*
- 2 *tablespoons peanut or corn oil*
- 2 *slices fresh gingerroot*
- 1 *scallion, cut into 2-inch-long sections*
- ½ *tablespoon sugar*
- ¼ *cup soy sauce*
- 1 *cup chicken broth*
- 6 *dried mushrooms, soaked in warm water until soft, and then cut into halves*

Preparation:

Use a heavy cleaver or kitchen shears to cut the chicken with bone and skin into 2 x 1-inch pieces to make about 4 cups. Reserve the back, a breastbone, wing tips, and skinned neck for soup stock.

Boil fresh chestnuts in water for 10 minutes. Take a few at a time from the hot water, and using a sharp paring knife, shell them to make about 2 cups peeled chestnuts.

Cooking:
Heat a saucepan to very hot. Add peanut oil and brown the chicken pieces lightly. Add ginger and scallion and stir-fry together for 1 minute. Add sugar and soy sauce and stir 2 more minutes. Add chicken broth and bring to a boil. Cover and cook over medium-low heat for 20 minutes. Add mushrooms and chestnuts, mix, and cook for 15 minutes more. Stir once during this time. Serve hot.

Yield: 4 servings or up to 10 when served with other dishes.

Note: Dried chestnuts may be used instead of fresh ones: Soak ½ pound dried chestnuts in cold water overnight. Cut off the spoiled parts. Rinse and cover with cold water, bring to a boil, and then simmer for 30 minutes. Add 1 tablespoon sugar and continue to simmer for 30 minutes more. Use higher heat to reduce the water in the pan, stirring to avoid scorching, as there will be very little water left. Add to the chicken and cook together for 15 minutes more.

Fu Jung Chi
STIR-FRIED CHICKEN VELVET

  1 *whole chicken breast, skinned and boned*
 ¼ *cup cold water*
  1 *tablespoon cornstarch*
1½ *teaspoons salt*
  1 *teaspoon sugar*
  1 *tablespoon dry sherry*
 ¼ *teaspoon monosodium glutamate*
  6 *egg whites*

  4 *dried mushrooms*
20 *fresh snow pea pods*
 ¼ *cup sliced (1½ x 1 x ⅛ inch) bamboo shoots*
 ¼ *cup sliced (1½ x 1 x ⅛ inch) cooked Smithfield ham*
  2 *cups peanut or corn oil*
 ½ *cup chicken broth*
  2 *teaspoons cornstarch combined with 2 tablespoons*
    water

Preparation:
Remove and discard as much of the membrane and tendons from the chicken breast as possible and cut the chicken into small strips.

Use a fine-holed plate in a meat grinder and grind the chicken into a mixing bowl 2 or 3 times or until the chicken is a smooth paste (it is fine enough when the paste feels smooth when rubbed between your fingers). Gradually add the cold water about ½ tablespoon at a time while mixing the chicken paste in one direction. Add cornstarch, salt, ½ teaspoon sugar, sherry, and monosodium glutamate. Continue mixing. The chicken mixture should be light and creamy smooth. Beat the egg whites until slightly foamy. Combine the egg whites with the chicken mixture and mix well. The chicken velvet can be made ahead of time up to this point and refrigerated as long as overnight.

Wash and soak the mushrooms in ½ cup warm water for 30 minutes. Cut off and discard stems and cut each mushroom in half. Snap off the tips and stems of the fresh snow pea pods. Blanch in boiling water for 1 minute, rinse in cold water, and drain well. Set these items on a large plate with the sliced bamboo shoots and ham.

Cooking:
Have a strainer over a pot near the cooking area. Heat a wok until it is very hot. Add the peanut oil and heat to about 280° over medium-high heat. Mix the chicken velvet and pour into the oil. Gently stir and turn with a spatula. As soon as the chicken velvet turns white, pour the oil and chicken into the strainer and drain.

Heat the same wok with 2 tablespoons of the drained oil. Add snow pea pods, mushrooms, bamboo shoots, ham, and ½ teaspoon sugar. Stir-fry for 2 minutes. Add the drained chicken velvet and chicken broth. Stir gently while heating over high heat. Stir the cornstarch mixture well and slowly pour into the wok. Stir until chicken and vegetables thicken and are coated with a light, clear glaze. Serve at once on a heated platter.

Yield: 4 servings or up to 8 when served with other dishes.

Note: To use up the egg yolks, see recipe for Stir-Fried Egg Yolks (page 94).

Kuei Fei Chi Ch'ih

BRAISED CHICKEN WINGS

貴妃雞翅

8 *large chicken wings (about 2 pounds)*
½ *teaspoon salt*
3 *tablespoons soy sauce*
2 *teaspoons sugar*
4 *dried mushrooms*
½ *cup roll-cut bamboo shoots*
1 *scallion, cut into 2-inch-long sections*
1 *1-inch piece fresh gingerroot, crushed with flat side of cleaver*
1 *tablespoon peanut or corn oil*
2 *tablespoons dry sherry*
½ *cup chicken broth*

Preparation:
Cut each chicken wing at the joint and discard the wing tips. Cut off and discard some of the thicker skin that has fat attached. Wash wings and dry well. Combine the salt, soy sauce, and sugar, and marinate the wings in this mixture for 30 minutes.

Wash and soak the dried mushrooms in warm water for 30 minutes. Remove and discard the stems. Cut each mushroom into halves. Set aside on a plate along with the bamboo shoots, scallion, and gingerroot.

Cooking:
Drain the chicken wings and reserve the marinade for later. Heat a heavy saucepan over medium heat until it becomes very hot. Add the peanut oil, ginger, then the wings. Stir-fry to seal. Splash on the sherry, stir for 30 seconds, and then add the reserved marinade and stir to coat the wings. Add the scallion, bamboo shoots, and mushrooms and stir together for 2 more minutes. Add the chicken broth, cover, bring to a boil, and let cook over medium-low heat for about 30 minutes, stirring twice. Serve hot.

Yield: 4 servings or up to 8 when served with other dishes.

Chiao Hua Chi

叫化雞

BEGGAR'S CHICKEN

   1 *3-pound (approximately) broiler chicken*
   2 *tablespoons salt*
   1 *tablespoon Szechuan peppercorns*
   2 *whole star anise, broken into small pieces*
   1 *½-inch piece gingerroot*
   1 *teaspoon cornstarch*
   1 *tablespoon cold water*
  ½ *cup julienne strips of lean pork*
  ½ *cup julienne strips of bamboo shoots*
   2 *scallions, finely shredded*
  ¾ *cup Tientsin preserved vegetables*
   3 *tablespoons plus 2 teaspoons peanut or corn oil*
   1 *tablespoon dry sherry*
  ½ *teaspoon sugar*
  ¼ *teaspoon monosodium glutamate*
   1 *egg yolk combined with 1 teaspoon water*

Dough:
   1 *teaspoon active dry yeast*
   1 *cup lukewarm water*
   2 *tablespoons sugar*
  ½ *teaspoon salt*
 3½ *cups all-purpose flour*

   1 *egg yolk combined with 1 teaspoon water*

Preparation:
Use a paring knife to slash the thick part of the legs from the inside
of the chicken a few times. Rub the chicken inside and out with salt.
Set in a large container. Add the Szechuan peppercorns and star
anise. Press the gingerroot through a garlic press and add the ginger
juice. Marinate the chicken for 30 minutes or longer. Turn over
twice during this time.

Combine the cornstarch and water and mix thoroughly. Then add
the pork strips and mix well. Place the bamboo shoots, scallions, and
pork strips on a plate along with the Tientsin preserved vegetables.

Heat a wok until it is very hot. Add the peanut oil and pork strips
and stir-fry over medium heat until the pork strips separate. Splash
on the sherry, sugar, and monosodium glutamate. Add the scallions,

preserved vegetables, and bamboo shoots. Stir-fry together with the pork for 2 minutes. Set aside to cool to use as a filling.

Remove and discard the Szechuan peppercorns and star anise from the chicken. Smear the entire chicken with about 2 teaspoons oil. Stuff the pork mixture inside the chicken cavity. Use a large piece of heavy aluminum foil to wrap the chicken securely. Smooth down the foil corners.

Making the dough:
Dissolve the yeast in lukewarm water. Add the sugar, salt, and yeast-water mixture to the flour in a large mixing bowl. Stir and mix well. Knead well into a soft dough. Cover and let rise for ½ hour. On a lightly floured surface knead the dough again. Roll out the dough until it is large enough to wrap around the entire chicken. Seal and mold smoothly. Set the chicken on an oiled roasting pan. Brush the surface of the dough that is wrapped around the chicken with the egg yolk mixture. The chicken is now ready to be baked.

Cooking:
Bake the chicken in preheated 325° oven for 1½ hours, then reduce the heat to 225° and continue baking for 1 more hour.

To serve:
Cut through the dough and foil, remove the chicken, and place on a large heated platter. Discard the foil. Pour the juice onto the chicken. The chicken will be chopstick tender. Serve hot, along with the baked dough on a separate platter.

Yield: 6 to 8 servings or up to 12 when served with other dishes.

Note: The surface of the wrapped chicken can be decorated for special occasions. Roll out thinly any extra overlapping dough. Cut into strips and lay these crisscrossed on top of the dough-covered chicken (or make any other design that you prefer).

Hao Yu Pao Chi
CHICKEN IN CASSEROLE, CANTONESE STYLE

6 *dried mushrooms*
1 *3-pound (approximately) fryer or broiler chicken*

Marinade:
1 *teaspoon salt*
1 *teaspoon sugar*
2 *tablespoons cornstarch*
3 *tablespoons light soy sauce*
1 *tablespoon dark soy sauce*
2 *tablespoons oyster sauce*
1 *teaspoon sesame oil*

3 *tablespoons peanut or corn oil*
4 *cloves garlic, crushed*
1 *scallion, cut into 1-inch pieces*
4 *thin slices gingerroot*

Preparation:
Wash and soak the mushrooms in ½ cup warm water for 30 minutes. Remove and discard the stems; cut each mushroom in half and set aside.

Clean and wash the chicken with water. Cut through the chicken skin and small bones and cut the chicken into 1-inch pieces. Put the chicken pieces into a large mixing bowl. Reserve the large backbone, tips of the wings, and the neck (minus its skin) for making soup stock. Combine the marinade ingredients and add along with the cut-up mushrooms to the chicken pieces. Toss well. Marinate the chicken and mushroom pieces for 30 minutes.

Cooking:
Heat a heatproof casserole or a heavy pot until hot. Add the peanut oil and then the garlic, scallion, and ginger and stir-fry for 1 minute. Add the marinated chicken and mushroom pieces. Stir-fry for 2 minutes. Cover and let cook over medium-low heat for about 30 minutes or until the chicken pieces are tender. Stir once or twice during cooking to prevent sticking. Juice will come out of the chicken, so it is not necessary to add water. Serve hot.

Yield: 6 servings or up to 10 when served with other dishes.

Ning Meng Chi

LEMON CHICKEN

檸檬雞

1 3-pound chicken or 2 whole chicken breasts
1 teaspoon salt
1 tablespoon light soy sauce

Sauce:
1 cup chicken broth
1 teaspoon salt
3 tablespoons sugar
1 tablespoon cornstarch

Batter:
½ cup flour
2 tablespoons cornstarch
¼ teaspoon baking powder
⅛ teaspoon baking soda
¼ teaspoon salt
¼ teaspoon sugar
½ cup water

2 cups peanut or corn oil

1 scallion, split and cut into 2-inch-long sections
2 large lemons, thinly sliced
4 or 5 lettuce leaves

Preparation:
Cut the chicken into quarters, or if breasts are used, cut into halves. Bone the chicken, leaving some skin. Mix the chicken with the salt and light soy sauce and marinate for about 15 minutes.

Combine the sauce ingredients in a bowl and set aside near cooking area.

Combine the batter ingredients. Using a wire whisk, mix the batter until smooth.

Cooking:
Heat the oil in a wok or a deep fryer to about 365° degrees. While the oil is heating, add 1 tablespoon of the warm oil to the batter, blend well, and then coat the chicken pieces with the batter. Deep

fry the chicken 2 pieces at a time for about 7 to 8 minutes (5 minutes for the breasts) or until golden brown and crispy. Keep warm in the oven.

Heat 2 more tablespoons of the warm oil in a wok. Add the scallion and stir, then add the sliced lemon. Stir-fry for 30 seconds. Mix the sauce ingredients very well, making sure that the cornstarch is in suspension and the sugar dissolves. Add the sauce to the wok and stir until it thickens and forms a clear glaze. Keep hot on low heat.

Take the chicken out of the oven and cut each quarter into ¾ x 2-inch pieces. Arrange on a large platter with the lettuce leaves. Pour the hot sauce over it. Serve hot.

Yield: 4 servings or up to 8 when served with other dishes.

Hsiang Ku La Ch'ang Cheng Chi
香菇臘腸蒸雞

STEAMED CHICKEN WITH SAUSAGE

6 *dried mushrooms*
2 *Chinese sausages*
6 *thin slices fresh gingerroot*
1 *3-pound (approximately) broiler or fryer chicken*

Marinade:
1 *teaspoon salt*
2 *teaspoons cornstarch*
2 *tablespoons light soy sauce*
1 *tablespoon peanut or corn oil*

Preparation:
Wash and soak the mushrooms in ½ cup warm water for 30 minutes. Cut off and discard the stems, then cut the mushrooms into halves. Cut each sausage diagonally into 5 or 6 pieces. Set aside on a plate along with the mushrooms and ginger slices.

Clean and wash the chicken. Cut through the chicken's skin and small bones and cut the chicken into 1-inch pieces. Put the chicken pieces in a mixing bowl. Reserve the backbone, wing tips, and neck (minus its skin) for making soup stock.

In a bowl, combine and mix the marinade ingredients and then add the marinade to the chicken. Mix and toss to coat chicken pieces evenly.

Cooking:

Take a plate with a rim or a pie plate 1 inch smaller in diameter than a steamer. Place the chicken pieces in not more than two layers on the plate. Set the mushrooms, sausages, and ginger in between the chicken pieces.

Set plate in a preheated steamer, cover, and steam over high heat for 30 minutes. Serve hot on the same plate on top of a large platter.

Yield: 6 servings or up to 10 when served with other dishes.

Lung Ch'uan Feng Yi
PRINCESS CHICKEN

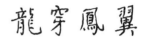

12 *large chicken wings*
½ *teaspoon salt*
 1 *teaspoon soy sauce*
 4 *medium dried mushrooms*
12 *2 x ¼ x ⅛-inch strips cooked Smithfield ham*
12 *2 x ¼ x ⅛-inch strips bamboo shoots*
 1 *scallion, cut into 2-inch sections*
 2 *slices gingerroot*

Sauce:
½ *teaspoon sugar*
 1 *teaspoon cornstarch*
 2 *teaspoons soy sauce*
 1 *tablespoon oyster sauce*
 2 *tablespoons cold water*

 2 *tablespoons peanut or corn oil*
½ *cup chicken broth*

Preparation:

Clean and wash the chicken wings. Cut off the wing tips and third sections; reserve for another time. Only the center portions of the wings are used in this dish. To bone the center section, chop off a small piece of bone at each end so that only two straight bones are left. They can be easily removed. Marinate these 12 boneless wing sections with salt and soy sauce for 30 minutes.

Wash and soak the dried mushrooms in ½ cup warm water for 30 minutes. Cut off and discard the stems, then cut each mushroom into three strips. Set aside on a plate with the strips of ham and bamboo shoots, scallion, and ginger. Combine the sauce ingredients in a cup and set aside near the cooking area.

Take 1 piece each of mushroom, ham, and bamboo shoot and thread into the center of each wing where the two bones were. Repeat until all the wings are stuffed.

Cooking:
Heat a wok. Add the peanut oil and stir-fry the ginger and scallion first, then add the stuffed wings and cook, stirring gently, for 3 to 4 minutes. Add the chicken broth. Cover and let cook over moderate heat for 15 minutes or until the wings are tender, stirring once during cooking to turn the wings. Mix the sauce ingredients thoroughly and pour into the wok while stirring until the sauce thickens and coats the wings with a clear glaze.

Yield: 2 servings or up to 6 when served with other dishes.

Kung Pao Chi Ting
CHICKEN WITH PEANUTS

宮保雞丁

2 *whole chicken breasts or 4 legs, skinned and boned*
1 *egg white*
1 *tablespoon cornstarch*
1 *tablespoon soy sauce*
1 *tablespoon cold water*
2 *scallions, cut into ¼-inch-long sections*
    (*about ½ cup*)
8 *whole dried red chili peppers*

Sauce:
1 *teaspoon sugar*
½ *teaspoon salt*
1 *teaspoon cornstarch*
1 *tablespoon soy sauce*
1 *teaspoon distilled white vinegar*
1 *teaspoon sesame oil*
2 *tablespoons water*

2 *cups peanut or corn oil*
½ *cup skinless roasted peanuts*

Preparation:
Cut chicken into ½-inch cubes. You will have about 1½ cups. Combine the egg white, cornstarch, soy sauce, and 1 tablespoon water

and add to chicken cubes, using your hand to mix well. Set aside for 30 minutes.

Wipe the dried chili peppers clean with a wet towel. Remove the tips and set aside on a plate with the scallions. Combine the sauce ingredients in a cup. Set aside near the cooking area.

Cooking:
Place a strainer over a pot near the cooking area. Heat a wok over moderate heat until it is very hot. Add the peanut oil and heat to about 300°. Mix the chicken again and add to the hot oil. Raise the heat to high and stir the chicken until it separates or until most of the chicken has changed color but is not yet completely cooked. Pour the oil and chicken into the strainer to drain. As soon as the oil has drained away, transfer the chicken to a plate.

Heat the same wok. Add 2 tablespoons of the drained oil, brown the chili peppers until they turn dark red, then add the scallions and cooked chicken and stir-fry for 1 minute. Stir the sauce mixture well and add it to the chicken while stirring over high heat until it thickens and coats the chicken with a clear glaze. Add the peanuts and mix well. Serve hot.

Yield: 4 servings or up to 8 when served with other dishes.

Variation: Beef or pork may be used in place of chicken. Without the peanuts this dish becomes the favorite chicken dish of General Tsu of Hunan, Boneless Chicken with Hot-and-Sour Sauce.

Note: You may use 6 tablespoons of oil instead of 2 cups. Use a slotted spoon to remove chicken, and use remaining oil in the wok to cook the chili peppers and scallions.

Yu Hsiang Chi Szu
FISH-FLAVORED CHICKEN

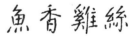

This dish has not only a peppery flavor but also a sweet-and-sour one. The sauce is usually cooked with fish dishes, although it is characteristically served with Szechuan dishes. Because Szechuan is located in the mountainous inland region of China, fish is not readily available and is considered a delicacy. Perhaps that is why its people sometimes substitute pork or chicken for fish—thus Fish-Flavored Chicken.

1 *whole chicken breast, skinned and boned*
½ *egg white*
¼ *teaspoon salt*
2 *teaspoons cornstarch*
1 *tablespoon cold water*
2 *teaspoons finely minced gingerroot*
1 *scallion, finely shredded*
1 *clove garlic, thinly sliced*

Sauce:
¼ *teaspoon cayenne pepper*
1 *teaspoon sugar*
1 *teaspoon cornstarch*
⅛ *teaspoon monosodium glutamate*
1 *teaspoon distilled white vinegar*
1 *tablespoon soy sauce*
1 *tablespoon cold water*

2 *bunches watercress*
1 *cup peanut or corn oil*
1 *tablespoon gin*
Salt and sugar to taste

Preparation:
Slice the chicken with the grain ⅛ inch thick. Cut again into 2-inch-long julienne strips. Use your hand to mix the chicken well with the egg white, salt, cornstarch, and water. Set aside for at least 30 minutes.

Place the ginger, scallion, and garlic on a plate. In a small bowl combine the sauce ingredients. Mix well and set aside. Pick over, wash, and drain the tender parts of the watercress and cut into 2-inch-long sections. Discard the tough stems. You will have about 6 cups watercress.

Cooking:
Heat a wok over high heat until it smokes. Add 2 tablespoons peanut oil and the watercress all at once to cover the inner surface of the wok. Stir to coat the watercress with oil. Splash in the gin; cover for 10 seconds. Season with salt and sugar to taste. Dish out onto one side of a serving plate. Keep hot in the oven.

Place a strainer over a pot near the cooking area. Heat a clean wok over moderate heat until very hot. Add the remaining peanut oil and heat to about 280°. Add the chicken and stir quickly. The shredded chicken should separate into pieces within a minute. Pour the oil and chicken into the strainer. Heat the same wok over high heat with 2 tablespoons of the drained oil. Add the ginger, scallion, and garlic. Stir-fry for 30 seconds, then add the cooked chicken. Mix the sauce mixture well to make sure the cornstarch is completely in suspension. Pour over the chicken and stir over high heat. The sauce will thicken and coat the chicken with a clear glaze. Dish out onto the other side of the plate with the watercress. Serve hot.

Yield: 2 to 3 servings or up to 6 when served with other dishes.

Note: You may use 5 tablespoons of the oil to cook the chicken. Use a slotted spoon to remove the chicken, and use the remaining oil in the wok to cook the vegetables.

Chiang Pao Chi Fu
CHICKEN WITH BEAN SAUCE

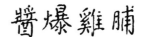

2 *whole chicken breasts, skinned and boned*

Marinade:
1 *tablespoon cornstarch*
1 *tablespoon soy sauce*
2 *tablespoons cold water*

½ *cup diced sweet red or green pepper*
½ *cup diced water chestnuts*
½ *cup diced canned, cooked fresh, or soaked dried mushrooms*
½ *cup roasted cashew nuts*
4 *tablespoons peanut or corn oil*
3 *tablespoons* hoisin *sauce*

Preparation:
Cut the chicken into ½-inch cubes to make about 1½ cups. Use your hand to mix them well with the marinade ingredients. Set aside.

Set the diced pepper, water chestnuts, mushrooms, and cashew nuts on a large plate.

Cooking:
Heat a wok. Add 1 tablespoon peanut oil and stir-fry the pepper, water chestnuts, and mushrooms over medium-high heat for 2 to 3 minutes. Dish out onto a plate.

Heat a clean wok over moderate heat until very hot. Add 3 table-spoons peanut oil. Mix the chicken cubes again and add to the hot oil, stirring quickly over high heat to separate the chicken pieces. Continue stirring until most of the chicken has changed color, about 1 minute. Add the *hoisin* sauce, stir, and mix. Add the cooked vegetables and mix. Cook with the chicken only long enough to heat through. Dish out and garnish with the cashew nuts. Serve hot.

Yield: 4 servings or up to 8 when served with other dishes.

Cha Pa Kuan
PEKING-STYLE FRIED CHICKEN

炸八塊

1 3-pound (approximately) broiler or fryer chicken or
    4 chicken legs (about 2 pounds)
1 egg white
1 tablespoon cornstarch
½ teaspoon five-spice powder
¼ teaspoon monosodium glutamate
¼ cup soy sauce
1 scallion, cut into 2-inch-long sections
1 ½-inch piece gingerroot
2 cups peanut or corn oil
2 teaspoons sesame oil
Roasted Salt and Szechuan Peppercorns (page 208),
    to taste

Preparation:
Wash and dry the chicken thoroughly. Cut the chicken, along with the skin and bone, into 1½ x 1-inch pieces and place in a large mixing bowl. Reserve the large backbone, wing tips, and neck (minus its skin) to make soup stock.

Add the egg white to the cut-up chicken. Mix well, then sprinkle on the cornstarch, five-spice powder, monosodium glutamate, and soy sauce. Crush the scallion sections and add to the chicken. Press the ginger in a garlic press and add the juice to the chicken. Toss and mix with your hand to make sure the chicken is evenly coated. Let stand for 30 minutes, turning over twice during this time.

Cooking:
Heat a wok until it is very hot (about 375°) and add the peanut oil. Put half the chicken pieces in and stir to separate the pieces. Deep

fry for about 4 to 5 minutes. Use a large strainer to lift out the chicken. When the oil is hot again, put the chicken back in the wok and refry for another 2 minutes. Drain and keep warm in the oven. Fry the remaining pieces in the same manner. Sprinkle the sesame oil over the fried chicken. Serve hot with Roasted Salt and Szechuan Peppercorns (page 208).

Yield: 4 servings or up to 8 when served with other dishes.

Hsün Chi

SMOKED CHICKEN

    1 4-*pound* (*approximately*) *roasting chicken*
    4 *tablespoons coarse salt*
    1 *tablespoon Szechuan peppercorns*
 ¼ *cup hickory chips* (*see note*)
    2 *tablespoons black tea leaves*
    2 *teaspoons sesame oil*

Preparation:
Clean the chicken by rinsing it with water. Drain and dry well. Brown the salt and peppercorns in a dry frying pan over moderate heat until the salt turns slightly brown and the peppercorns smell fragrant. Use a spoon to sprinkle the hot salt and pepper on the inside and outside of the chicken. With your hand rub it in thoroughly and evenly. Place the chicken in a container with a cover and store in the refrigerator overnight or for up to 2 days for a more concentrated flavor.

Cooking:
Use a steamer or pot with a cover that is large enough to hold a deep dish that can hold the chicken. Fill the large pot with water at least 1½ inches deep. Place a rack or ovenproof glass above the water. Set the chicken dish on the rack. Cover tightly, bring water to a boil, and steam for 45 minutes. Take the chicken out to cool and dry completely. Save the chicken liquid for other uses, such as soup stock or gravy.

Smoking:
Line the inside of a wok and its domed cover with aluminum foil. Sprinkle hickory chips and black tea over the foil that covers the bottom inner surface of the wok. Place an oiled rack in the wok. Lay the chicken on it. Cover the wok with the domed cover and smoke

over moderate heat for 15 minutes. Turn off the heat and let stand for 5 minutes to allow the smoke to settle down before removing the cover. If the hickory chips and tea leaves are not fully burned and the chicken's skin is not brown in color, continue smoking for 5 to 10 minutes.

Remove the chicken and brush with sesame oil. Cut the chicken into small pieces (see "How to Chop Chicken or Duck," page 15). Smoked Chicken can be made in advance and will keep for days in the refrigerator.

Yield: 6 servings or up to 12 when served with other dishes.

Note: A good brand of hickory chips is Hickory Farm of Ohio. If hickory chips are unobtainable, ¼ cup raw rice, ¼ cup black tea leaves, and 1 tablespoon sugar may be used instead. Smoke for 5 minutes only.

Variation: Smoked duck may be prepared in the same manner. Deep fry the whole duck, and then cut the duck into small serving pieces. Serve with Lotus Leaf Buns (p. 267).

Hung Shao Ya
RED-COOKED DUCK

紅燒鴨

   1 *5-pound (approximately) fresh or frozen duck*
   1 *teaspoon salt*
   6 *tablespoons dark soy sauce*
   1 *whole star anise*
   2 *scallions, cut into 2-inch-long sections*
1½ *tablespoons sugar*
   4 *cups water*
 ¼ *cup dry sherry*
   2 *teaspoons sesame oil*

Preparation:
Cut off the extra skin and excess fat from the body of the duck. Rinse the duck with water, including the giblets and neck (with its skin removed), drain, and dry well. Set in a Dutch oven or a large pot. Sprinkle the salt inside the duck and smear 1 tablespoon dark soy sauce on the outside of the duck. Let stand for 1 hour, turning over once during this time.

Remove the top rack from the oven and oil the rack. Pour about 1 inch water into a broiler pan, and place the broiler pan on the lowest level in the oven. Preheat the oven to 400°. Take the duck out of the pot, but save the pot with its marinade for later use. Place the duck breast side up on the removed oven rack and roast the duck at the middle level for 30 minutes or until the skin is browned. Turn off the oven and open the door. Let the duck cool for 10 minutes for easier handling.

Cooking:

Set an asbestos pad (heat-tamer) on a burner and on it place the pot containing the marinade. Add the star anise, scallions, sugar, 5 tablespoons soy sauce, and water (or enough to half cover the duck). Bring the sauce to a boil, stirring well. Add the sherry, the roasted duck breast side down, giblets, and neck. Let boil for 5 minutes. Cover and turn down the heat to medium-low and cook for 1 hour. Turn the duck over and continue cooking for 1½ hours or until the duck is very tender. Baste with the sauce a few times during cooking. Carefully take the whole duck out and lay on a large platter breast side up. Keep warm in the oven. Discard the star anise and skim the fat off the liquid. Add the sesame oil, mix well, and then pour the liquid onto the duck. (If there is too much liquid, boil down to about ¾ cup.) Serve hot.

Yield: 6 servings or up to 10 when served with other dishes.

Variations: Add 6 to 8 large soaked dried mushrooms to the duck during the last hour of cooking. Add 6 shelled hard-boiled eggs to the pot during the last hour of cooking. Add 2 cups stir-fried chopped onion or 6 cups stir-fried spinach or watercress to the platter with the duck before serving.

Hung Men Ch'u Ku Ya
BONELESS DUCK WITH VEGETABLES   紅燜出骨鴨

1 *recipe Red-Cooked Duck (page 78)*
2 *cups chicken broth or water*
1 *pound washed tender spinach or watercress*
2 *teaspoons cornstarch combined with 2 tablespoons water*

Follow the recipe for Red-Cooked Duck. After the duck has cooked for about 1½ hours, carefully take the whole duck out and lay it on a large deep dish breast side down. Slit the backbone skin and remove all the bones except those in the wings. Arrange the duck so that the giblets and most of the meat are at the center. Remove and discard the star anise and scallions from the sauce. Skim off the fat. Reduce the liquid to about ½ cup by boiling, then pour onto the boneless duck.

Before serving, use a regular steamer and steam the duck over medium heat for 45 minutes. Use rubber gloves to lift the duck dish. Pour the liquid into a small saucepan. More liquid will accumulate during the steaming. Add enough water to make 1 cup. Invert the duck onto a large platter. Keep warm in the oven.

Bring the liquid (about 1 cup) to a boil and keep simmering. Meanwhile parboil the spinach in chicken broth or water. Drain vegetables well. Stir the cornstarch and water very well, and add to the liquid. Stir and cook over moderate heat until the sauce thickens and boils again. Arrange the cooked spinach around the duck. Pour the hot sauce over the duck and vegetable. Serve hot.

Yield: 6 servings or up to 10 when served with other dishes.

Chiang Ya

GLAZED DUCK

  1 *5-pound (approximately) fresh or frozen duck*
¼ *cup plus 1 teaspoon salt*
  2 *whole star anise*
  1 *scallion, cut in half*
  2 *tablespoons red rice*
  3 *cups water*
  2 *tablespoons light soy sauce*
  3 *tablespoons crushed rock sugar*
  1 *tablespoon sesame oil*
  1 *tablespoon dry sherry*

Preparation:
Rinse the duck, drain, and dry well. Rub thoroughly with ¼ cup salt inside and out and let stand for 2 to 3 hours.

Place star anise, scallion, and red rice in a piece of double-thickness cheesecloth. Tie into a loose bundle. Set aside.

Cooking:
Rinse the salted duck under cold water. Drain and set breast side down in a large pot. Add the water and herb and spice bundle. Put an asbestos pad (heat-tamer) on a burner and set the pot over it.

Bring the liquid to a boil, cover, and cook over medium heat for 30 minutes. Turn the duck over and add the soy sauce, rock sugar, and 1 teaspoon salt and cook for 30 minutes. Turn the duck once more. Add the sesame oil and sherry and cook for 10 minutes. Turn off the heat and let the duck sit in the pot, covered, for 30 minutes. Take the duck out, discard the spice bundle, and leave the liquid in the pot. Skim off most of the fat and reduce the liquid by boiling down to ¼ cup. Keep stirring to avoid scorching. The concentrated gravy is used to obtain a glazed look as well as for added seasoning.

The duck may be served whole. Brush the duck with hot gravy and carve it at the dinner table, or let the duck cool and cut it up into small pieces, then arrange it to reconstruct an entire duck on a large platter (see "How to Chop Chicken or Duck," page 15). Brush the reduced hot gravy onto the duck.

Yield: 4 servings or 12 servings as an appetizer.

Kuo Shao Ya
PRESSED DUCK

锅烧鸭

  1 *5-pound fresh or frozen duck*
  1 *tablespoon salt*
  4 *thin slices gingerroot*
  1 *scallion, cut in half*
1½ *tablespoons light soy sauce*
  ½ *cup frozen peas or snow pea pods*
  ½ *cup canned sliced mushrooms*
  1 *tablespoon cornstarch combined with 3 tablespoons water*

Batter:
  2 *eggs*
  ⅓ *cup cornstarch or water chestnut flour*
  ½ *teaspoon baking powder*

  2 *cups peanut or corn oil*
  2 *cups shredded lettuce (covered and refrigerated)*
  ¼ *cup finely chopped toasted almonds*

Preparation:
Cut off the extra skin around the neck joint of the duck and remove excess fat from the body. Rinse the duck with water, drain, including the giblets and neck (with its skin removed), and dry well.

Remove the tips of the wings and reserve for making soup stock, along with the giblets and neck. Rub salt on both inside and outside of duck. Leave in a cool place overnight.

Place the ginger and scallion on top of the duck and steam over high heat in a deep dish for 1 hour or until the meat is tender. Remove the duck from the dish and let cool. Skim the fat off the liquid (about 1 cup) from the steaming dish and set aside for later use.

Remove the bones of the duck, keeping the skin intact, and divide into 4 pieces. Press boned duck with a heavy object between 2 layers of waxed paper in the refrigerator at least 4 hours.

Place the reserved duck broth, light soy sauce, peas, and mushrooms in a small saucepan. Set on the stove. Set the chopped almonds and cornstarch combined with water near the cooking area.

Beat the eggs and add the cornstarch and baking powder. Mix into a thin, smooth batter. Add 2 teaspoons of the heated deep-frying oil (see below) to the batter and mix well just before frying.

Cooking:
Heat the peanut oil to 375°. Coat the duck pieces with batter. Fry the duck pieces two at a time on both sides until brown and crispy, about 5 minutes. Keep warm in the oven. Fry remaining pieces in the same manner. While duck pieces are frying, turn the heat on under the saucepan with the broth and bring it to a boil. Mix the cornstarch with water very well and slowly stir it in until the broth thickens and begins to boil again. Keep hot.

Line a warm serving platter with shredded lettuce. Cut the fried duck into 1½ x ¾ -inch pieces and place on top of lettuce. Pour the sauce onto the duck. Garnish with the chopped almonds. Serve hot.

Yield: 4 servings or up to 8 when served with other dishes.

Note: The duck may be fried ahead of time and the pieces reheated in hot deep fat or a preheated 450° oven for about 7 to 8 minutes. Serve with the hot sauce.

Hsiang Su Ya

SZECHUAN CRISPY DUCKLING

香酥鴨

1 4-pound (approximately) fresh or frozen duckling
4 slices fresh gingerroot, crushed
1 scallion, cut into 2-inch-long sections and crushed
   with the side of a cleaver
2 tablespoons coarse salt
1 tablespoon Szechuan peppercorns
1 teaspoon five-spice powder
1 tablespoon soy sauce
2 tablespoons flour
4 cups peanut or corn oil
Lotus Leaf Buns (page 267)

Preparation:
Cut off the extra skin around the neck joint and remove excess fat
from the body of the duck. Rinse the duck with water, including the
giblets and neck (with its skin removed), drain, and dry well.
Remove the tips of the wings and reserve along with giblets and
neck for making soup stock.

Press down hard on the duck to break the rib bones and backbone.
Use a paring knife to slash the thick part of the legs from the inside
of the duck a few times. Rub the crushed ginger and scallion onto
the duck inside and out. Discard the ginger and scallion.

Roast the salt and peppercorns in a dry frying pan over moderate
heat until the salt is slightly brown and the pepper smells fragrant.
Allow to cool and mix in five-spice powder. Rub this mixture onto
the inside and outside of the duck. Keep the duck in a covered container or wrapped in foil in the refrigerator overnight.

Brush off the peppercorns, place duck on a plate with a rim, and
steam over moderate heat for 2 hours. The duck will be very tender.
Pour out the liquid (reserve for gravy), and allow the duck to cool
completely. Then rub the duck all over with soy sauce and allow to
dry thoroughly.

Sprinkle the flour to coat the duck and set it aside while you heat
the oil in a large wok or deep fryer to about 350°. Fry the duck for
about 10 minutes on each side or until golden brown and crisp.
While frying, move and turn the duck occasionally to insure even
frying.

Cut the duck into small pieces through the skin and bone (see "How to Chop Chicken or Duck," page 15). Serve hot in sandwich fashion on hot Lotus Leaf Buns (page 267), sprinkled with Roasted Salt and Szechuan Peppercorns (page 208) to taste.

Yield: 6 servings or up to 10 when served with other dishes.

Pei Ching Ya　　　　　　　北京鴨
PEKING DUCK

Peking Duck, an important dish, is usually served in the latter part of formal dinners and banquets. The skin is the essential part of the dish. When Peking Duck is properly prepared, the skin is crispy, fluffy, and not greasy. At the same time, the meat remains juicy and tender. As the name indicates, this special way of preparing roast duck originated in Peking.

In Peking many restaurants specialize in serving Peking Duck. For simple dinners one eats the duck's skin and meat first along with Mandarin Pancakes, followed by a soup made of celery cabbage cooked in the stock from the leftover duck bones. For a banquet only the skin and the meat are served with hot Mandarin Pancakes along with sweet bean sauce and scallions. In Canton the serving of Peking Duck is a little different. There they serve the duck's skin with steamed bread and bean sauce, followed by another course of stir-fried duck meat with bamboo shoots, mushrooms, and vegetables wrapped in a neat little pancake that is eaten with the fingers.

The following recipe for Peking Duck and soup can be served at home as a simple duck dinner.

  1 *5-pound (approximately) fresh or frozen duck*
10 *cups water*
  1 *½-inch piece gingerroot, crushed*
  1 *scallion, cut in half*
  3 *tablespoons honey*
  2 *tablespoons dry sherry*
  1 *tablespoon distilled white vinegar*
  3 *tablespoons cornstarch combined with ½ cup water*

Sauce:
  1 *teaspoon sesame oil*
 ¼ *cup* hoisin *sauce*

2 *teaspoons sugar*
2 *tablespoons water*

10 *small scallions*
20 *Mandarin Pancakes* (*page* 87) *or thinly sliced*
    white bread without crusts, steamed and served hot
½ *pound cut-up celery cabbage* (*tender parts*)
    or lettuce
Salt
Pinch of monosodium glutamate

Preparation:
Cut off the two joints of the wings from the duck and set aside along with the giblets and the neck (minus its skin). Cut off only the thin part of extra neck skin around the neck joint and leave the thick part attached to the neck area. Remove excess fat from the body of the duck. Rinse with water, drain, and dry well. Tie one end of a string around the neck bone of the duck. Use wooden picks or sticks to prop the third joints of each wing away from the body. Suspend the duck from the string in a cool airy place for at least 4 hours. In a saucepan combine the wings, giblets, neck, and 4 cups water. Bring to a boil and remove the scum. Let simmer for 1 hour. Set aside and reserve for later use.

In a large wok combine 6 cups water, ginger, scallion, and honey. Boil for 2 minutes. Add the sherry and vinegar, and stir in the cornstarch and water mixture. Bring to a boil again. Holding the duck by its string, lower it into the boiling liquid. With the string in one hand and a large spoon in the other, turn the duck from side to side until every part of the skin has been moistened. Lift the duck and repeat the dipping once more. Remove the duck and hang it again in a cool and airy place for 4 hours. To speed up drying or during hot weather, the duck can be hung in front of an air conditioner or electric fan for 2 to 3 hours each time.

To make the sauce:
Combine sesame oil, *hoisin* sauce, and sugar in a small saucepan. Stir and cook for 1 minute. Add water and stir and cook some more. Pour into a small sauce dish. Set aside; it is ready for use.

To make scallion brushes:
Use only the white parts of the scallions. Cut the scallions down to 3-inch-long pieces and trim off the roots. Use the sharp point of a knife to make lengthwise slits about 1 inch long on each end, then

cut each scallion in two. Place in a bowl of ice water for 10 minutes or until the cut parts curl up like brushes. Arrange on a dish. They are ready to use.

Cooking:

Remove the top rack from the oven and oil it. Set a broiler pan on the lower level. Pour 1 to 2 inches water into the pan. Preheat oven to 350°. Untie the duck and remove the wooden picks. Place the duck breast side up on the removed rack. Roast the duck in the middle level of the oven (about 4 inches above the broiler pan) for 30 minutes. Then turn it breast down and roast for 45 minutes. Return duck to its original position and roast for a final 30 minutes or until dark brown.

Steam the Mandarin Pancakes (see following recipe) or bread 10 minutes before the duck is done.

Carving:

Use a sharp knife to cut off the wings and drumsticks. Remove the crisp skin from the breast, side, and back; scrape off the fat, if any, between the skin and meat; then cut skin into 2 x 3-inch pieces. Arrange in a single layer on a heated platter. Remove the meat from its carcass. Slice into 2 x ½-inch pieces and arrange with wings and drumsticks on another heated platter. You may keep them warm in the oven for a few minutes. Eat as soon as possible.

Making soup:

Break or cut up the duck carcass into small pieces. Put carcass pieces into the pan that contains the wings, giblets, and neck. Bring it to a boil and cook for 10 minutes. Strain out the solid material and skim off the fat. Add celery cabbage to the strained stock. Let it simmer while serving the carved duck until the cabbage is very soft; lettuce may be used, but add it to the soup just before serving. Season with salt and monosodium glutamate. This is an excellent soup to end the meal.

To serve:
Place the platters of duck meat and skin, the heated pancakes, the dish of sauce, and the scallion brushes in the center of the table. Traditionally, each guest spreads out a pancake on his plate, dips a scallion in the sauce, and brushes the center part of the pancake with it. The scallion is then placed in the middle of the pancake with one piece each of duck skin and meat, the pancake is folded over the scallion and duck and tucked under them, one end is folded over to enclose the filling, and the whole pancake is rolled into a neat cylinder that can be picked up with the fingers and eaten. The meal is finished with the soup, which will be just ready to be served.

Yield: 4 servings or up to 10 when served with other dishes.

Pao Ping
MANDARIN PANCAKES

    2 *cups all-purpose flour*
  ⅞ *cup boiling water*
    1 *tablespoon peanut or corn oil*

Preparation:
Place the flour in a large bowl and gradually pour in the boiling water while stirring with chopsticks. Add 1 teaspoon peanut oil and stir until all the flour is damp and mealy. Let the dough cool down, then knead together until it is soft and smooth (add flour if it is too sticky). Cover the dough in the bowl with a damp cloth and let set for 15 minutes.

Knead the dough again for 2 minutes and divide into 2. Keep one half covered in the bowl and roll the other evenly ⅕ inch thick. Using a round cookie cutter, cut out pancakes 2 inches in diameter. Knead scraps into the remaining half of dough. Roll out and cut out more pancakes. The total number of pancakes should be about 28 to 30. Lightly and evenly brush 2 teaspoons peanut oil on one side

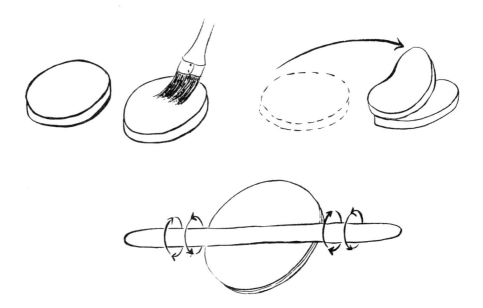

of half the pancakes. Lay an unoiled pancake on each oiled one. Roll each double pancake out on both sides, working from the center out, to about a 6-inch diameter. Cover with a cloth while you are working with the rest of dough.

Cooking:

Preheat a heavy frying pan over medium heat. Fry each pancake until it begins to bubble and small brown spots appear, then turn over. This takes less than 1 minute on each side. Remove from the pan and pull the 2 pancakes apart while still hot. Stack the thin pancakes while you cook the rest. When finished, keep the pancakes covered with a damp cloth until ready to serve.

The stacked pancakes can be wrapped in foil and frozen for future use. Before serving, steam the pancakes in a covered steamer or a colander placed over a covered pan of boiling water for 10 to 15 minutes or until pancakes are hot and pliable.

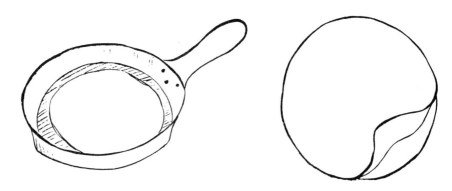

Mandarin Pancakes are served with Peking Duck and with Mu Shu Pork.

Yield: 28 to 30 Mandarin Pancakes.

Cha Ju Ke
FRIED SQUAB

炸乳鴿

2 *squabs*
3 *to 4 cups Brown Master Marinade (page 100)*
2 *cups peanut or corn oil*
1 *lemon, cut into wedges*
2 *teaspoons Roasted Salt and Szechuan Peppercorns*
   (page 208)

Preparation:
Clean the squabs. Tie one end of a string around the neck bone of each squab. Blanch squabs in boiling water for 2 minutes. Rinse, drain, and dry well.

Bring the Brown Master Marinade to a boil. Add the squabs and bring to a boil again. Cover and cook over low heat for 20 minutes. With the strings, turn the squabs twice to cook evenly. Turn heat off. Let squabs sit in the liquid, covered, for 5 minutes. Drain. Suspend the squabs by the strings in a cool airy place for at least 2 hours to dry the skin. (Reserve master marinade for reuse.)

Cooking:
In a wok or deep fryer heat the peanut oil to about 350°. Holding the squabs by the strings or setting them in deep fryer basket, fry and turn the squabs in the oil for about 5 minutes or until all sides of each squab are dark brown and well fried. Cut each squab into 6 pieces. Serve with lemon wedges and Roasted Salt and Szechuan Peppercorns on the side to use as a dip.

Yield: 2 servings or up to 6 when served with other dishes.

Note: The squab's head and giblets are delicacies; for those who like them, do not discard them. Cook them with the squabs and try them.

Ch'a Yeh Tan

茶葉蛋

TEA EGGS

Tea Eggs are convenient foods for snacks, appetizers, buffets, and best of all, for picnics. Save the egg container to pack the cooked eggs. Let the diner remove the shell himself before eating. The white will be marbled with fine dark lines and be a surprise at the picnic table. The eggs will also have a surprisingly delicious tea flavor.

12 *eggs*
 2 *tablespoons salt*
⅛ *teaspoon monosodium glutamate*
 2 *tablespoons soy sauce*
 2 *whole star anise*
 3 *black tea bags*

Place the eggs in a 1½- to 2-quart pot. Cover the eggs with water, bring to a rapid boil, cover the pot, and turn off the heat. Let stand for 20 minutes.

Pour off the hot water and tap the eggs lightly with a spoon just enough to crack them, then fill the pot with cold water. Gently tap the eggs again one by one with the back of a spoon to finely crack the shell all over. Do not peel. Return eggs to the pot and add 4 cups cold water (just enough to cover), the salt, monosodium glutamate, soy sauce, star anise, and tea bags. Bring to a boil, then reduce heat to lowest setting. Cover pot and cook for 2 to 3 hours. Turn off the heat and leave the eggs in the liquid overnight. Drain, discarding everything but the eggs. Serve hot or cold.

The eggs will keep up to 2 weeks in the refrigerator if kept in a covered container.

The eggs may be cooked on the lowest heat overnight to enhance the flavor and may be served hot for breakfast; however, make sure the heat is very low and use a pot with a tight-fitting lid.

Tan Chüan

EGG AND PORK ROLLS

蛋捲

4 *eggs*
1 *teaspoon dry sherry*

Filling:
½ *pound finely ground pork (about 1 cup)*
 2 *teaspoons cornstarch*
 1 *teaspoon salt*
½ *tablespoon soy sauce*
 2 *tablespoons cold water*

Preparation:
Beat the eggs thoroughly with the sherry and set aside.

Combine the filling ingredients in a mixing bowl. Use a spoon to mix and stir very well in one direction until meat holds together. Set aside.

Heat an 8-inch skillet until very hot. Turn heat down to low and let skillet cool off. Brush pan with a little oil. Pour ¼ of the beaten eggs into the pan and swirl around to make an 8-inch-diameter egg pancake. Before the pancake gets too dry, transfer to a plate. Repeat in this manner to make three more pancakes.

Divide meat filling evenly into 4 portions and spread 1 portion over each of the egg pancakes. Wet your hand and spread the filling evenly and thinly. Roll up tightly to seal. (To seal well, apply a few drops of leftover beaten egg from the egg bowl.) Set on a large flat plate.

Cooking:
Steam the 4 Egg and Pork Rolls on a plate in a steamer over low heat for 15 minutes. Let cool in the covered steamer for 5 minutes.

Cut the rolls into slanted slices to serve as is, or heat and serve hot on top of cooked vegetables.

Yield: 8 servings as an appetizer or 2 servings if served alone.

Variation: Finely chopped beef may be used instead of pork.

Fu Jung Tan

EGG FU JUNG

      4 *dried mushrooms*
    ⅓ *cup julienne strips of bamboo shoots*
    ½ *cup julienne strips of Chinese roast pork*
      2 *cups fresh bean sprouts, washed and drained*
      1 *scallion, finely shredded*
      5 *tablespoons peanut or corn oil*
      6 *large eggs*
  1½ *teaspoons salt*
    ⅛ *teaspoon pepper*
    ⅛ *teaspoon monosodium glutamate*
    ½ *teaspoon sesame oil*

Preparation:
Wash and soak the dried mushrooms in ½ cup warm water until soft. Drain, remove the stems, and finely shred. Set aside on a plate with bamboo shoots, roast pork, bean sprouts, and scallion.

Heat 2 tablespoons peanut oil in a wok over high heat. Stir-fry the scallion, bean sprouts, bamboo shoots, mushrooms, and roast pork for 2 minutes. Dish out and let cool. Beat the eggs thoroughly. Add meat and vegetable mixture to the beaten eggs, then add the salt, pepper, monosodium glutamate, and sesame oil. Mix well.

Cooking:
Heat a wok until very hot. Add 3 tablespoons peanut oil. Before the oil reaches the smoking point, pour the egg mixture into the wok. Using a spatula, push the eggs back and forth, then flip and turn them so that the pieces will be slightly brown outside yet soft inside. Serve hot.

Yield: 4 servings for brunch or up to 6 when served with other dishes.

Variations: Stir-fried fresh mushrooms or canned mushrooms may be used instead of dried mushrooms. Ham or stir-fried seasoned fresh meat may be used instead of roast pork.

Yu Hsiang Hung Tan

FISH-FLAVORED EGG PATTY

魚香烘蛋

1 tablespoon dried tree ears
2 cups hot water
3 tablespoons finely chopped water chestnuts or
   bamboo shoots
1 tablespoon chopped scallion
1 teaspoon minced gingerroot
½ teaspoon minced garlic

Sauce:
½ teaspoon sugar
1 teaspoon cornstarch
½ tablespoon soy sauce
1 teaspoon distilled white vinegar
¼ cup cold water

4 eggs
1 teaspoon salt
¼ teaspoon monosodium glutamate
1 teaspoon cornstarch
¼ cup cold water
5 tablespoons peanut or corn oil
¼ pound ground pork (about ½ cup)
2 teaspoons hot brown bean sauce

Preparation:
Soak the tree ears in hot water until soft. There will be about ½ cup tree ears. Wash the tree ears several times and finely chop. Set on a plate with water chestnuts, scallion, ginger, and garlic.

Combine the sauce ingredients in a cup and set aside near cooking area.

Beat the eggs with salt and monosodium glutamate until well combined. Mix cornstarch with cold water in a cup. Slowly add to the eggs while beating. Continue beating until fluffy.

Cooking:
Heat a 9-inch frying pan over moderate heat until very hot and add
3 tablespoons peanut oil to coat the entire pan. Pour egg mixture
into the pan. Cover and let cook over medium heat for about 3 minutes or until the eggs begin to puff up. Lower the heat and continue
cooking until the bottom side of the egg patty is golden in color and
completely firm. Use a spatula to turn it over. Cook for less than 1
minute. Transfer to a cutting board and cut into 1½-inch diamond-
shape pieces. Set on a serving plate. Keep warm in the oven.

Heat the same pan over moderate heat. Add 2 tablespoons peanut
oil and stir-fry the ground pork until it separates. Add hot brown
bean sauce, minced ginger, garlic, and scallion. Stir and mix for 1
minute, then add the chopped tree ears and water chestnuts. Stir
and cook some more. Mix the sauce ingredients again, then add to
the meat, stirring over high heat until the sauce thickens and coats
the meat with a clear glaze. Pour mixture over the eggs. Serve hot.

Yield: 2 servings or up to 6 when served with other dishes.

Liu Huang Tsai   溜黄蛋
STIR-FRIED EGG YOLKS

15 *dried shrimps, about ½ inch in diameter*
 2 *tablespoons dry sherry*
 3 *water chestnuts, fresh or canned*
 1 *tablespoon finely minced cooked Smithfield ham*
 8 *egg yolks*
 1 *teaspoon salt*
¼ *cup chicken broth*
 3 *tablespoons peanut or corn oil*

Preparation:
Soak the dried shrimps in sherry for 30 minutes, drain, and chop
finely. Reserve the sherry. Chop the water chestnuts and set aside
with the shrimps and ham on a plate.

Beat the egg yolks until they are a light yellow color. Add the salt
and chicken broth; beat again. Add the chopped shrimps, the reserved sherry, and the water chestnuts and mix well. This dish may
be prepared up to this point ahead of time, but add the shrimps
close to cooking time.

Cooking:

Heat a wok until very hot; add the peanut oil to coat the wok. Reduce heat to medium. Beat the egg mixture again and slowly pour into the wok. When the eggs are barely set on the bottom, push back and forth until they solidify but are still soft in texture and not dry. Transfer to a dish and garnish top with the minced ham. Serve hot.

Yield: 2 servings or up to 4 when served with other dishes.

8 MEAT

NAME OF DISH	NATURE OF DISH
Food Cooked in Master Marinade 2 kinds: Brown Master Marinade and White Master Marinade	Food cooked in master mariande is tasty and not greasy. Master marinade can be used for a variety of meats. It is easy to cook and it can be used repeatedly. Brown Master Marinade —soy sauce with spices; White Master Marinade—salt with spices. Latter lighter in flavor. Both are excellent for appetizers or for main dishes.
Stir-Fried Pork with Broccoli	A typical Chinese dish—less meat and a lot of vegetable
Steamed Ground Pork, Steamed Ground Pork with Chinese Sausage, Steamed Ground Pork with Salted Duck Eggs, Steamed Ground Pork with Salty Fish	A basic dish like meat loaf
Steamed Spareribs with Ground Rice	Spareribs coated with toasted cream of rice, then steamed
Lion's Head	Large meatballs with vegetables resembling lion's head
Honey Ham with Chestnuts	Smithfield ham cooked with rock sugar and chestnuts; lotus seed variation
Soy Sauce Pork	Braised fresh belly of pork in soy sauce; good with plain rice
Shredded Pork with Preserved Vegetable	Shredded pork with red-in-snow (salted vegetable)
Meat-Stuffed Wheat Gluten	A typical Chinese dish with both meat and vegetable protein
Stir-Fried Liver with Onion	Quick stir-fried pork or beef liver with onion
Pork with Scallion Sauce	Marinated thinly sliced boneless pork chop, panfried and served with scallion sauce
Spicy Chiang	Diced pork, pressed bean curd, and other ingredients cooked in brown bean sauce
Chinese Roast Pork	Marinated pork strips, roasted by hanging in oven; can be eaten hot or cold, or can be cooked with other ingredients
Sweet-and-Sour Pork	Pork coated with batter and deep fried, served with sweet-and-sour sauce (or use the sauce as a dip)

COOKING METHOD	LAST-MINUTE COOKING TIME REQUIRED	REGION OF COOKING BY ORIGIN OR POPULARITY
Submerging food in concentrated marinade and boiling	see chart with recipe	National, but more advanced in southern region, particularly Brown Master Marinade; the eastern region uses more White Master Marinade
Quick stir-frying	10 minutes	National and regional, depending on vegetables available and use
Steaming over medium-high heat	30 minutes	Mainly eastern and southern
Steaming over high heat	2 hours, 15 minutes	Mainly eastern or western; latter with more hot pepper
Slow simmering	1 to 2 hours	Eastern—Yangchow
Steaming and boiling	10 to 15 minutes	Eastern—with Kinhwa ham Western—with Yunnan ham
Braising in soy sauce	1½ hours	Eastern—Shanghai
Stir-frying meat and vegetable separately, then combining and cooking together	10 minutes	Eastern—Ningpo
Cooking in a wok or large frying pan	15 minutes	Eastern—Shanghai
Blanching and quick stir-frying	15 minutes	Eastern—Shanghai
Panfrying in very hot shallow oil until crisp and brown	15 minutes	Eastern—Fukien
Stir-frying and cooking together	20 minutes	Eastern—Soochow
Roasting in oven	1 hour, 15 minutes	Southern—Canton
Deep frying and stir-frying	30 minutes	Southern—Canton

NAME OF DISH	NATURE OF DISH
Spareribs with Salted Black Beans	Braised spareribs with preserved black beans, served hot with plain rice
Stuffed Peppers	Fresh hot peppers, stuffed with pork and shrimp; hot and tasty
Stir-Fried Pork with Bean Milk Skin	Dried bean milk skin soaked to soften and stir-fried with sliced pork; an all-protein dish
Spicy Pork with Bean Curd	This is an all-protein dish, easy to cook, and goes well with plain rice
Twice-Cooked Pork	A typical twice-cooked Szechuan dish; boil the pork first and stir-fry at the last minute.
Pearl Balls	Meatballs coated with glutinous rice; good-looking and easy to cook in a steamer
Pork Kidney with Spicy Sauce	A dish with a hot or plain spicy sauce; usually, the former version is served cold and the latter is served hot
Mu Shu Pork	A typical northern dish, served with Mandarin Pancakes
Braised Soy Sauce Beef	A basic braised beef that goes well with plain rice (may be served as appetizer); star anise variation
Onion Steak	A basic stir-fried beef dish; can lead to many other dishes by using different combinations of ingredients; pepper steak variation
Glazed Beef with Tomato	Marinated beef partially cooked and stir-fried at the last moment
Curry Beef	A spicy dish for serving plain rice
Ground Steak with Smoked Oysters	Served in a lettuce-leaf package; smoked oysters are considered a delicacy
Thin Steak with Vegetables	Steaks are panfried with a prepared sauce, served on lettuce and tomato; a substantial, easy-to-cook dish
Ants on the Tree	A fancy name for a fancy dish—ground beef-steak on cellophane noodles; light and tasty, with a hot bean sauce
Dried Spicy Beef	The beef is dried and has a concentrated flavor; good for appetizers and snacks
Spicy Beef with Rice Noodles	A typical Szechuan dish, dry and hot; can be served hot or at room temperature
Lamb with Leeks, Hunan Style	Typical Hunan cooking—lamb with leeks and hot, peppery condiments
Stir-Fried Lamb with Scallions	Both lamb and scallions are typically northern ingredients; beef may be substituted for lamb
Jellied Lamb	A good dish to serve cold; goes well with drinks

COOKING METHOD	LAST-MINUTE COOKING TIME REQUIRED	REGION OF COOKING BY ORIGIN OR POPULARITY
Braising and simmering	10 minutes	Southern—Canton
Browning and cooking in a frying pan	15 minutes	Southern—Canton
Quick stir-frying	10 minutes	Southern—Canton
Stir-frying	10 minutes	Western—Szechuan
Simmering and stir-frying at the last minute	10 minutes	Western—Szechuan
Steaming over medium-high heat	20 minutes	Western—Szechuan
Blanching and stir-frying	10 minutes	Western—Szechuan (with hot spicy sauce, served cold); northern (with plainer sauce, served hot)
Stir-frying	10 minutes	Northern—Peking
Slow simmering	2 hours	Eastern—Shanghai
Quick stir-frying over high heat	10 minutes	Southern—Canton
Blanching the meat and stir-frying at the last moment	5 minutes	Southern—Canton
Simmering over low heat	2 hours	Southern—Canton
Stir-frying over moderate heat	5 minutes	Southern—Canton
Panfrying and boiling sauce	10 minutes	Southern—Canton
Stir-frying with sauce	10 minutes	Western—Szechuan
Stir-frying, simmering, and baking	2 hours	Western—Szechuan
Deep frying, then stir-frying vegetables and meat	10 minutes	Western—Szechuan
Preliminary deep frying and finally quick stir-frying	10 minutes	Western—Hunan
Quick stir-frying over very high heat	5 minutes	Northern—Peking
Cooking over low heat, then chilling until jellied	none	Northern—Peking

Lu Wei

滷味

FOOD COOKED IN MASTER MARINADE

Lu is a spice-flavored concentrated marinade in which many foods are cooked simply by submerging them into the *lu* and boiling them. In China this method of cooking is usually used by small restaurants and delicatessens. They cater to those who wish to buy small amounts of different kinds of meats as appetizers to go with wine or as cold dishes. The foods can also be served hot with added sauce or cooked with vegetables.

Each shop has its own special *lu*. Some stores are famous for their good cooked foods because of their good sauces. Whatever goes into their marinade is a secret. The two recipes I have given for master marinade are similar to those prepared in the food shops.

There are two types of master marinade: One is made with soy sauce—*Hung Lu*—and is called Brown Master Marinade, and the other is made with salt—*Pai Lu*—and is called White Master Marinade.

Since salt is used instead of soy sauce in White Master Marinade, no color is added to the food and it is lighter in flavor than food cooked with soy sauce.

Food that is cooked in a master marinade is always cooked whole or in big chunks. You may use either marinade and cook in the same way.

Food cooked in Brown Master Marinade is lighter in flavor than food that is red cooked (stewed in soy sauce) and is usually served cut up and cold. It is good as an appetizer as well as a main dish. It is ideal for serving at buffet dinners.

Brown Master Marinade

Spices:
   2 *whole or 16 pods star anise*
   1 *piece dried tangerine peel, about 2 inches in diameter*
   1 *teaspoon fennel seeds*
   1 *stick Chinese cinnamon bark, about ½ x 4 inches*

1 *cup dark soy sauce*
½ *cup light soy sauce*
¼ *cup sugar*
¼ *cup dry sherry*
¼ *teaspoon monosodium glutamate*
5 *cups water*

White Master Marinade

Use the same ingredients as for the brown master marinade except for the dark and light soy sauces; use ⅓ cup of salt instead.

Cooking:
Place the spices in a double layer of cheesecloth. Tie into a bundle. To an enamel or earthenware pot add all the ingredients, including the bundle of spices. Stir and bring to a boil. Let simmer for 10 minutes.

To start any tasty master marinade, use a pot just large enough to hold the marinade and a 4- to 5-pound chicken. Bring the marinade to a boil. Add the chicken and bring to a boil again. Cook over medium-low heat for 35 to 45 minutes (do not overcook the chicken). To cook evenly turn the chicken 2 or 3 times. Turn off the heat and let the chicken cool in the liquid with the cover on for about 20 to 30 minutes. Then remove and brush with sesame oil. For other meats, follow the chart below.

Cut the chicken into small pieces or carve it. It may be served warm or cold with ½ cup hot sauce. It can also be served hot: Just heat up ½ cup sauce, pour over the cut-up chicken, drain, heat the sauce again, and pour over the chicken again until the chicken is warm. Never reheat the chicken directly over heat or in the oven, for it will dry out. The remaining liquid with the spice bundle is the basic master marinade. It may be reused. The more it is used, the better tasting it will become. Keep in the refrigerator for weeks or freezer for months.

Each time the marinade is used, supplemental seasonings (not spices) should be added: Approximately add ⅙ to ¼ of the seasoning ingredients, including the water, depending upon how much food is in the pot. By the fifth use, the spices should be replaced.

Following are other possible meats to use, the special cooking method for each, and cooking and cooling times for each. The same sauce can be reused to cook all these meats.

INGREDIENTS	SPECIAL INSTRUCTIONS	COOKING TIME	COOLING TIME
4- to 5-pound chicken	Preferably fresh killed	35–45 minutes	20–30 minutes
5-pound duck	Remove excess fat	45 minutes	30 minutes
2 squabs	Blanch in water first	20 minutes	15 minutes
12 eggs	Hard-boil and shell	30 minutes	15 minutes
2 pounds fresh pork belly or butt, shoulder, callas, knuckle	Blanch in water first; can be reheated in the sauce to serve hot (the belly is the best; do not be scared of the fat and skin).	2 hours or until tender	30 minutes
2 pounds beef shin	Blanch in water first	2 hours	30 minutes
2 pounds chicken or duck gizzards or liver	Blanch in water first	45 minutes (20 minutes for liver)	15 minutes
1 to 2 pounds pork liver	Blanch in water first	45 minutes	15 minutes
1 to 2 pig tripes	Remove all the fat, rub with salt and flour to clean, rinse well, repeat, then blanch in water	1½ hours	30 minutes
Cuttlefish	Use body only; blanch in water first	45 minutes	15 minutes
20 to 30 dried mushrooms	Wash and soak to soften and remove stems	30 minutes	10 minutes
10 squares pressed white bean curd	Cook at the lowest heat (slowly bring to simmer with the marinade)	30 minutes	20 minutes

Note: Lamb and game meats should have a separate master marinade because these meats have strong flavors.

Chieh Lan Ch'ao Jou Pien
STIR-FRIED PORK WITH BROCCOLI   芥蘭炒肉片

This typical stir-fried dish consists of a little meat and a lot of vegetable. You can cut up the vegetable and season the meat ahead of time, or if you wish to save a few minutes to avoid a last-minute rush, you may parboil the vegetable and mix it in with the meat at the last minute. Do not make the dish ahead of time and reheat it.

> 1 *bunch broccoli (about 2 pounds)*
> 2 *center-cut pork chops, cut ½-inch thick, with bones and most of the fat removed (the bones may be reserved for soup stock)*

Marinade:

> 1 *teaspoon cornstarch*
> ¼ *teaspoon sugar*
> 1 *tablespoon soy sauce*
> 1 *tablespoon water*

> 4 *tablespoons peanut oil*
> 1 *teaspoon salt*
> ½ *teaspoon sugar*
> ¼ *cup chicken broth or water*
> 1 *teaspoon cornstarch combined with 2 tablespoons water*

Preparation:

Prepare broccoli following the instructions in Stir-Fried Broccoli (page 189). You should have about 6 cups. Set aside. Slice the pork into 2 x 1 x ⅛-inch pieces. Combine with the marinade ingredients. Use your hand to mix well. Set aside.

Cooking:

Heat a wok over moderate heat until very hot. Add 2 tablespoons peanut oil, mix the pork again, and add to the oil. Stir-fry until the pork begins to separate into slices and the color of all the meat has changed. Dish out.

Heat a clean wok and add 2 tablespoons peanut oil. Stir-fry the broccoli for 2 to 3 minutes. Add salt and sugar. Mix well. Add the broth and cover the wok. Let cook over high heat for 1 to 2 minutes, stirring once during cooking. Add the cooked meat, stir, and mix. Mix the cornstarch and water very well and slowly pour into the wok, stirring until the sauce thickens and a clear glaze coats the broccoli and meat. Serve hot.

Yield: 2 servings or up to 6 when served with other dishes.

Variations: Any vegetable can be used instead of broccoli: cauliflower, green beans, celery cabbage, brussels sprouts, broccoli rab, cabbage, endive, cucumber, zucchini, or squash. Sliced beef or chicken may be used in place of the pork.

Cheng Jou Ping

蒸 肉 餅

STEAMED GROUND PORK

This steamed ground pork dish is similar to the Western meat loaf. It is easy to cook, subtle in flavor, and good for family meals with plain rice. There are many variations of this dish.

1 *pound ground pork (about 2 cups)*
1 *teaspoon salt*
1 *tablespoon soy sauce*
2 *eggs*

Preparation:
In a mixing bowl combine the ground pork, salt, soy sauce, and eggs. Stir the mixture in one direction until the meat holds together.

Transfer the meat mixture to a soup plate or an 8-inch pie plate. Smooth the surface evenly. The meat is now ready to be cooked. It can be kept in the refrigerator for several hours and removed ½ hour before cooking.

Cooking:
Set up a steamer and bring the water to a boil over medium-high heat. Steam the meat in the plate for 25 minutes. Turn off the heat and let stand for 5 minutes. Lift the hot dish from the steamer and set on a plate. Serve hot.

Yield: 4 servings or up to 8 when served with other dishes.

Variation: Ground veal or beef may be used instead of pork. Add 1 tablespoon peanut oil with other seasonings while mixing.

La Chang Cheng Jou Ping

臘腸蒸肉餅

STEAMED GROUND PORK WITH CHINESE SAUSAGE

1 *recipe Steamed Ground Pork (above)*
2 *Chinese sausages*

Use the recipe for Steamed Ground Pork, except slice the sausages crosswise into ¼-inch pieces and arrange on top of meat mixture before steaming. Steam according to directions. Serve hot.

Yield: 4 servings or up to 8 when served with other dishes.

Shien Tan Cheng Jou Ping 鹹蛋蒸肉餅
STEAMED GROUND PORK WITH SALTED DUCK EGGS

1 *pound ground pork*
1 *tablespoon light soy sauce*
1 *fresh egg*
2 *salted duck eggs*

In a mixing bowl mix the ground pork, soy sauce, and fresh egg in one direction. Separate the whites from the yolks of the salted duck eggs. Mix the salted egg whites with the meat mixture, then transfer to a soup plate or 8-inch pie plate.

Smooth the meat mixture down evenly. Make 4 dents in the meat for the duck egg yolks. Cut each yolk in half. Put a half in each space, round side up. Steam according to directions in Steamed Ground Pork (page 104). Serve hot, with white rice.

Yield: 4 servings or up to 8 when served with other dishes.

Hsien Yü Cheng Jou Ping 鹹魚蒸肉餅
STEAMED GROUND PORK WITH SALTY FISH

The Chinese have many different kinds of preserved fish. Most of them are salty but very tasty. The Ningponese are well-known for their preference for salty fish. I can predict that you will eat more rice when you have this dish, but remember to take very small portions of the fish to begin with.

1 *recipe Steamed Ground Pork (page 104)*
1 *section preserved salty fish, about 3 x 4 inches, either*
    canned, in a jar, or dried

Follow recipe for Steamed Ground Pork until the pork mixture is in a soup plate ready for steaming.

Wash and clean the fish well. Soak in cold water for ½ hour. Drain. Cut into ½-inch strips. Lay on top of meat and egg mixture and steam according to directions. Serve hot, with plain rice.

Yield: 4 servings or up to 8 when served with other dishes.

Fen Cheng P'ai Ku
STEAMED SPARERIBS WITH GROUND RICE

粉蒸排骨

1 *scallion*

Marinade:
⅛ *teaspoon ground Roasted Szechuan Peppercorns (page 208)*
⅛ *teaspoon cayenne pepper*
½ *teaspoon salt*
1 *teaspoon sugar*
2 *tablespoons soy sauce*
2 *tablespoons water*

1½ *pounds spareribs (ask the butcher to chop the spareribs across the bones into 1¼-inch-long sections) or 1 pound pork butt cut into 1 x 1½ x ¼-inch pieces*
½ *cup cream of rice*

Preparation:
Trim and wash the scallion, cut it into 1½-inch-long sections, and finely shred. Put in a large mixing bowl and add the marinade ingredients. Stir well to dissolve the salt and sugar. Set aside.

Cut the spareribs between each rib, leaving some fat, until all the ribs are separated. You will have about 3 cups. Wash and drain. Add to the bowl with the marinade. Let stand for 20 minutes. Turn and mix several times where marinating.

Toast the cream of rice in a dry frying pan for 5 minutes or until slightly brown. Let cool. Then coat each sparerib with the toasted cream of rice. Arrange with scallion shreds on a large soup plate or on a 9-inch pie plate, making 2 layers at the most. Pour the extra marinade on top. The dish is now ready to be cooked. It can be kept in the refrigerator, covered, for a few hours, but take it out ½ hour before cooking.

Cooking:
Place the dish of ribs in a steamer and steam over medium-high heat for 1½ hours or until the pork is tender. Make sure there is enough water. Have a kettle of boiling water ready on the stove to add to the steamer when it needs more water.

Check after 1 hour of steaming; if some cream of rice coating the ribs is still dry, turn meat around and continue steaming for another half hour. Serve hot.

Yield: 4 servings or up to 8 when served with other dishes.

Variation: To make Steamed Beef with Ground Rice, use ¾ pound sliced flank steak instead of pork. Add ¼ teaspoon baking soda, 2 tablespoons water, ¼ cup oil, and ¼ teaspoon cayenne to the marinade. Preferably, steam directly in a bamboo steamer lined with vegetable leaves, such as *bok choy*, lettuce, or cabbage. Steam for 15 minutes only.

Shih Tzu Tou
LION'S HEAD

獅 子 頭

- 2 *tablespoons cornstarch*
- 2 *tablespoons cold water*
- 1 *pound ground boneless pork butt with some fat (about 2 cups)*
- 3 *tablespoons soy sauce*
- 1 *egg*
- 1 *pound Chinese celery cabbage or* bok choy (6 *cups*)
- 1 *tablespoon peanut oil*
- 1 *teaspoon sugar*
- ½ *cup meat stock or water*

Preparation:
In a large mixing bowl combine cornstarch with cold water and mix well. Add the ground pork to the cornstarch mixture and mix well. Add 2 tablespoons soy sauce and the egg. Stir with chopsticks or spoon in one direction until the meat holds together. Set aside.

Trim the wilted ends from the cabbage and cut off and discard the root end. Separate the leaf stalks and wash well. Drain and dry well. Cut each stalk lengthwise into ½-inch pieces, then crosswise into 3-inch-long sections (to make about 6 cups). On the bottom of a 2- to 3-quart heatproof casserole (preferably earthenware) arrange about ¼ of the cut-up cabbage in one layer. Set aside.

Cooking:
Heat a 10-inch skillet to a very high temperature over moderate heat. Add peanut oil to coat the pan. Wet your hand with cold water and divide the meat into 4 portions, rolling each into a round ball. Put them into the skillet one at a time and fry until light brown. Gently remove the meatballs and place on the bed of cabbage in the casserole.

Stir-fry the remaining cabbage in the same skillet for 2 minutes. Add the sugar and 1 tablespoon soy sauce and pour the stock over the meatballs. Cover the casserole tightly, slowly bring to a simmer, and cook for 5 minutes. Continue to simmer for 1 hour on the stove or bake in a preheated 300° oven for 1 hour.

Serve hot directly from the casserole, or transfer the meatballs and vegetables with sauce to a deep dish.

Yield: 4 servings or up to 8 when served with other dishes.

Note: When reheating this dish, always bring it to a simmer slowly. Place an asbestos pad on the burner to avoid scorching.

Variations: To make Lion's Head with Water Chestnuts add 4 large water chestnuts, peeled and finely chopped, to the ground meat. For Lion's Head with Ham add ½ cup finely chopped ham to the ground meat. Cook in the same manner. Also, veal or beef may be used instead of pork. Add 2 tablespoons oil to the meat mixture in addition to the other ingredients.

Mi Chih Huo T'ui
HONEY HAM WITH CHESTNUTS

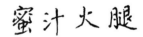

  1 *pound cooked Smithfield ham with some fat*
 ¼ *cup crushed rock sugar*
 ½ *cup hot water*
  1 *pound fresh chestnuts*
  1 *teaspoon cornstarch combined with 2 tablespoons*
      water

Preparation:
Slice the ham into 1½ x 2 x ¼-inch pieces. Arrange in a large soup plate or a shallow bowl with the slices overlapping. Sprinkle 3 table-spoons rock sugar on the sliced ham, then add hot water. Steam over medium-high heat for 30 minutes.

Boil fresh chestnuts in water for 10 minutes. Take a few at a time from the hot water, and using a sharp paring knife, shell them (you will have about 2 cups).

Set the partially cooked chestnuts in another bowl. Pour ⅔ of the sauce from the already-steamed ham over the chestnuts. Add 1 tablespoon rock sugar to the chestnuts and steam for about 1 hour or until they are very soft. Pour the chestnuts and liquid into the bowl with the ham. This dish can be prepared ahead of time up to this stage.

Cooking:
Before serving, steam the whole dish in its bowl for about 10 to 15 minutes, then pour the liquid out into a small saucepan. Keep ham and chestnuts hot in the steamer.

Cook the liquid until it is reduced to ¼ cup, mix the cornstarch and water, then add to the pan, stirring until the sauce thickens. Invert the ham and chestnuts onto a large platter with a rim, maintaining the dome shape. Pour the hot sauce on top. Serve hot.

Yield: 6 servings or up to 12 when served with other dishes.

Note: If canned chestnuts are used, omit the separate cooking.

Variation: Honey Ham with Lotus Seeds. Lotus seeds have a smooth texture and fragrant flavor. Used instead of chestnuts, they produce a delicate variation to this dish. It is important that they be freshly dried so that the texture and flavor after cooking will be better. In a saucepan cover ½ cup dried lotus seeds with hot water and bring to a boil. Cover and simmer until just soft, 1 to 3 hours, depending on the quality of the seeds; the stale ones will need longer cooking. Drain, add 2 tablespoons rock sugar, and steam for 1 hour or until soft and smooth. Pour the seeds and liquid onto the cooked ham, and steam together before serving.

Hung Shao Chu Jou
SOY SAUCE PORK

紅燒豬肉

1½ *pounds fresh lean pork belly*
  1 *scallion*
  1 *tablespoon peanut oil*
1½ *tablespoons sugar*
  ¼ *cup soy sauce*
  2 *tablespoons dry sherry*
  1 *cup hot water*

Preparation:
Cut the pork belly with skin into 1 x 2-inch chunks. Trim and wash the scallion and cut into 2-inch-long sections. Set aside with the pork.

Cooking:

Heat a heavy pot until very hot. Add 1 tablespoon oil and the pork pieces. Stir-fry the pork until the pork pieces are sealed. Add the sugar, then the soy sauce. Stir and mix for 3 to 4 minutes, add the sherry and scallion, stir, and mix some more. Add the hot water, cover, and bring to a boil. Cook over medium-low heat for 30 minutes, then over low heat for 1 hour or until the pork pieces are tender. There should be very little sauce left. Let set for 2 minutes. Skim the fat from the sauce. The dish can be reheated over low heat on a stove or in an oven. Serve hot with plain rice or steamed buns.

Yield: 6 servings or up to 10 when served with other dishes.

Note: Fresh boneless pork butt may be used instead of pork belly.

Variation: To make Soy Sauce Pork with Bamboo Shoots or Mushrooms add 1 cup sautéed roll-cut bamboo shoots or 6 to 8 sautéed dried mushrooms (washed and soaked until soft, with stems removed) 1 hour before the meat is done. You may add both ingredients to the pork. Adjust the seasoning.

Hsien Ts'ai Ch'ao Jou Szu   鹹菜炒肉絲
SHREDDED PORK WITH PRESERVED VEGETABLE

½ *pound lean pork*
 4 *large dried mushrooms*
½ *cup shredded bamboo shoots*
 1 *cup chopped red-in-snow preserved vegetable*
 4 *tablespoons peanut or corn oil*
 1 *tablespoon dry sherry*
½ *teaspoon sugar*
½ *tablespoon light soy sauce*

Preparation:

Slice the pork to a ⅛-inch thickness, then cut again into 2-inch-long julienne strips to make about 1 cup. Set aside.

Wash and soak the mushrooms in ½ cup warm water for 30 minutes. Drain the mushrooms but save the liquid (¼ cup). Remove and discard the stems and finely shred the mushrooms. Set on a plate with the shredded bamboo shoots and chopped red-in-snow preserved vegetable.

Cooking:
Heat a wok until very hot. Add 2 tablespoons peanut oil, then the pork strips. Stir-fry until the pork shreds separate. Splash sherry over the meat and add sugar and light soy sauce. Stir for 1 minute and remove food from wok.

Heat the same wok. Add 2 tablespoons peanut oil. Add the bamboo shoots, mushrooms, and preserved vegetable and stir-fry for 2 minutes. Put back the cooked pork, add the reserved ¼ cup mushroom water, cover, and cook over high heat for about 2 minutes, stirring once during this time. Serve hot or warm.

Yield: 4 servings or up to 8 when served with other dishes.

Yu Mien Chin Chien Jou
MEAT-STUFFED WHEAT GLUTEN   油麵筋嵌肉

½ *pound fried wheat gluten (about 16 balls, 1½ to 2
     inches in diameter)*

Filling:
½ *pound ground pork*
 1 *teaspoon salt*
 1 *tablespoon soy sauce*
 2 *teaspoons sesame oil*
¼ *cup minced bamboo shoots*
 2 *tablespoons water*

 1 *tablespoon peanut or corn oil*
 1 *cup chicken broth*
 1 *tablespoon soy sauce*

Preparation:
Soak fried wheat gluten in 1 quart boiling water for 5 minutes. Squeeze and stir with a large spoon. Pour the hot water off and replace with warm water. Gently squeeze and wash off most of the oil, changing water about 2 or 3 times. Press each wheat gluten ball dry and set aside.

Combine the filling ingredients and stir with chopsticks or a spoon in one direction until the meat holds together. Divide into 16 portions. Make a hole in each gluten ball for the stuffing. Stuff 1 portion of meat into each wheat gluten ball. Set aside.

Cooking:
Heat a large frying pan and add the oil. Set stuffed gluten balls in the pan. Add broth and soy sauce. Bring to a boil, then lower the heat to medium and cook, covered, for 10 minutes. Serve hot.

Yield: 4 servings or up to 8 when served with other dishes.

Variations: Ground beef, shrimp, or fish can be used as filling. This dish can be cooked with vegetables, such as snow pea pods, mushrooms, *bok choy*, or celery cabbage. For example, 2 minutes before the dish is done, add 20 cleaned, blanched snow pea pods and some cornstarch and water mixture to thicken the liquid.

Ch'ao Chu Kan
STIR-FRIED LIVER WITH ONION

炒猪肝

¾ *pound pork, calf, or beef liver*
½ *egg white*
1 *tablespoon cornstarch*
1 *tablespoon soy sauce*
3 *medium onions*

Sauce:
½ *teaspoon sugar*
¼ *teaspoon monosodium glutamate*
⅛ *teaspoon pepper*
1 *tablespoon soy sauce*
1 *tablespoon dry sherry*

4 *tablespoons peanut oil*

Preparation:
Remove the thin membrane and veins from the liver. Slice the liver into 2 x 1 x ⅛-inch pieces to make about 1 cup. Set in a mixing bowl, add the egg white, cornstarch, and soy sauce and mix well with your hand. Set aside for 15 minutes.

Cut both ends off the onions and peel them. Cut the onions lengthwise into ½-inch wedges to make about 2 cups. Separate the layers. Combine the sauce ingredients in a small cup. Set aside.

Bring 1 quart water to a boil in a large pot. Mix and add the marinated liver, stirring gently to separate the pieces in the water. Bring just to a boil again. Turn off the heat and drain immediately. Cool the liver in 1 quart of cold water for 10 seconds. Drain well. Set aside.

Cooking:
Heat a wok until hot over high heat. Add 2 tablespoons peanut oil and stir-fry the onions quickly for about 1 minute. Do not let them brown. Remove and set aside.

Heat the same wok with 2 tablespoons peanut oil. Add the partially cooked liver. Stir-fry over medium-high heat for about 2 minutes. Mix the sauce and add to the liver, stirring to blend well. Add the cooked onion and stir to heat through. Serve hot.

Yield: 3 servings or up to 6 when served with other dishes.

Variation: Chicken livers are good substitutes for the pork, beef, or calf liver.

Hsiang Yu P'ai Ku
PORK WITH SCALLION SAUCE

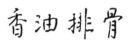

6 ¼-inch-thick center-cut pork chops (*about 1½ pounds*)

Marinade:
½ teaspoon salt
1 teaspoon sugar
1 teaspoon sesame oil
½ tablespoon soy sauce

Sauce:
½ teaspoon salt
3 tablespoons sugar
3 tablespoons distilled white vinegar
2 tablespoons soy sauce

¼ cup cornstarch
½ cup peanut oil
1 scallion, finely chopped

Preparation:
Remove the bone and most of the fat from each pork chop. Pound each chop with the back of a cleaver, then cut into 3 pieces, about 2 x 1 inch each. There should be about 2 cups of meat.

In a mixing bowl combine pork pieces with marinade ingredients and mix well. Set aside for 30 minutes.

In a small saucepan combine the sauce ingredients. Set on the stove.

Lightly coat the pork pieces with cornstarch and set on a plate. Have a platter with a rim ready.

Cooking:
Heat a skillet until very hot. Add the peanut oil, and when the oil gets hot, about 375°, put half of the pork in the pan and fry on both sides until crisp and brown. Remove to platter. Repeat with the other half of the pork.

Heat the sauce in the saucepan, add the chopped scallion, and pour over the fried pork. Serve hot.

Yield: 4 servings or up to 8 when served with other dishes.

Ch'ao Chiang
SPICY CHIANG

 6 *dried mushrooms*
 1 *pound boneless pork*
 2 *medium green peppers*
 2 *pieces seasoned pressed bean curd*
 ½ *cup diced bamboo shoots*
 ¼ *cup peanut oil*
 1 *tablespoon dry sherry*
 ¼ *cup brown bean sauce or 2 tablespoons brown bean*
    sauce plus 2 tablespoons hot bean sauce (for hot
    food lovers)
 1 *tablespoon sugar*

Preparation:
Wash and soak the mushrooms in 1 cup warm water for 30 minutes. Drain and save the water (½ cup). Cut off and discard the mushroom stems. Dice each mushroom into ¼-inch pieces. Set on a large plate. Cut the pork into ¼-inch pieces. Set on same plate as mushrooms.

Wash the green peppers. Remove seeds and pits and dice into ¼-inch pieces. Dice seasoned bean curd. Set peppers, bean curd, and bamboo shoots on a plate.

Cooking:
Heat a wok until very hot. Add 2 tablespoons peanut oil, then the pork. Stir-fry until the pork separates and the color has changed. Sprinkle the sherry into the wok. Add the mushrooms, stir, and cook for 1 more minute. Add the bean sauce and sugar. Stir and cook some more. Remove from heat and dish out.

Heat 2 tablespoons peanut oil. Add bamboo shoots and green peppers. Stir-fry until the peppers turn dark green. Add the bean curd, pork, and mushrooms and the reserved ½ cup mushroom water. Cover, bring to a boil, and let cook over medium heat for 10 minutes. Stir once or twice during this time. Serve hot or cold. This dish can be kept in the refrigerator for up to two weeks.

Yield: 6 servings or up to 10 when served with other dishes.

Note: Spicy Chiang makes a delicious sandwich meat.

Ch'a Shao

CHINESE ROAST PORK

  2 *pounds boneless pork butt or tenderloin*
  2 *cloves garlic, crushed*
  1 *teaspoon salt*
  1 *tablespoon sugar*
½ *teaspoon five-spice powder*
¼ *cup soy sauce*
  1 *tablespoon ground brown bean sauce*
  2 *tablespoons chicken broth or water*
¼ *cup corn syrup*

Preparation:
Cut the pork into four 6 x 1½ x 1½-inch irregular strips. Combine the crushed garlic, salt, sugar, five-spice powder, soy sauce, ground bean sauce, and chicken broth. Mix to blend well. Marinate the pork strips in the mixture for at least 2 hours, turning several times.

Cooking:
Preheat the oven to 325°. Fill the broiler pan with 1 inch of water and place pan in lowest part of the oven to catch drippings and prevent smoking.

Take 4 S-shaped metal curtain hooks and insert the curved tip of each into one end of a pork strip. Use the other end of the hook to

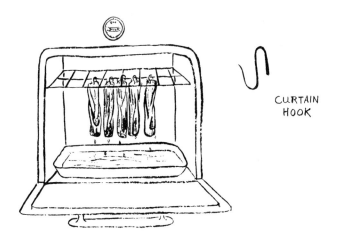

CURTAIN
HOOK

suspend the pork from the uppermost rack of the oven, directly above the broiler pan. Roast the pork for 1 hour. Increase the heat to 425° and continue roasting for 5 to 10 minutes.

Pour the corn syrup into a dish. Remove the pork strips from the oven and immediately dip the hot pork into the corn syrup, turning on all sides for even coating. Slice the strips and serve hot.

Yield: 6 servings or up to 10 when served with other dishes.

Ku Lu Jou

SWEET-AND-SOUR PORK

咕嚕肉

1 *pound pork tenderloin or boneless pork butt*

Marinade:
1 *tablespoon soy sauce*
½ *teaspoon sugar*
¼ *teaspoon salt*
⅛ *teaspoon freshly ground black pepper*
½ *teaspoon cornstarch*

2 *tablespoons peanut or corn oil*
1 *clove garlic, thinly sliced*
1 *green pepper, cored, seeded, and cut into*
   ½ *-inch cubes*
1 *peeled carrot, cut into julienne strips*
4 *tablespoons cider vinegar*
4 *tablespoons sugar*

2 *tablespoons tomato catsup*
1 *tablespoon soy sauce*
½ *cup chicken broth*

Batter:
½ *cup flour*
2 *tablespoons cornstarch*
¼ *teaspoon baking soda*
⅛ *teaspoon baking powder*
¼ *teaspoon salt*
¼ *teaspoon sugar*
½ *cup cold water*

2 *cups peanut or corn oil*
1 *tablespoon cornstarch combined with 3 tablespoons
    water*

Preparation:
Cut the pork into 1-inch cubes. Blanch in 1 quart boiling water for 2 minutes, drain, and run under cold water. Drain again and dry well. Combine the marinade ingredients, add the pork, and set aside.

In a saucepan heat the peanut oil. Add the garlic, green pepper, and carrot and stir-fry for 2 minutes. Remove and set aside near the cooking area. Add the vinegar, sugar, catsup, soy sauce, and chicken broth to the same saucepan. Stir to dissolve and set on burner to be heated later.

Combine the batter ingredients. Use a wire whisk to mix the batter until smooth.

Cooking:
Heat a wok. Add the oil and heat to about 365°. When heating, take about 1 tablespoon warm oil from the wok and add to the batter. Mix well. Mix the marinated pork again, drain, and add to the batter. With a spoon, drop half of the coated pork cubes, one by one, into the hot oil and fry for 4 to 5 minutes. The pork cubes should be crisp and brown. Fry the rest of the batter-dipped pork. Keep warm in the oven.

Bring the sauce to a boil while stirring. Add the cornstarch and water mixture and stir until the sauce clears and thickens. Add the cooked vegetables. Mix to blend. Serve either poured over the fried pork or in a sauce bowl.

Yield: 4 servings or up to 8 when served with other dishes.

Note: The fried pork can be reheated by frying for 2 to 3 minutes in 400° oil or by heating 5 minutes in a preheated 450° oven.

Variation: Add ½ cup canned pineapple chunks for extra tartness.

Tou Shih P'ai Ku

豆豉排骨

SPARERIBS WITH SALTED BLACK BEANS

1 *2-pound (approximately) rack lean spareribs (ask*
the butcher to chop the spareribs across the bones
into 1½-inch-long sections)
1 *tablespoon sugar*
3 *tablespoons soy sauce*
2 *cloves garlic*
1 *tablespoon salted black beans*
2 *tablespoons peanut or corn oil*
2 *tablespoons dry sherry*
1 *cup water*
1 *teaspoon cornstarch combined with 2 tablespoons*
water

Preparation:
Trim the fat from the spareribs and separate each rib. Place in a mixing bowl. Sprinkle sugar and soy sauce on the spareribs. Mix and toss well. Let marinate for 10 minutes.

Crush the garlic. Coarsely chop the salted black beans. Set these items on a plate.

Cooking:
Drain the spareribs, reserving the marinade. Heat a wok or pot until very hot. Add the peanut oil, then garlic, and spareribs. Stir-fry until spareribs are lightly browned on both sides. Add the salted black beans, sherry, the reserved marinade, and water. Bring to a boil, cover the pot, and reduce heat to low. Simmer for about 1 hour. Stir 2 or 3 times during cooking. There should be about ½ cup sauce left. At this stage the dish can be set aside to be reheated.

Before serving, push the meat to the sides of the pot and skim and discard the floating fat from the gravy. Heat up the ribs on low heat. Mix the cornstarch and water well and pour into the sauce.

Stir until it thickens and becomes clear. Mix with ribs to coat. Serve hot, with plain rice.

Yield: 4 servings or up to 8 when served with other dishes.

Variation: 2 tablespoons brown bean sauce may be used instead of the salted black beans.

Niang Ch'ing Chiao
STUFFED PEPPERS

醸青椒

8 *fresh hot chili peppers (about 4 inches long and*
    1 to 1½ inches wide)
1 *tablespoon cornstarch*

Filling:
½ *pound ground pork (about 1 cup)*
¼ *pound fresh shrimps, shelled, deveined, and finely*
    chopped; or 15 ½-inch-diameter dried shrimps,
    soaked and finely chopped
1 *tablespoon finely chopped pork fat or 1 strip*
    blanched fatty bacon, finely chopped
1 *small egg*
1 *teaspoon finely minced scallion*
1 *teaspoon finely minced gingerroot*
1 *tablespoon cornstarch*
1 *tablespoon light soy sauce*
¼ *teaspoon salt (if dried shrimps are used, omit the salt)*
¼ *teaspoon sugar*
Pinch of pepper and monosodium glutamate
1 *tablespoon dry sherry*

Sauce:
¼ *cup chicken broth*
½ *tablespoon light soy sauce*
½ *teaspoon sugar*

2 *tablespoons peanut oil*

Preparation:
Wash the peppers. Split each into halves and remove the seeds and pith. Sprinkle cornstarch onto the insides of the peppers.

Combine the filling ingredients and stir them well in one direction. Divide the filling mixture into 16 portions. Fill each pepper half with a portion. Smooth top with wet spatula. Set aside on a large plate.

Combine the sauce ingredients in a cup and set aside.

Cooking:
Preheat a large skillet. Add the peanut oil and lay the filled peppers in upside down. Brown them over moderate heat for 5 minutes.

Carefully turn the peppers and cook the other sides for 3 to 4 minutes. Stir the sauce ingredients and pour into the pan. Bring to a boil, cover, and let cook for 2 minutes. Carefully move the peppers meat side up to a serving plate. Serve hot.

Yield: 4 servings or up to 8 when served with other dishes.

Erh Chu Ch'ao Jou Pien   二 竹 炒 肉 片
STIR-FRIED PORK WITH BEAN MILK SKIN

¼ *pound* erh chu (*dried bean milk skin*)
 4 *dried mushrooms*
 3 *¾-inch-thick loin pork chops* (*about 1 pound*)

Marinade:
 2 *tablespoons soy sauce*
 2 *teaspoons cornstarch*
½ *teaspoon sugar*

 3 *tablespoons peanut or corn oil*
 1 *tablespoon dry sherry*
 1 *teaspoon salt*

Preparation:
Soak the bean milk skin in hot water for ½ hour or until soft and creamy in color. Cut into 1 x 2-inch rectangles. Rinse in water and drain well.

Wash and soak the dried mushrooms in ½ cup warm water for 30 minutes. Drain the mushrooms and reserve the liquid (¼ cup). Remove and discard the mushroom stems and cut mushrooms in halves. Set aside with bean milk skin on a plate.

Remove bones and most fat from each pork chop, reserving the bones for soup stock. Slice the pork into 2 x ¾ x ⅛-inch pieces to make about 1 cup. Combine the marinade ingredients. Add the pork to the marinade and use your hand to mix well. Set aside.

Cooking:
Heat a wok until very hot. Add the peanut oil, then the pork. Stir-fry until the pork slices separate. Splash the sherry over the pork, then stir and mix well. Add mushrooms and bean milk skin, stir, and cook together for 1 minute, then add salt and the reserved mushroom water. Cover the pan and cook for 5 minutes. Stir once during this time. Serve hot.

Yield: 4 servings or up to 6 when served with other dishes.

Ma P'o Tou Fu
麻婆豆腐
SPICY PORK WITH BEAN CURD

Spicy Pork with Bean Curd is very good when served on top of plain rice, as you would serve meat sauce on spaghetti.

¼   *cup dried tree ears*
 4   *3 x 3 x ¾ -inch pieces fresh firm bean curd or 2 pieces*
        4 x 4 x 1½ -inch Chinese or Japanese fresh tender
        bean curd
½   *teaspoon salt*
¼   *pound ground pork or beef (about ½ cup)*

Marinade:
½   *teaspoon sugar*
 1   *teaspoon cornstarch*
 1   *tablespoon soy sauce*
 1   *tablespoon water*
 1   *clove garlic*
 1   *tablespoon minced scallion*
⅛   *teaspoon ground Roasted Szechuan Peppercorns (page 208)*
 3   *tablespoons peanut oil*
 1   *tablespoon hot brown bean sauce*
¼   *teaspoon monosodium glutamate*
½   *cup chicken broth*
 2   *teaspoons cornstarch combined with 2 tablespoons*
        water
 1   *teaspoon sesame oil*

Preparation:

Soak the tree ears in 2 cups hot water for 30 minutes or until soft. Rinse under cold water several times, drain, and squeeze dry. You will have about 1 cup. Break them into smaller pieces if large.

Cut bean curd into ½-inch cubes. Sprinkle with the salt. Set aside. Combine the pork with the marinade ingredients and mix well in one direction until meat holds together. Set aside.

Cut the garlic into thin slices. Set aside along with the minced scallion, Szechuan Peppercorns, and tree ears.

Cooking:

Heat a wok until very hot over moderate heat and add the peanut oil. Stir-fry the garlic and scallion, then add the pork. Stir to separate the pork pieces, about 2 minutes. Add tree ears, hot bean sauce, and monosodium glutamate. Mix well. Drain the bean curd. Add to the wok and gently mix with the pork. Add chicken broth, cover, and slowly bring to a boil. Let cook together for 2 minutes over medium-high heat, stirring once during this time. Mix the cornstarch and water mixture well. Add to the wok while gently stirring until it thickens and the contents are coated with a clear glaze. Sprinke with the Roasted Szechuan Peppercorns and sesame oil. Serve piping hot.

Yield: 4 servings or up to 8 when served with other dishes.

Hui Kuo Jou   回鍋肉
TWICE-COOKED PORK

  1 *pound boneless pork butt*
½ *pound cabbage*
  1 *clove garlic*
  2 *scallions*

Sauce:
  1 *teaspoon* hoisin *sauce*
  1 *teaspoon brown bean sauce*
  2 *teaspoons hot brown bean sauce*
½ *teaspoon sugar*
  2 *tablespoons water*

  2 *tablespoons peanut oil*

Preparation:

Put the pork butt in a pot. Cover with water to 1 inch above the meat. Bring to a boil, remove scum, cover, and simmer for 45 minutes. Remove from water and let cool. Save the broth for a later use. When the pork is cooled, slice into 2 x 1 x ⅛-inch pieces. Spread on a large plate in a single layer to dry for 10 minutes.

Cut cabbage into 2 x 1-inch pieces to make about 2 cups, packed. Set on a large plate. Thinly slice the garlic and set on plate with cabbage. Trim the scallions, split, and cut into 2-inch-long sections. Set on plate with cabbage.

Combine sauce ingredients in a small cup. Set aside along with the meat and vegetables.

Cooking:

Heat a wok over moderate heat. Add the peanut oil, then the sliced pork. Stir-fry for about 3 to 4 minutes. Add garlic and scallions. Stir together with pork for 2 more minutes. Add cabbage and stir and cook a few minutes more. Mix the sauce well and add to the pork. Stir and blend over high heat. This dish has no gravy but should still be slightly moist. Serve hot.

Yield: 4 servings or up to 8 when served with other dishes.

Chen Chu Jou Wan
PEARL BALLS

珍珠肉丸

⅔ cup glutinous rice (sweet rice), washed and soaked
    in cold water for 1 hour
1 pound finely ground pork
1 small egg
1½ teaspoons salt
¼ teaspoon sugar
⅛ teaspoon monosodium glutamate
1 tablespoon light soy sauce
1 tablespoon cornstarch combined with 2 tablespoons
    water
4 water chestnuts, minced
1 tablespoon minced scallion

Preparation:

Drain the rice and allow to dry completely, then spread it out on a dry clean cloth.

In a mixing bowl combine the pork, egg, salt, sugar, monosodium glutamate, soy sauce, and cornstarch and water mixture. Using chopsticks or a spoon, mix in one direction until the meat holds together, then add water chestnuts and scallion and mix some more.

Set up a steamer with a rack or plate 1 inch smaller in diameter than the pot for steaming. Lightly oil the steamer rack or the plate. Scoop up about 1½ tablespoons of the pork mixture with your wet hands and shape into a ball about 1 inch in diameter. Evenly roll one meatball at a time in the rice, then place the ball directly on the steamer rack or plate. Leave a ½-inch space between each ball. Cover and refrigerate until ready to cook.

Cooking:
Bring the water in the steamer to a boil. Set the steamer rack in place and steam the Pearl Balls over medium-high heat for 20 minutes. Serve hot.

Yield: 30 1½-inch-diameter Pearl Balls; 8 to 12 servings as an appetizer.

Variation: Beef may be used instead of pork; add 2 tablespoons oil to the meat mixture in addition to the other ingredients.

Ma La Yao Pien
PORK KIDNEY WITH SPICY SAUCE

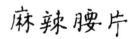

1 *pound pork kidneys (about 4 to 5 large ones)*
¼ *cup dried tree ears or 1 cup thinly sliced cucumber (peeled and seeded)*
½ *teaspoon salt (if cucumber is used)*
1 *tablespoon peanut oil*
2 *teaspoons minced fresh gingerroot*
¼ *teaspoon ground Roasted Szechuan Peppercorns (page 208)*
½ *teaspoon cayenne pepper*

Sauce:
2 *tablespoons soy sauce*
2 *teaspoons distilled white vinegar*
1 *teaspoon sugar*
2 *teaspoons sesame oil*
⅛ *teaspoon monosodium glutamate*

Preparation:

Pull away the thin membrane, if any, on the outside of each kidney. Lay the kidneys flat on a cutting board and split in two through the center. Carefully cut away and discard the cores (dark red and white parts). Holding the knife almost parallel to the board, slice the kidneys into 2 x 2 x 1/16-inch pieces. Put the kidney pieces in a large bowl of cold water. Change the water 3 or 4 times until it comes out clear.

Soak the tree ears in 2 cups hot water for 30 minutes, then wash several times. Drain and squeeze dry. Set aside. If cucumber is used, sprinkle with salt and let set for 30 minutes, then squeeze out the saltwater.

Heat the peanut oil in a saucepan and add the ginger, Szechuan Peppercorns, and cayenne pepper. Turn off the heat and add the sauce ingredients. Set aside.

Cooking:

Drain the soaked kidneys. In a large pot bring 2 quarts water to a boil. Have a colander ready. Blanch the kidney pieces for about 30 seconds or until they are just cooked and have no trace of blood. Drain and quickly run cold water over them. Drain well. Put in a mixing bowl and add tree ears and sauce mixture. Mix well and serve cold.

The kidneys can be served hot with another sauce, which makes this dish typically northern:

2 *tablespoons peanut oil*
1 *teaspoon minced fresh gingerroot*
1 *tablespoon minced scallion*

Sauce:

2 *tablespoons chunky-style peanut butter*
   diluted with 2 tablespoons hot water
1 *tablespoon light soy sauce*
¼ *teaspoon salt*
1 *teaspoon sugar*
1 *teaspoon hot brown bean sauce*
⅛ *teaspoon monosodium glutamate*

1 *tablespoon coarsely chopped coriander leaves*

Heat the peanut oil in a saucepan and add ginger and scallion. Stir and cook for 30 seconds. Add the sauce ingredients. Stir and cook until a hot thin sauce forms. Put the blanched kidneys in the sauce. Mix for 30 seconds and dish out. Serve hot, garnished with coriander.

Yield: 6 servings or up to 10 when served with other dishes as an appetizer.

Mu Shu Jou   木樨肉
MU SHU PORK

This northern Chinese egg dish is usually served with homemade pancakes (see the recipe for Mandarin Pancakes, page 87).

30 *dried tiger lily buds*
¼ *cup dried tree ears*
 2 *scallions*
½ *pound boneless pork*

Marinade:
 1 *teaspoon cornstarch*
½ *teaspoon sugar*
 1 *tablespoon soy sauce*
 1 *tablespoon water*

 4 *tablespoons peanut oil*
 3 *large eggs, broken into a bowl*
 1 *teaspoon salt*
¼ *teaspoon monosodium glutamate*
 2 *teaspoons sesame oil*

Preparation:
Soak the tiger lily buds and tree ears in separate bowls with plenty of hot water for ½ hour. Pick off and discard the hard ends, if any, of the tiger lily buds. Pile buds together, then cut into three sections to make about ½ cup, packed. Clean and wash tree ears under cold water several times. Drain and squeeze dry, cut or break into small pieces, and set with tiger lily buds on a plate. Trim the scallions, cut into 2-inch-long sections, and finely shred them to make about ½ cup. Set on the same plate.

Cut the pork into very thin slices, then cut again into julienne strips 1½ inches long to make about 1 cup. Combine the pork with the marinade, stirring in one direction so that the meat holds together. Set aside.

Cooking:
Heat a wok until very hot. Add 2 tablespoons peanut oil, and when the oil starts to smoke, turn heat down to moderate. Beat the eggs well and pour into the wok. Slowly push the eggs back and forth until dry, breaking them up with a spatula. Dish out. Heat 2 tablespoons peanut oil in the same wok. Add the shredded scallions and stir-fry for 30 seconds, then add the pork. Stir-fry until the pork turns color and separates into shreds. Add tiger lily buds, tree ears, salt, and monosodium glutamate. Stir and mix over high heat for 2 minutes. Add the eggs. Stir and cook some more. Add sesame oil and stir to blend well. Serve hot as a filling for 12 hot Mandarin Pancakes (page 87) or with steamed buns or plain rice.

Yield: 4 servings or up to 6 when served with other dishes.

Variation: 1½ cups finely shredded cabbage may be used instead of the tiger lily buds and tree ears.

Hung Shao Niu Jou   紅燒牛肉
BRAISED SOY SAUCE BEEF

This dish has a concentrated flavor and should always be accompanied by mildly flavored dishes, such as salad dishes or vegetables with meat. It is also a good idea to put half of the dish away for another meal. If stored in the refrigerator, use within the week, or if stored in the freezer, it may be kept up to a month.

 2 *pounds boneless shin of beef or chuck*
 2 *scallions, cut into 2-inch-long sections*
 4 *thin slices fresh gingerroot*
 1 *whole or 8 pods star anise*
 1 *tablespoon sugar*
½ *teaspoon salt*
 3 *tablespoons soy sauce*
 2 *tablespoons dry sherry*
 1 *cup water*

Preparation and cooking:
Trim the beef and save the fat. Cut the beef into 1-inch chunks. Heat a heavy pot until very hot, add the cut-up beef fat, and let

brown over moderate heat. About 2 tablespoons beef drippings should be rendered. If there is no fat on the beef, use 2 tablespoons peanut oil. Add half of the beef chunks, stir to seal well on all sides, and remove. Stir and seal the remaining beef. Put all the beef back into the pot and add the scallions, ginger, star anise, sugar, salt, soy sauce, sherry, and water. Mix well together and bring to a boil. Cover and cook over medium-low heat for 30 minutes. Reduce the heat to low and let simmer for about 1½ hours or until the meat is tender. Stir a few times.

There should be about ¾ cup liquid left with the beef. If there is more liquid, uncover the pot, turn heat up to high, and reduce it. Discard the star anise. Serve the heat on a platter with its sauce. Serve hot, with rice or steamed buns.

Yield: 6 servings or up to 12 when served with other dishes.

Variations: Add 2 to 3 roll-cut peeled carrots to the beef for the last 20 minutes of cooking. Add 2 to 3 dried whole red chili peppers to give this dish a peppery flavor.

For Star Anise Beef, the beef may be cooked in one piece with 2 whole star anise 1 hour longer. Let cool and keep in the refrigerator until firm, then thinly slice and serve as an appetizer with the jellied sauce.

Yang Ts'ung Niu Jou   洋葱牛肉
ONION STEAK

Flank steak is a comparatively less expensive and easy-to-slice cut of meat. This particular dish is one of the first stir-fried dishes to be taught in beginning Chinese cooking classes. It usually becomes a favorite, as it lends itself to many variations, using vegetables that are in season. Because the recipe has so many uses, it is advisable to watch price specials on flank steak and cut up the steak into 1½-inch-wide strips. Wrap each strip individually in freezer paper. Allow 10 to 15 minutes thawing time before slicing the strips into ¼-inch-thick slices. The slices are cut across the grain through the fibers to make the meat tender.

1 *pound flank steak*

Marinade:
  1 *tablespoon cornstarch*
  ½ *teaspoon sugar*
2½ *tablespoons soy sauce*
  1 *tablespoon water*

  4 *thin slices fresh gingerroot*
  3 *medium onions*
  4 *tablespoons oil*

Preparation:
Trim the fat from the flank steak and cut steak lengthwise into 1½-inch strips. Slice each strip across the grain into ¼-inch-thick pieces to make about 2 cups. Combine the marinade with the steak pieces. Use your hand to mix so that the steak will soak up the marinade. Set aside for 30 minutes. Set the fresh ginger with the steak.

Cut off both ends of the onions and peel. Cut the onions into ½-inch wedges and separate the layers to make about 3 cups. Set aside.

Cooking:
Heat a wok over high heat and add 1 tablespoon oil. Add the onion and stir-fry in the oil for about 2 minutes. Do not let the onion brown and wilt. Remove cooked onion and set aside. Wash the wok and dry over the fire.

Heat the wok until very hot. Add 3 tablespoons oil and the ginger. Mix the beef slices again and add to the hot oil, quickly stirring over high heat to separate the beef pieces. Cook until the meat just turns color. Add the cooked onion. Stir, let heat through, and mix with meat thoroughly. Do not overcook the meat. Serve hot.

Yield: 4 servings or up to 8 when served with other dishes.

Note: For extra-tender beef, dissolve ½ teaspoon baking soda in 1 tablespoon cold water and mix with 2 cups cut-up beef. This mixture may be kept in the refrigerator for as long as overnight. Add the marinade 30 minutes before cooking.

Variation: For Pepper Steak, use 2 cups cubed green pepper instead of the onions.

Fan Chia Hua Niu
GLAZED BEEF WITH TOMATO

番 茄 滑 牛

Translations of food names from Chinese to English invariably sound strange to the American. For instance, this recipe appears on most restaurant menus as Slippery Beef. An unusual cooking procedure is used to give the beef a unique coating and texture. After marinating in an egg white, cornstarch, and soy sauce mixture, the beef slices are blanched, then cooled quickly and drained well before the final stir-frying with tomatoes. This is a typical Cantonese dish.

1 *pound flank steak or top sirloin*
1 *egg white*
3 *tablespoons cornstarch*
2 *tablespoons soy sauce*
3 *medium tomatoes*
4 *thin slices gingerroot*
3 *tablespoons peanut oil*

Sauce:
1 *tablespoon soy sauce*
1 *tablespoon oyster sauce*
1 *teaspoon sugar*

Preparation:
Slice the beef into 1½ x 1 x ¼-inch pieces to make about 2 cups and place in a large mixing bowl. Add the egg white, cornstarch, and soy sauce. Mix well with your hand and set aside for 30 minutes.

Dip the tomatoes in boiling water for 10 seconds. Peel and cut each into 6 to 8 wedges. Remove the seeds and set tomatoes aside on a plate. Set the ginger on the same plate.

In a large pot bring 1 quart water to a rolling boil. Add the marinated beef and stir gently to separate the pieces. Turn off heat and drain meat immediately. Cool in 1 quart cold water. Drain well again. The meat can sit for several hours at this stage.

Cooking:
Heat a wok over medium heat until very hot. Add the oil, ginger, and tomatoes and stir-fry for 1 minute. Turn heat to high and add drained beef. Stir and mix. Add the sauce ingredients to the beef. Keep over high heat and stir until the sauce coats everything well. Serve hot.

Yield: 4 servings or up to 8 when served with other dishes.

Note: Pork or chicken may be used instead of beef. Other vegetables, such as onions, broccoli, or cauliflower may be used instead of tomatoes.

Chia Li Niu Jou
CURRY BEEF

咖哩牛肉

2 *pounds shin of beef*
2 *medium onions (about ½ pound)*
4 *cloves garlic*
3 *tablespoons peanut oil*
1 *to 1½ tablespoons imported Madras curry powder*
        (to taste)
2 *tablespoons light soy sauce*
2 *teaspoons salt*
1 *tablespoon sugar*
1 *cup beef broth*

Preparation:
Cut beef into 2 x 1-inch chunks. Cut off both ends of onions and split lengthwise in two. Cut each onion half lengthwise into ½-inch wedges to make about 2 cups, packed. Crush and peel the garlic. Set aside with the onions.

Cooking:
Heat a heavy pot. Add 1 tablespoon oil, then the onion and garlic. Stir-fry for 2 minutes. Transfer to a dish. Heat the same pot and add 2 tablespoons oil and the curry powder. Stir to mix. Add the beef. Stir-fry together for 2 to 3 minutes to seal the beef and coat with curry powder. Put the cooked onion and garlic back in the pot and add soy sauce, salt, sugar, and beef broth. Cover and bring to boil. Let cook on medium-low heat for 30 minutes. Turn down heat to low and let cook for 1½ hours or until the beef is tender. There should be about ¾ cup liquid left; if there is more, turn heat to high and cook uncovered to reduce the sauce. Serve hot, with plain rice.

Yield: 6 servings or up to 12 when served with other dishes.

Variation: Beef chuck or short ribs may be used instead of shin of beef. Also, chicken may be used instead of beef.

Hao Wei Niu Jou Sung
GROUND STEAK WITH SMOKED OYSTERS

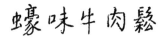

16 *lettuce leaves (bibb, Boston, or iceberg)*
¾ *pound ground top round steak (about 1½ cups)*

Marinade:
  2 *tablespoons soy sauce*
  1 *tablespoon dry sherry*
  2 *teaspoons cornstarch*
  1 *tablespoon peanut oil*

  1 *3¼-ounce can smoked oysters*
  ¾ *cup thawed frozen peas*
  3 *tablespoons peanut oil*
  1 *tablespoon oyster sauce*
  ½ *tablespoon cornstarch combined with 2 tablespoons*
      water

Preparation:
Wash lettuce leaves under cold water. Spread out to dry. Trim into
16 pieces of uniform size (4-inch-diameter cups). Keep in a plastic
bag and refrigerate until serving time.

Combine ground steak with marinade and mix well in one direction.
Set aside. Drain and finely chop the oysters and set aside on a plate
with the peas.

Cooking:
Heat a wok until very hot and add peanut oil. Add beef and stir-fry
over moderate heat until the meat separates and loses its red color.
Add oysters, oyster sauce, and peas. Stir and mix. Mix the cornstarch
and water mixture well, add to the meat, and stir until the sauce
thickens and coats the meat with a clear glaze. Transfer meat to a
heated plate and serve with lettuce leaves.

Each guest should be instructed to take a lettuce cup and place
about 2 tablespoons of the steak with smoked oysters on it. One end
of the leaf is folded over the meat about 1 inch to enclose the filling
and prevent it from dropping out. Then the whole leaf is rolled into
a cylinder and is eaten with the fingers.

Yield: 4 servings or up to 8 when served with other dishes.

Chung Shih Niu P'ai

THIN STEAK WITH VEGETABLES

中式牛排

1 *pound fillet of beef*

Marinade:
 1 *tablespoon cornstarch*
½ *egg white*
½ *teaspoon salt*
⅛ *teaspoon pepper*
 1 *tablespoon soy sauce*
 1 *tablespoon peanut oil*

 6 *tablespoons peanut oil*
½ *cup minced onion*

Sauce:
 3 *tablespoons Worcestershire sauce*
 2 *tablespoons tomato catsup*
 2 *tablespoons chicken stock*
 1 *tablespoon sugar*
½ *tablespoon soy sauce*

 1 *tomato, sliced*
 5 *to 6 lettuce leaves*

Preparation:
Slice fillet into 2 x 2 x ⅕-inch pieces. Combine the marinade ingredients with beef in a mixing bowl. Mix well with your hand and set aside for 30 minutes.

Heat 2 tablespoons peanut oil in a small saucepan. Stir-fry the minced onion until wilted. Turn off the heat and add the sauce ingredients. Set on stove to be heated at the end.

Cooking:
Heat a large skillet. Add 4 tablespoons peanut oil and panfry the steak 6 to 7 pieces at a time for about 1 minute on each side over medium-high heat. Keep warm in the oven.

Bring the sauce to a boil in the saucepan. Arrange the tomato and lettuce on a heated platter. Place the cooked steak on top, then pour the hot sauce over the steak. Serve hot, with plain rice.

Yield: 4 servings or up to 8 when served with other dishes.

Ma Yi Shang Shu
ANTS ON THE TREE

螞蟻上樹

1 2-ounce package cellophane noodles

Marinade:
  1 *tablespoon soy sauce*
  2 *teaspoons cornstarch*
  1 *tablespoon water*
  1 *tablespoon oil*

½ *pound ground beef*
  3 *tablespoons peanut oil*
  2 *tablespoons minced scallion*
  4 *teaspoons hot brown bean sauce*
  1 *teaspoon sugar*
  1 *cup beef or chicken broth*

Preparation:
Soak cellophane noodles in warm water for 20 minutes or until they are soft. Drain and cut into 4-inch-long pieces.

Combine marinade ingredients and add to ground beef. Mix well in one direction until the meat has thoroughly soaked up the marinade.

Cooking:
Heat a wok over moderate heat until very hot. Add the peanut oil, then the scallion and the beef. Quickly stir-fry until the meat separates. Add the hot bean sauce and sugar. Stir and mix well. Add the cellophane noodles, stir, and blend with the meat. Add broth and bring to a boil. Cover and let cook together for 5 minutes until the broth is all absorbed. Mix and stir twice during this time. Serve hot.

Yield: 4 servings or up to 6 when served with other dishes.

Variation: Ground pork may be used instead of beef.

Wu Hsiang Niu Jou Kan
DRIED SPICY BEEF

五香牛肉乾

This is a chewy form of beef that has a concentrated flavor and is served as a snack or appetizer. It will keep in a jar for a week or in the refrigerator for months. Pieces can be individually wrapped in plastic wrap and carried around as a snack.

1 *pound top or eye round beef*
2 *tablespoons peanut or corn oil*
2 *tablespoons sugar*
½ *cup water*
1 *scallion, cut into 2-inch-long sections*
2 *whole star anise*
½ *teaspoon cayenne pepper or crushed red chili*
    pepper (to taste)
½ *teaspoon salt*
⅛ *teaspoon monosodium glutamate*
2 *tablespoons dark soy sauce*

Preparation and Cooking:
Cut beef into ½-inch cubes. Heat a heavy saucepan until very hot. Add the peanut oil, then the beef cubes, and sugar. Stir-fry over high heat until the beef pieces are seared and sugar-coated, about 2 to 3 minutes. Add water, scallion, star anise, cayenne pepper, salt, monosodium glutamate, and soy sauce. Bring to a boil. Turn heat to medium-low, cover, and cook for 45 minutes, stirring 2 or 3 times during cooking.

During the last 10 minutes of cooking, make sure that all the liquid has evaporated, but do not let the meat burn. Discard the scallion and star anise. Spread beef in a baking dish. Place in a preheated 200° oven for 1 hour. Turn off heat and let cool in the oven. Keep in a covered jar.

Yield: 80 cubes.

Kan Pien Niu Jou Szu
SPICY BEEF WITH RICE NOODLES

乾扁牛肉絲

This is a typical Szechuan dish and should be kept dry and hot. It can be served hot or at room temperature.

1 *pound sirloin or flank steak*

Marinade:
2 *teaspoons sugar*
¼ *teaspoon monosodium glutamate*
3 *tablespoons soy sauce*
1 *tablespoon cold water*

1 *ounce rice or cellophane noodles*
2 *cups oil*
2 *cups julienne strips of celery*
½ *cup julienne strips of carrot*
½ *cup julienne strips of fresh hot chili peppers*
1 *teaspoon finely minced gingerroot*
1 *teaspoon crushed dried red peppers (to taste)*
1 *teaspoon sesame oil*

Preparation:
Slice the steak with the grain to a thickness of ⅛ inch. Cut again with the grain into 2-inch-long julienne strips. Combine the beef with the marinade ingredients in a mixing bowl. Mix well with your hand and set aside for 30 minutes.

Cooking:
Loosen the dried noodles, then deep fry them in 2 cups *very hot* (about 400°) oil for 5 seconds on both sides. (Oil can be reused.) Crush the noodles into smaller pieces and lay them in one thin layer on a platter.

Heat a wok and add 2 tablespoons of the used oil. Stir-fry the celery, carrots, and hot pepper for 2 minutes. Remove. Heat the same wok, add 3 tablespoons oil, and add the crushed dried red peppers first, then the beef and ginger. Stir-fry over high heat for about 5 minutes or until the meat is dry and no liquid is left. Lower the heat and stir for another 2 to 3 minutes. Add the cooked vegetables. Stir together for 1 minute and add sesame oil. Mix well, then pour over fried noodles.

Yield: 4 servings or up to 10 when served with other dishes.

Variation: If fresh hot chili peppers cannot be obtained, use sweet peppers instead and increase the quantity of crushed dried red peppers to 2 teaspoons. Rice noodles have more flavor than cellophane noodles. The rice noodles can be prepared ahead of time. To keep them crispy, put them in a tightly sealed tin.

Hunan Yang Jou
LAMB WITH LEEKS, HUNAN STYLE

湖南羊肉

¾ pound lean lamb, either from the leg or
    center-cut chops

Marinade:
1 small egg white
¼ teaspoon salt
2 teaspoons cornstarch
1 teaspoon oil
1 tablespoon water

Sauce:
3 tablespoons dry sherry
3 tablespoons soy sauce
1 teaspoon sugar
1 teaspoon sesame oil
2 teaspoons cornstarch
2 tablespoons water

⅓ cup sliced bamboo shoots (2 x 1 x ⅛-inch pieces)
4 dried mushrooms, soaked until soft, stems removed,
    and cut into ½-inch strips
2 to 3 dried hot chili peppers, coarsely chopped
4 cloves garlic, thinly sliced
1½ cups leeks, finely shredded into 2-inch-long sections
1 tablespoon hot brown bean sauce
2 cups peanut oil

Preparation:
Slice the lamb into 2 x 1 x ⅛-inch pieces to make about 1½ cups. Add the marinade ingredients one at a time while mixing with your hand so that the meat will soak up the marinade. Set aside.

Combine the sauce ingredients in a cup and set aside near the cooking area. Place the bamboo shoots, mushrooms, hot chili peppers, garlic, and leeks on a large plate.

Cooking:
Place a strainer over a pot near the cooking area. Heat a wok until very hot, add the peanut oil, and heat to about 300°. Deep fry the lamb, bamboo shoots, and mushrooms. Keep stirring until the lamb slices separate. As soon as the lamb loses its redness, pour contents of wok into strainer and drain.

Reheat 2 tablespoons of the drained oil in the same wok. Add the dried hot peppers and garlic and stir-fry. Then add the leeks and stir to mix. Add the hot bean sauce, cooked lamb, mushrooms, bamboo shoots, and sauce ingredients. Stir over high heat until a clear glaze coats the ingredients. Serve hot.

Yield: 4 servings or up to 8 when served with other dishes.

Variation: Beef may be used in place of lamb.

Ts'ung Pao Yang Jou

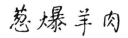

STIR-FRIED LAMB WITH SCALLIONS

¾ *pound boneless lean lamb, either from the leg or*
     center-cut chops

Marinade:
 2 *teaspoons cornstarch*
½ *teaspoon sugar*
 2 *tablespoons soy sauce*
 1 *tablespoon cold water*

 2 *bunches scallions*
 2 *cloves garlic, thinly sliced*

Sauce:
 1 *tablespoon soy sauce*
 1 *tablespoon dry sherry*
 1 *teaspoon distilled white vinegar*
 2 *teaspoons sesame oil*

 4 *tablespoons peanut oil*

Preparation:
Slice lamb into 2 x 2 x ⅛ -inch pieces to make about 1½ cups. Combine the marinade ingredients with the lamb in a mixing bowl. Use your hand to mix them well. Set aside.

Trim the roots and tips of each scallion. Cut into 2-inch-long sections and shred finely to make about 2 cups. Set garlic aside with the scallion.

Combine the sauce ingredients in a small bowl. Leave near cooking area.

Cooking:
Heat a wok until it is very hot, then add the peanut oil. When oil is hot, add the sliced garlic and lamb, stirring constantly until the

lamb pieces separate and change color. Add the shredded scallions and stir-fry over high heat with the lamb for 1 minute. Add the sauce. Stir and blend with lamb for another minute. The heat should remain high at all times. Serve hot.

Yield: 4 servings or up to 8 when served with other dishes.

Variation: Beef may be used instead of lamb.

Yang Kao
JELLIED LAMB

羊 羔

1 *pound boneless lamb*
2 *scallions, cut into halves*
2 *cloves garlic*
1 *½-inch piece gingerroot*
1 *10½-ounce can beef broth*
1 *whole or 8 pods star anise*
2 *teaspoons sugar*
3 *tablespoons soy sauce*
2 *tablespoons dry sherry*
1 *envelope (1 tablespoon) unflavored gelatin,*
   soaked in ½ cup cold water

Preparation and Cooking:
Cut the lamb into 8 large chunks and place in a pot, cover with water, and bring to a boil for 2 to 3 minutes. Rinse the lamb and discard the water. Return the lamb to the pot and add the scallions, garlic, ginger, beef broth, star anise, sugar, soy sauce, and sherry. Cook over low heat for 1½ hours or until the meat is very soft.

Take the lamb out and cool. Cut into small (about ¼-inch) pieces. Put the meat in a mold (oblong or square). Discard the scallion, garlic, ginger, and star anise. Strain the liquid with a fine sieve (a paper towel may be used over a coarser sieve). Add enough water to the strained liquid to make 1 cup. Pour back into the pot. Add the softened gelatin, heat, and stir, making sure the gelatin dissolves. Pour the sauce mixture into the mold. Refrigerate 4 hours or until the liquid jells. Scrap fat off the top and unmold. Slice into 2 x 1 x ¼-inch pieces. Serve cold.

Yield: 4 servings or up to 12 as an appetizer.

9 Fish and Shellfish

NAME OF DISH	NATURE OF DISH
Steamed Fish with Salted Black Beans	A tasty and easy-to-cook dish
Steamed Fish with Ginger Sauce	Fried ginger sauce gives the steamed fish extra flavor without frying the fish
Carp with Hot Bean Sauce, Szechuan Style	Tender texture, tasty and appetizing; timing is important
West Lake Carp, Chekiang	Delicious and subtle
Squirrel Fish	Whole fish, a Chinese preference; boned, tasty, and easy to enjoy. Winter carp may be prepared in the same manner and is a Honan recipe
Fish with Soybean Milk Skin Rolls	Deep-fried party dish with fish fillet filling
Spiced Crispy Sea Bass	Hot, spicy, and crispy whole sea bass
Puffed Fish Fillet with Seaweed	Easy to cook; goes well with drinks
Smoked Fish	Actually deep fried (eastern style), although called smoked, and can be cooked beforehand and used as a cold dish or appetizer; the northern style dish, after being deep fried, uses a smoking method like that used for smoked chicken
Braised Fish with Scallions	Small fish bones are cooked with vinegar, become tasty and edible.
Fillet of Fish with Wine Rice Sauce	The special cooking method and the wine rice sauce make all the difference

Phoenix-Tail Shrimp
   with Sweet-and-Sour Sauce
   with Roasted Salt and Szechuan Peppercorns
	A popular dish and easy to cook; two dips add a different taste

Shrimp Paste: Basic Recipe	A basic recipe for many shrimp dishes, using a meat grinder or cleaver to chop the shrimp
Fried Shrimp Balls	The fried shrimp balls can be cooked ahead of time and reheated in oven
Poached Shrimp Balls	Less oily than fried method and have a subtler taste
Shrimp Puffs	Excellent with drinks and as an appetizer
Shrimp Balls with Vegetables	Stir-fried poached shrimp balls with assorted vegetables

COOKING METHOD	LAST-MINUTE COOKING TIME REQUIRED	REGION OF COOKING BY ORIGIN OR POPULARITY
Steaming on high heat	10 to 15 minutes	Eastern and southern
Steaming the fish on high heat and stir-frying the ginger sauce	10 to 15 minutes	Eastern—Fukien Southern—Canton
Poaching the fish in plain water; stir-frying the sauce ingredients	15 minutes	Eastern and western—Szechuan
Poaching and stir-frying	15 minutes	Eastern—Hangchow, West Lake
Deep frying boneless fish with sauce	10 to 15 minutes	Eastern—Shanghai Northern—Honan
Deep frying	5 minutes	Eastern—Ningpo
Deep frying whole fish; stir-frying sauce	10 minutes	Western—Hunan
Deep frying with batter	15 minutes	Eastern—Ningpo
Deep frying and smoking ahead of time	none	Northern—Peking Eastern—Soochow
Braising over low heat for a long time and serving cold	none	Northern—Shantung
Stir-frying with wine rice sauce	10 minutes	Northern—Shantung
Deep frying with batter	15 minutes	Northern—Shantung Southern and eastern
	none	Eastern and southern
Deep frying	15 minutes	Eastern—Shanghai
Poaching in water	10 minutes	Southern—Canton
Deep frying	10 minutes	Southern—Canton
Stir-frying with vegetables	10 minutes	Southern—Canton

NAME OF DISH	NATURE OF DISH
Crab Meat with Bean Curd	Tasty, nutritious, and easy to cook
Stir-Fried Shrimp	Small, delicate shrimp; a typical Shanghai dish
Soochow Cabbage Stew with Shrimps	A Soochow (Kiangsu) specialty; good for a one-dish meal
Shrimp Sampan	A very fancy dish; good for a party, with or without wine
Shrimp in Shells, Szechuan Style	Shrimp in shell dish, with wine rice and hot bean sauce
Diced Shrimp with Croutons	The fried croutons should soak up the sauce and still remain a little crispy
Seafood Sizzling Rice	Shrimp with lobster or crab and other ingredients, poured over hot rice patties to make a sizzling noise—a dramatic dish
Stir-Fried Fresh Scallops	Cook with care to get the right delicate texture
Steamed Clam-Egg Custard	Natural flavor and subtle taste
Drunken Crabs	Saltwater crabs marinated in wine, always served cold and raw
Squid with Preserved Vegetable	A typical Chinese dish; goes well with rice
Stir-Fried Lobster with Black Bean Sauce	A popular dish, cooked with salted black beans; shelled and precooked shrimps, scallops, or cut-up crabs may be used instead of lobster
Fried Oysters	Deep-fried oysters with a light batter; rich and tasty
Chinese Cabbage with Abalone in Cream Sauce	Cabbage cooked in cream sauce, soft and smooth; abalone or ham add extra flavor
Stir-Fried Clams with Chinese White Turnip	Shucked clams stir-fried with turnip or leeks; a subtle family meal with rice
Conch, Dipping Method	A Canton delicacy that needs a special cooking technique and timing
Dried Scallops and Seaweed	Needs careful attention in preparation and cooking

COOKING METHOD	LAST-MINUTE COOKING TIME REQUIRED	REGION OF COOKING BY ORIGIN OR POPULARITY
Stir-frying and cooking over moderate heat	10 minutes	Eastern—Shanghai Northern—Shantung
Preliminary deep frying and finally quick stir-frying	10 minutes	Eastern—Shanghai
Stir-frying separately, then cooking together; last-minute stir-frying	10 minutes	Eastern—Soochow
Deep frying in oil	5 minutes	Southern—Canton
Stir-frying	10 minutes	Western—Szechuan
Deep frying the croutons and stir-frying the shrimp	5 minutes	Northern—Tsinan
Stir-frying the shellfish and deep frying the rice patties	10 minutes	Western—Szechuan
Preliminary deep frying and finally quick stir-frying	10 minutes	Eastern—Shanghai
Steaming over low heat	30 minutes	Eastern—Ningpo
Marinating in prepared liquid	none	Eastern—Ningpo
Quick stir-frying	10 minutes	Eastern—Shanghai
Stir-frying the lobster and the sauce ingredients	10 minutes	Southern—Canton
Deep frying batter-coated oysters	10 minutes	Southern—Canton
Stir-frying the cabbage and steaming before serving	15 minutes	Southern—Canton
Stir-frying	15 minutes	Southern—Canton
Dipping in boiling broth, then quickly stir-frying	10 minutes	Southern—Canton
Steaming, then deep frying at the last minute	5 minutes	Northern—Peking

STEAMING FISH

The Chinese method of steaming fish is extremely easy. The food is tasty because not a drop of sauce is lost in the pot, and the steam seals in the flavor. The cooking is odorless because the steam does not transmit the fishy flavors. The fish must be fresh, and thick fish, such as sea bass, yellow pike, or red snapper, should weigh about 1½ pounds. Most important of all, the fish should be whole, with head and tail intact. If you have never eaten the head or tail, please try it. I can assure you that you will like it.

General Rules for Steaming Fish

Use only very fresh fish that weigh about 1½ pounds, including head and tail, or double the recipe and use two fish in the same dish. Always lay them in one layer head to head, not on top of each other. Choose the dish to fit the pot or Chinese steamer that you are using to steam. The dish should be at least 1 inch smaller in diameter than the pot to allow the steam to rise. It should also be deep, like a soup or pie plate, for the rim is needed to hold the sauce. To improvise a steamer, the perfect shape would be an oval roasting pan with domed cover. Use a high rack to raise the dish. Fill the pan with water about 1½ to 2 inches deep but at least 1 inch below the dish. Bring the water to a boil first to avoid steam burns, turn off the heat, then put the fish in the dish. Cover. Turn heat on medium high and steam for 15 minutes with sea bass, red snapper, yellow pike, striped bass, or whiting; for flatter fish, such as gray sole, flounder, or butterfish, 8 to 10 minutes is sufficient. Wear rubber gloves to remove the fish from the steamer when done. Either transfer to a heated serving platter or put the dish with the steamed fish on top of another platter. The latter is the preferred way of serving steamed fish, since it is best eaten when it is very hot.

To test whether the fish is done or not, push a pair of chopsticks into the thickest part of the fish. If the flesh is soft and there is no resistance to the prodding, the fish is done. Otherwise, continue steaming for 2 to 3 minutes.

Tou Shih Cheng Yü
STEAMED FISH WITH SALTED BLACK BEANS

豆豉蒸魚

1 tablespoon salted black beans
1 scallion
1 tablespoon finely shredded fresh gingerroot
1 1½-pound (approximately) sea bass, with
   head and tail
1 teaspoon salt
½ teaspoon sugar
1 tablespoon dry sherry
1 tablespoon soy sauce
1 tablespoon peanut or corn oil

Preparation:
Coarsely chop the salted black beans. Split the scallion and cut into 2-inch-long sections. Set the beans, scallion, and ginger aside on a plate.

Clean and wash the fish, then dry with paper towels. Cut 3 or 4 slashes crosswise on both sides of fish. Sprinkle fish inside and out with the salt. Place the entire fish in a dish with a rim and sprinkle the sugar, sherry, soy sauce, and peanut oil all over the top of the fish.

Cooking:
In a steamer bring water to a boil. Place the fish and dish on steaming rack. Cover tightly and steam over high heat for about 15 minutes. Remove dish and place on top of another larger platter to serve. Serve hot.

Yield: 2 to 3 servings or up to 6 when served with other dishes.

Yu Lin Yü

STEAMED FISH WITH GINGER SAUCE

油淋魚

Although this fish is steamed, it has a fried flavor.

1 *2-pound (approximately) gray sole, with head*
   and tail
1 *tablespoon dry sherry*
2 *scallions*
2 *tablespoons finely shredded gingerroot*
3 *tablespoons peanut or corn oil*
3 *tablespoons light soy sauce*
½ *teaspoon sugar*

Preparation:
Ask the fish dealer to trim off the fins and part of the side fat of the sole. Cut the whole fish into 5 or 6 pieces through the backbone. Wash the fish and pat dry with paper towels. Arrange the fish pieces into a fish shape in a dish with a rim and sprinkle the sherry on top.

Split the scallions and cut into 2-inch-long sections. Set the scallions and ginger aside on a plate.

Cooking:
In a steamer bring water to a boil. Place fish with dish on steaming rack. Cover tightly and steam over medium high heat for about 10 minutes.

Heat a wok until hot. Add the peanut oil and the shredded ginger. Turn heat to moderate and let the ginger cook in the oil for 1 minute, then add shredded scallion; stir-fry for 10 seconds. Add the soy sauce and sugar and remove from heat.

Take the fish and plate out. If a lot of liquid has accumulated in the plate, pour off so that about 2 to 3 tablespoons remain. Pour the hot ginger and scallion sauce over the fish. Serve hot.

Yield: 2 to 3 servings or up to 6 when served with other dishes.

Variation: For Steamed Fish, Hunan Style, use as seasonings 1 tablespoon salted black beans, 4 dried chili peppers, 1 tablespoon soy sauce, 1 teaspoon sugar, ¼ teaspoon monosodium glutamate, and the same amounts of gingerroot, scallions, and sherry. Fry the chili peppers until dark, add the shredded ginger, black beans, and scallions, and then cook in the same manner.

Tou Pan Chi Yü

CARP WITH HOT BEAN SAUCE, SZECHUAN STYLE

豆瓣鯽魚

Poaching a fresh winter carp gives it finer texture. There are two different kinds of sauce that make its cooking in western and eastern China distinctively different: hot bean sauce and sweet-and-sour sauce, respectively.

   1 1½- to 2-pound (approximately) whole live carp
        (preferably winter carp)
  ½ cup finely chopped scallions
   2 cloves garlic, thinly sliced
   2 tablespoons finely chopped gingerroot

Sauce:
   3 tablespoons hot brown bean sauce
1½ tablespoons soy sauce
   2 tablespoons dry sherry
  ½ teaspoon salt
  ½ tablespoon sugar
1½ cups Rich Meat Stock (page 221)
1½ tablespoons cornstarch

   3 tablespoons peanut or corn oil
   2 teaspoons sesame oil

Preparation:
Ask the fish dealer to scale the fish and remove the gills, stomach, and other organs through the head of the fish, leaving the fish stomach whole and closed. This will keep the carp body from breaking when poached. If this cannot be done, only the appearance of the fish will be altered.

Set aside the scallions, garlic, and ginger on a plate. Combine the sauce ingredients in a small bowl and set aside near the cooking area.

Cooking:
In a large roasting pan bring to a boil enough water to cover the fish. Place the fish in the water and bring to a boil again. Cover and turn off heat. Let sit for 20 minutes. To test whether the fish is done or not push a pair of chopsticks into the thickest part of the fish. If red liquid does not flow and the flesh is soft, the fish is done. Otherwise, bring water to a boil again. Cover and turn off heat. Let sit for 5 minutes more.

Heat a wok and add the peanut oil. Stir-fry the ginger, garlic, and scallions for 1 minute. Mix the sauce ingredients well and pour into the wok. Stir until the sauce thickens and forms a clear glaze. Stir in the sesame oil. Keep warm over low heat.

Drain off the poaching water and carefully slide the cooked fish onto a large oval platter with a rim. Pour the hot sauce over the fish. Serve hot, with plain rice.

Hsi Hu Ts'u Yü

西湖醋魚

WEST LAKE CARP, CHEKIANG

1 1½- to 2-pound (approximately) whole live carp
    (preferably winter carp)
⅓ cup finely shredded young gingerroot (if old ginger-
    root is used, use 2 tablespoons, finely chopped)

Sauce:
  1 teaspoon salt
  3 tablespoons sugar
  1 tablespoon soy sauce
  2 tablespoons dry sherry
¼ cup wine vinegar
  1 cup Rich Meat Stock (page 221)

  3 teaspoons peanut or corn oil
½ teaspoon white pepper

Preparation:
Have the carp prepared as described in the recipe for Carp with Hot Bean Sauce, Szechuan Style (page 147).

Soak the shredded ginger in cold water for 30 minutes. Drain and pat dry. Combine the sauce ingredients in a small bowl.

Cooking:
Poach the whole fish in the same manner as for Carp with Hot Bean Sauce. Heat the peanut oil in a saucepan. Mix the sauce ingredients well and pour into the saucepan. Stir until the sauce thickens. Keep warm over low heat. Slide the drained cooked fish onto a large oval platter with a rim. Sprinkle on the pepper and shredded ginger, then pour the hot sauce over it. Serve hot.

Yield: 4 servings or up to 8 when served with other dishes.

Variations: Sea bass, striped bass, or yellow pike may be used instead of carp.

Sung Shu Yü
SQUIRREL FISH

松鼠魚

  2 *sea bass or yellow pike, without heads (about
      1½ pounds each)*
 ¼ *cup plus 1½ tablespoons cornstarch*
  2 *cups peanut oil*
 ½ *cup canned sliced mushrooms*
  1 *small onion, cut into quarters, with layers separated*
  1 *small carrot, scraped and sliced with a
      serrated knife*
  4 *water chestnuts, sliced*
 ¼ *cup thawed frozen peas or ¼ cup diced green pepper*
  1 *clove garlic, thinly sliced*

Sauce:
  1 *teaspoon salt*
 ¼ *cup sugar*
 ¼ *cup distilled white vinegar*
  2 *tablespoons catsup*
  1 *tablespoon soy sauce*
  1 *teaspoon sesame oil*
  1 *cup chicken broth*

 ¼ *cup water*

Preparation:
Wash and dry the fish. Lay the fish on its side, and with a cleaver or sharp knife split it in half, cutting along the backbone; cut off the backbone at the base of the tail. Score the flesh side of the fillets with crisscrossing diagonal cuts ½ inch apart and almost down to the skin. The fish should be separated into two fillets with skin intact and joined at the tail. Dredge with ¼ cup cornstarch to cover the entire surface of the fish as well as inside the scores. Set aside.

Heat a wok or deep fryer, add the peanut oil, and heat to 385°. Shake the fish to remove any excess cornstarch and lower them into the hot oil. Ladle the hot oil over the top of the fish, then gently shift the fish once or twice to make sure they are evenly fried. Fry the fish until the flesh is firm and brown, about 5 to 6 minutes. Lift fish out and place skin side down on a platter. Keep the oil in the wok; the fish will be fried again.

Set aside the mushrooms, onion, carrot, water chestnuts, peas, and garlic on a large plate.

Heat a small saucepan, add 2 tablespoons of the oil from the wok, and stir-fry the garlic first, then the carrot and onion, stirring for 2 minutes. Add the water chestnuts, mushrooms, and peas and cook some more. Turn off the heat and dish out. Add the sauce ingredients to the saucepan and mix well. Leave the saucepan on the burner to be heated at the end.

Cooking:
Heat the oil until very hot again (385°) and refry the fish for about 2 to 3 minutes or until crisp outside. Lift out fish skin sides down onto a heated platter. Keep warm in the oven.

Bring the sauce to a boil. Mix 1½ tablespoons cornstarch with the water and slowly add to the sauce, stirring until sauce thickens. Add the cooked vegetables just to heat through. Pour over the fish and serve hot.

Yield: 6 servings or up to 10 when served with other dishes.

Variation: Winter carp can be cooked in the same manner. This dish becomes Sweet-and-Sour Whole Carp and is a Honan recipe.

Fu Yi Huang Yü
FISH WITH SOYBEAN MILK SKIN ROLLS

腐衣黄魚

Filling:
½ *pound fillet of pike, gray sole, or flounder*
½ *teaspoon salt*
¼ *teaspoon sugar*
⅛ *teaspoon monosodium glutamate*
Dash of white pepper
 1 *teaspoon dry sherry*

 6 *pieces* fu-yi (*very thin dried soybean milk skin*),
     about 10 x 14 *inches and in half-moon shapes*

½ *egg, lightly beaten*
2 *tablespoons flour*
¼ *teaspoon salt*
2 *teaspoons minced scallion*
3 *tablespoons cold water*
2 *cups peanut or corn oil*
Roasted Salt and Szechuan Peppercorns (*page* 208)

Preparation:
Cut the fillet into 1½-inch-long julienne strips. Combine the cut fish with the rest of the filling ingredients and mix. Refrigerate for 30 minutes.

Handle the bean milk skin carefully; any broken pieces can be patched up. Place each sheet between damp cloths. Set aside for 15 to 20 minutes or until they are soft enough to handle.

Using a wire whisk, mix egg with flour, salt, scallion and water into a thin paste. Set aside.

On a tray or table loosely stack the bean milk skins, three at a time, so that each rounded edge is extending 2 inches beyond the next one. Brush each skin lightly with the paste. Divide the fish filling into 2 portions. Take one portion of filling and place it along the straight side of the bean milk skin. With your hands, shape it into a 10-inch cylinder or sausage. Loosely cover the filling with the straight side of the bean milk skin, tuck in both ends, and roll until the skin is entirely rolled up. Repeat procedure with remaining stack of bean milk skins and filling. At this stage the rolled bean skins can be kept in the refrigerator, covered, for a few hours.

Cooking:
Using a sharp cleaver, chop each roll diagonally into 1½-inch-long sections. Heat the oil to about 365°. Fry a few pieces of roll at a time for 3 to 4 minutes or until golden and crispy. Drain well. Serve hot, with Roasted Salt and Szechuan Peppercorns.

Yield: 16 3 x 1½-inch pieces bean milk skin rolls

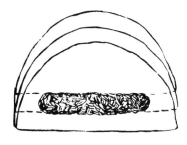
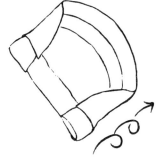

Tsui P'i Yü

SPICED CRISPY SEA BASS

脆皮魚

1 1½- to 2-pound (approximately) whole sea bass,
   with head and tail
½ cup cornstarch
6 cups peanut or corn oil

Sauce:
2 whole dried red chili peppers, coarsely chopped
4 cloves garlic, thinly sliced
¾ cup finely minced scallions
3 tablespoons finely minced gingerroot
¼ cup dried mushrooms, soaked in warm water until
   softened, stems removed, and finely minced
⅓ cup finely minced bamboo shoots
½ cup Wine Rice, storebought or homemade
   (see Wine Rice, page 298)
⅓ cup dry sherry
2 tablespoons hot brown bean sauce
2 tablespoons soy sauce

1 teaspoon cornstarch combined with 2 tablespoons
   water

Preparation:
Clean the fish and dry well with paper towels. Lay the fish flat and
cut slashes crosswise on both sides at a 45° angle to the table toward
the fish's head. Cut almost to the bone. Make the slashes about ¾
inch apart. Dredge with cornstarch to cover the entire surface of the
fish, as well as inside the slashes. Rub into the slashes, over the top,
and inside the fish. Set aside.

Heat a large wok, add the peanut oil, and heat until very hot, about
385°. Lifting the fish by the tail, dip the fish into the hot oil, lift up,
and dip again, making sure that the oil gets in between the slashes
on both sides of the fish. Then lay fish down in the oil. After a few
minutes, ladle the hot oil over the top of the fish. Gently shift the
fish once or twice to make sure it does not stick to the bottom of the
wok. When the fish looks crisp and golden and bubbles cease to
form on top of the oil and the sizzling noise stops (about 10 to 12
minutes), the fish is done.

Transfer the fish to a platter. You can prepare the fish up to this
point ahead of time and leave it at room temperature. Save the wok
with the oil; the fish will have to be refried.

Cooking:

Just a few minutes before serving, prepare the sauce ingredients: Place on a large plate the red chili peppers, garlic, scallions, ginger, mushrooms, and bamboo shoots. Combine the Wine Rice, sherry, hot bean sauce, and soy sauce in a cup.

Heat another wok or pan, and add 3 tablespoons of the oil that was used to fry the fish before. Add the dried red chili peppers and garlic, then the scallions. Stir-fry for 1 minute. Add the ginger, mushrooms, bamboo shoots, and the sauce mixture from the cup. Stir and cook for 1 more minute. Mix the cornstarch and water well. Pour over the sauce and stir until it thickens and forms a clear glaze. Add 2 tablespoons oil and mix into the sauce. Keep warm on the stove.

Heat the wok with the used frying oil until it is very hot and refry the fish for about 3 to 4 minutes. Place the fried fish sitting upright on its belly on a serving platter. With a towel, hold and press down gently on the neck of the fish so that the slashed belly sides protrude. Pour the hot sauce over the fish. Serve hot, with plain rice.

Yield: 6 servings or up to 10 when served with other dishes.

T'ai T'iao Huang Yü
苔 條 黄 魚

PUFFED FISH FILLET WITH SEAWEED

1 ¾ *-pound gray sole or flounder fillet*

Marinade:
  1 *teaspoon salt*
  1 *teaspoon dry sherry*
  ⅛ *teaspoon white pepper*
  ⅛ *teaspoon monosodium glutamate*

  ¾ *cup flour*
  ¾ *cup water (approximately)*
  2 *teaspoons baking powder*
  2 *cups peanut oil*
  2 *tablespoons* tai tiao *(green seaweed) or Japanese* aonoriko
  1 *teaspoon Roasted Salt and Szechuan Peppercorns (page 208)*

Preparation:

Cut fish fillet into 2 x 1-inch strips. Combine the marinade ingredients, mix well, add the fish strips, mix well, and set aside in the refrigerator.

Mix together in a bowl the flour and water until they form a smooth batter. The consistency should be such that the batter will form a thin coating on the fish. Add the baking powder. Mix again and set aside.

Cooking:
Heat a wok or deep fryer. Add the peanut oil and heat until a haze forms above it or until it reaches 350°. Add the seaweed and 1 tablespoon warm oil to the batter and blend well, then add the fish strips.

Put 8 to 10 pieces of batter-coated fish one by one into the hot oil. Fry until light brown on both sides. Remove and drain on paper towels. Keep warm in the oven while you fry the remaining fish. Serve hot. Sprinkle the Roasted Salt and Szechuan Peppercorns on the puffed fish.

Yield: 4 servings or up to 8 when served with other dishes; 10 servings as an appetizer.

Variation: For Puffed Fish Fillet, omit the seaweed.

Hsün Yü
SMOKED FISH

> 3 *pounds live carp (preferably winter carp; ask the fish dealer to clean the fish, split them in two with center bones, split the heads, and cut each half in two)*
> 2 *scallions, cut into 2-inch-long sections*
> 6 *thin slices fresh gingerroot*
> 2 *teaspoons salt*
> ¼ *cup soy sauce*
> ¼ *cup sugar*
> ¼ *cup dry sherry*
> 2¼ *cups peanut oil*
> ½ *teaspoon five-spice powder*

Preparation:
Rinse the fish, drain, and dry thoroughly with paper towels. Slice each half into ½-inch-wide pieces (you may ask fish dealer to do this for you). Put the sliced fish in a large bowl and marinate with the scallions, ginger, salt, and soy sauce. Mix well and let soak for at least 4 hours or preferably overnight.

Place the fish in a colander to drain. In a large deep dish combine the sugar, sherry, and 2 tablespoons peanut oil. Mix until the sugar dissolves. Set aside near the stove. Have a large skillet ready with 2 tablespoons peanut oil in it on the stove over low heat.

Cooking:
Heat a wok until very hot and add 2 cups peanut oil. Heat over moderate heat to about 350°. Put 5 or 6 pieces of fish in the oil. Do not crowd them. Fry one side at a time for about 10 minutes. Do not turn the fish before a dark brown crust has formed; if they are turned too soon, the fish will break. The fish will be quite dry. Take out and lay in the sherry-and-sugar–mixture dish. Turn on the other side, let soak in the sherry-sugar, then put in the heating skillet. Cook both sides for 2 to 3 minutes. Sprinkle on a little five-spice powder. Cook the remaining fish in the same manner. Before serving, cut the fish into smaller pieces. Serve cold.

Yield: 12 servings as an appetizer.

Note: The cooked fish can be kept in a covered container for weeks in the refrigerator and for months in the freezer.

Su Yü

BRAISED FISH WITH SCALLIONS

酥魚

2 *pounds whole butterfish (6 medium or 8 small)*
6 *scallions, cut into 4-inch-long sections*
1 *teaspoon salt*
2 *tablespoons sugar*
¼ *cup soy sauce*
6 *tablespoons distilled white vinegar*
2 *tablespoons peanut oil*
2 *tablespoons sesame oil*

Preparation and cooking:
Clean, wash, and dry the fish. Set the scallions aside with the fish.

Using an earthenware or pyroceram pot, put ⅓ of the cut-up scallions in the bottom, then a layer of fish on top of it. Continue alternating layers of fish and scallions. Season with the salt, sugar, soy sauce, vinegar, peanut oil, and sesame oil.

Put an asbestos pad (flame-tamer) on the burner. Place the pot on the pad and bring to a boil. Cook over low heat for about 2 hours.

Do not move the fish but baste with sauce several times. There should be very little sauce left when the dish is done. The small bones become so soft that you can eat all parts except the spine. Serve cold.

Yield: 6 servings or up to 10 when served with other dishes.

Tsao Liu Yü Pien
FILLET OF FISH WITH WINE RICE SAUCE

糟溜魚片

1 *pound gray sole, yellow pike, or sea bass fillets*

Marinade:
½ *egg white*
 1 *tablespoon cornstarch*
 1 *teaspoon salt*

¼ *cup dried tree ears*
 2 *cloves garlic*

Sauce:
½ *cup Wine Rice* (*page* 298)
 2 *tablespoons dry sherry*
½ *teaspoon salt*
½ *teaspoon sugar* (*if Wine Rice is very sweet, omit the sugar*)
 2 *teaspoons cornstarch*

 2 *cups peanut oil*

Preparation:
Remove any bones found in the centers of the fillets. Cut fillets lengthwise into 2 strips. Slice each half almost parallel with the grain but at a slight angle into 2 x 2-inch squares. Set the fish in a bowl and add the marinade. Mix well with your hand. This may be kept in the refrigerator for a few hours.

Soak the dried tree ears in 2 cups boiling water for 30 minutes. Clean and wash several times. Drain, squeeze dry, and set aside on a plate. Thinly slice the garlic. Set aside the garlic with the tree ears.

To make the sauce: Use a double layer of cheesecloth to squeeze the wine rice juice out; add water and squeeze some more to make

½ cup wine rice juice; discard the rice. Add sherry, salt, sugar, and cornstarch. Set aside.

Have a strainer over a pot near the cooking area. Heat a wok until very hot, add the oil and heat to about 280° to 300°. Add the fish and gently stir and cook until most of the color has changed. Pour the oil and fish into the strainer. Don't let fish drain too long because juices may run out too. Remove to a dish.

Heat the same wok. Add 2 tablespoons oil from the drained oil and stir-fry the garlic and tree ears. Stir the sauce ingredients well. Add to the pan, stirring until the contents are coated with a light, clear glaze. Add the cooked fish, then 1 tablespoon oil. Stir gently and cook just to heat through. Serve immediately.

Yield: 4 servings or up to 8 when served with other dishes.

Note: This dish can be prepared with 5 tablespoons of oil instead of 2 cups. Use a slotted spoon to remove fish pieces and use remaining oil in the wok to stir-fry the garlic and tree ears.

Variations: Use fillets of winter carp with skin and change the sauce: 2 teaspoons vinegar, 2 teaspoons soy sauce, ½ cup broth (instead of ½ cup Wine Rice); increase sugar to 2 teaspoons. This becomes the Honan dish, Sweet-and-Sour Boneless Carp. Fillet of Fish may be prepared without the garlic, tree ears, and sauce, but add 1 tablespoon chopped scallion and 1 teaspoon minced gingerroot while stir-frying the fish in the 5 tablespoons oil. Serve immediately.

Cha Ta Hsia

炸 大 蝦

PHOENIX-TAIL SHRIMP

1 *pound raw shrimp with shells (about 24 to 28)*
1 *teaspoon salt*
⅛ *teaspoon white pepper*
1 *teaspoon dry sherry*

Batter:
¾ *cup flour*
¾ *cup cold water*
2 *teaspoons baking powder*

2 *cups peanut or corn oil*
Sweet-and-Sour Sauce (page 159) or Roasted Salt and
 Szechuan Peppercorns (page 208)

Preparation:
Remove all but the tail sections of the shells of the shrimps. Split
the back sides with a knife and remove the sandy veins. Rinse, drain,
and dry well. In a small bowl combine the salt, pepper, and sherry.
Add the shrimps and blend well. Set aside in the refrigerator.

Combine the batter ingredients in a bowl and mix until smooth. To
test the consistency, dip a shrimp into the batter; it should be covered with a thin coating. Set aside.

Cooking:
Heat a wok or a deep fryer. Add the oil and heat until a haze forms
above it or it registers about 350°. Add 1 tablespoon of the hot oil to
the batter and mix well. Now hold the shrimps by the tail and dip
them one by one into the batter, but leave the tail parts uncovered.
Then place them in the hot oil and fry on both sides for about 2
minutes or until golden brown. Fry about 6 to 8 at a time. Drain.
Keep warm in the oven while you fry the remaining shrimps. Serve
hot. Accompany with Sweet-and-Sour Sauce or Roasted Salt and
Szechuan Peppercorns as dips.

Yield: 8 servings as an appetizer.

Note: The shrimps may be reheated in a 400° oven for about 7 to 8
minutes.

T'ien Suan Chih
SWEET-AND-SOUR SAUCE

甜酸汁

¼ cup sugar
¼ cup cider vinegar
2 tablespoons tomato catsup
1 tablespoon soy sauce
1 tablespoon peanut or corn oil
½ cup chicken broth
2 teaspoons cornstarch combined with 2 tablespoons
water

Combine sugar, vinegar, catsup, soy sauce, peanut oil, and chicken broth in a small saucepan. Stir and cook the sauce to boiling point. Mix the cornstarch and water well and add to the saucepan, stirring until the liquid thickens. Serve in a sauce bowl.

Hsia Chiu Jung
SHRIMP PASTE: BASIC RECIPE

蝦球茸

1 pound raw shrimp, shelled and deveined
¼ cup ground fresh pork fat or blanched fatty bacon
2 egg whites
1 tablespoon cornstarch
1½ teaspoons salt
⅛ teaspoon white pepper
1 tablespoon dry sherry
1 ½-inch piece fresh gingerroot

Preparation:
Use a fine-holed plate in a meat grinder to grind the shrimps and pork fat separately twice; or chop them into a fine paste with a cleaver.

Beat egg whites until foamy, add the ground pork fat, and beat together for about 2 minutes. Add the ground shrimps, cornstarch, salt, pepper, and sherry. Place the ginger in a garlic press and squeeze out the juice into the shrimp mixture. Beat another 2 minutes. The shrimp paste can be kept covered in the refrigerator for a few hours or overnight.

This shrimp paste can be used for Fried Shrimp Balls (below), Poached Shrimp Balls, Shrimp Puffs (page 161), Shrimp Balls with Vegetables (page 162), and Shrimp Ball Soup (page 231).

Note: If frozen shrimps are used, add ¼ teaspoon monosodium glutamate to the shrimp in addition to the other ingredients.

Cha Hsia Chiu
FRIED SHRIMP BALLS

炸蝦球

2 *cups peanut or corn oil*
1 *recipe Shrimp Paste* (*page* 159)
Roasted Salt and Szechuan Peppercorns (*page* 208)
    to taste

Preparation:
Have ready a small bowl of cold water, a measuring tablespoon, and a large plate lined with paper towels.

Heat a wok until very hot. Add the peanut oil and heat over medium heat to about 300°. With your left hand, take a handful of the shrimp paste and squeeze your fingers into a fist, forcing the paste up between your thumb and forefinger and forming a ball about the size of a walnut. With your right hand, use a measuring tablespoon dipped in the cold water (to prevent sticking) to scoop up the shrimp ball and drop it into the hot oil. Repeat until you have made all the balls. Fry for about 2 minutes or until they float to the top and become fluffy. Turn the balls to fry evenly. Do not overcook. Overfrying will shrink the shrimp balls. Transfer the balls to the paper-lined plate to drain. Serve hot with Roasted Salt and Szechuan Peppercorns.

Yield: 24 1-inch-diameter shrimp balls.

Note: The shrimp balls can be frozen and reheated in a preheated 350° oven.

Chu Hsia Wan

煮蝦丸

POACHED SHRIMP BALLS

1 *recipe Shrimp Paste* (*page* 159)

Preparation and Cooking:
Make shrimp balls, using the same technique as in the recipe for Fried Shrimp Balls (page 160). Instead of dropping shrimp balls into oil, drop them into a pot containing 4 cups cold water. Turn the heat to medium. When the water just begins to boil, gently stir once and turn heat to low and let simmer for 2 minutes. Drain and run under cold water.

Prepare a container with enough cold water to cover the shrimp balls. Keep the shrimp balls in the cold water until ready to use. They can be stored, covered in cold water, for up to 1 week in the refrigerator. They are now ready to be used in the recipes for Shrimp Ball Soup (page 231) and Shrimp Balls with Vegetables (page 162).

Yield: 24 1-inch-diameter Shrimp Balls.

Hsia Ho

蝦盒

SHRIMP PUFFS

10 *very thin slices of white bread* (*about* ⅛ *inch thick*)
½ *recipe Shrimp Paste* (*page* 159)
 2 *cups peanut or corn oil*

Using a 1½-inch-diameter round cookie cutter, cut each slice of bread into four round, crustless disks. Use a sandwich spreader to spread about 1 heaping tablespoon shrimp paste on each bread disk and top with another one. Deep fry Shrimp Puffs 7 or 8 at a time in 325° to 350° peanut oil for 1 to 2 minutes on each side. Remove and drain on paper towels. Keep warm in the oven while you fry the rest.

Yield: 20 Shrimp Puffs.

Note: Shrimp Puffs can be frozen and reheated in a 400° oven for about 7 to 8 minutes.

Ch'ao Hsia Wan
SHRIMP BALLS WITH VEGETABLES

炒蝦丸

  6 *dried mushrooms*
 ½ *cup sliced bamboo shoots*
  1 *scallion, cut into 2-inch-long sections*
  1 *cup snow pea pods, cut-up broccoli, or cut-up*
    bok choy
  3 *tablespoons peanut or corn oil*
 12 *Poached Shrimp Balls (page 161)*
  1 *teaspoon salt*
 ½ *teaspoon sugar*
 ⅛ *teaspoon monosodium glutamate*
 ½ *cup water*
  1 *teaspoon cornstarch combined with 2 tablespoons*
    water

Preparation:
Wash and soak the mushrooms in ½ cup warm water for 30 minutes. Drain and cut off and discard the stems. Cut each mushroom in half. Set aside on a large plate with sliced bamboo shoots, scallion, and green vegetable.

Cooking:
Heat a wok until hot. Add the peanut oil and stir-fry the bamboo shoots, mushrooms, and vegetables for 2 minutes. Add the scallion and Shrimp Balls, stir, and mix. Add the salt, sugar, monosodium glutamate, and water. Cover and let cook on medium-high heat for about 3 to 4 minutes. Stir the cornstarch and water well and slowly pour into the wok, stirring until all ingredients are coated with a light, clear glaze. Serve hot.

Yield: 2 servings or up to 6 when served with other dishes.

Hsieh Fen Tou Fu

CRAB MEAT WITH BEAN CURD

蟹 粉 豆 腐

A minimum of cooking time is required for this dish, if cooked crab meat is used and if all the ingredients are assembled before starting to cook.

  1 *cup fresh, frozen, or canned crab meat*
  2 *4 x 4 x 1½ -inch pieces tender bean curd (4 pieces*
        3 x 3 x ¾ -inch firm bean curd may be also used)
1½ *teaspoons salt*
  4 *tablespoons peanut or corn oil*
  1 *teaspoon finely chopped fresh gingerroot*
⅛ *teaspoon ground white pepper*
  2 *tablespoons finely chopped scallion*
½ *teaspoon sugar*
¼ *teaspoon monosodium glutamate*
½ *cup water*
  2 *teaspoons cornstarch combined with 2 tablespoons*
        water

Preparation:
Remove crab cartilage, if any, and break meat into small pieces. Set aside. Cut bean curd into 1 x 1 x ¾ -inch cubes. Sprinkle ½ teaspoon salt on bean curd. Set aside with crab meat.

Cooking:
Heat a wok until very hot and add 2 tablespoons peanut oil. Add the ginger, crab meat, and pepper and stir-fry for 1 minute. Dish out.

Drain the bean curd and discard the liquid. Heat the same wok and add 2 tablespoons peanut oil. Add the scallion and bean curd and gently stir-fry for 30 seconds. Add 1 teaspoon salt, sugar, monosodium glutamate, and water. Slowly bring to a boil and cook, covered, over moderate heat for 2 minutes.

Add the cooked crab meat and combine just to heat through. Mix the cornstarch mixture well and pour over the meat, gently lifting the crab meat and bean curd until they are coated with a clear glaze. Transfer to a platter or shallow bowl and serve piping hot.

Yield: 4 servings or up to 8 when served with other dishes.

Variation: Cooked shrimps may be used instead of crab meat, and this dish becomes Shrimp with Bean Curd.

Ch'ao Hsia Jen
STIR-FRIED SHRIMP

炒蝦仁

> 1 *pound small raw shrimp, or frozen miniature*
> *shrimp, shelled and deveined*
> 1½ *teaspoons salt*
> 1 *egg white*
> 2 *teaspoons cornstarch*
> 1 *cup lard, or peanut or corn oil*
> ½ *teaspoon sugar*
> 2 *teaspoons dry sherry*
> 1 *teaspoon sesame oil*
> 1 *teaspoon cornstarch combined with 2 tablespoons*
> *water*

Preparation:
Split each shrimp in two. Place in a bowl, add ½ teaspoon salt, egg white, and cornstarch. Use your hand to mix well. Let it marinate for at least 1 hour or at most overnight in the refrigerator. If frozen shrimp are used, thaw completely and dry them, then add ¼ teaspoon monosodium glutamate in addition to the other ingredients.

Cooking:
Place a strainer over a pot near the cooking area. Heat a wok. Add lard and let it just warm up to about 280°. Add the marinated shrimps and quickly stir to separate them. When most of the shrimps' color has changed, pour the shrimps and lard into the strainer to drain. As soon as the lard has drained away, set the shrimps on a dish.

Heat the same wok over high heat and add 2 tablespoons of the drained lard. Add the partially cooked shrimps, 1 teaspoon salt, and sugar. Stir and mix until thoroughly heated. Splash on the sherry and sesame oil. Mix the cornstarch and water well and slowly pour over the shrimp, stirring until the sauce thickens and forms a clear glaze. This last-minute cooking process should be completed within 2 minutes. The dish should be served at once.

Yield: 4 servings or up to 8 when served with other dishes.

Variation: Add ½ cup blanched fresh peas or thawed frozen peas and ¼ cup cooked Smithfield ham, cut into pea-size pieces, to the partially cooked shrimps and finish cooking as above.

Note: If the shrimps smell fishy, serve Chinese vinegar or wine vinegar in a small side dish along with them.

Hsia Jen Lan Hu

SOOCHOW CABBAGE STEW WITH SHRIMP   蝦仁爛糊

Soochow Cabbage Stew with Shrimps is a specialty from Soochow in the province of Kiangsu. It can be used as a one-dish meal. It is delicious served with plain rice and can be partly cooked ahead of time.

½ *pound raw shrimp, shelled and deveined*

Marinade:
 ½ *egg white*
 1 *teaspoon cornstarch*
 ½ *teaspoon salt*

 ½ *pound lean pork*
 2 *pounds celery cabbage*
 7 *tablespoons peanut or corn oil*
 2 *tablespoons dry sherry*
1½ *teaspoons salt*
 ½ *cup water*
 2 *tablespoons cornstarch combined with ¼ cup*
      water
 ¼ *cup diced cooked Smithfield ham*

Preparation:
Dice the cleaned shrimps. Put them in a mixing bowl, add the marinade ingredients, and use your hand to mix well. Refrigerate for 30 minutes or longer.

Cut the pork into ⅛-inch-thick slices and cut again into julienne strips to make about 1 cup. Set aside.

Rinse the entire cabbage with cold water. Separate the cabbage leaf stalks. Cut each stalk into 2-inch sections, then cut again lengthwise to a width of ¼ inch. Keep stalks and leaves separate. There will be about 12 cups cabbage all together.

Cooking:
Heat a wok until very hot. Add 2 tablespoons peanut oil. Stir-fry the sliced pork over medium heat until it separates into shreds and changes color, about 2 minutes. Sprinkle 1 tablespoon sherry over the pork and mix well. Remove the pork and set aside.

Heat a clean wok or pot. Add 3 tablespoons peanut oil. Stir-fry the cabbage stalks for about 3 minutes over medium heat. Add the cabbage leaves. Stir together for another 2 minutes or until they are wilted. Add salt and the cooked pork. Stir and mix well and add water. Cover, bring to boil, and let it cook over low heat for 20 minutes or until the cabbage is very soft. The stew can be made in advance and reheated. Finish the cooking at the last minute.

Stir the cornstarch and water thoroughly. Slowly pour into the cabbage stew, stirring until it thickens and comes to a boil again. Keep warm in the oven while making the shrimp topping.

Heat the wok until hot. Add 2 tablespoons oil and stir-fry the shrimps until they separate and are just cooked, about 1 minute. Sprinkle on 1 tablespoon sherry. Add the diced him. Remove from heat and pour over the cabbage stew. Serve hot.

Yield: 4 servings or up to 8 when served with other dishes.

Niang Ta Hsia
SHRIMP SAMPAN

釀 大 蝦

18 *large raw shrimp (about 1 pound)*

Filling:
½ *egg white*
 1 *teaspoon cornstarch*
½ *teaspoon salt*
¼ *teaspoon sugar*
 1 *teaspoon dry sherry*
 2 *tablespoons finely chopped pork fat or blanched finely chopped fatty bacon*
 2 *tablespoons finely chopped water chestnuts*

½ *teaspoon salt*
12 *2 x ½ x ⅛-inch strips cooked Smithfield ham*

Batter:
½ *cup flour*
¼ *cup cornstarch*
½ *teaspoon salt*
½ *cup chicken broth*
 2 *teaspoons baking powder*

 2 *cups peanut or corn oil*

Preparation:

Shell 6 shrimps and remove the sandy veins. Wash, drain, and dry well. Chop the shrimps into a smooth pulp and set in a mixing bowl. Add the filling ingredients. Mix very well. Set aside.

Take the remaining 12 shrimps and remove all the shells except those from the tail sections. Split each shrimp laterally with a knife along its underside, but do not cut through the back. Remove the sandy veins. Rinse and dry the shrimps and sprinkle them with salt.

Open each shrimp flat, with its cut side up. Along the center lay a strip of ham, then use a sandwich spreader to spread about 1 tablespoon of the shrimp mixture on top of the ham. Dip the spreader in cold water to smooth the top of the shrimp mixture. Set the shrimps in one layer on a plate.

Combine the batter ingredients and mix into a smooth batter. Set aside.

Cooking:

Heat a wok or deep fryer. Add the peanut oil and heat until a haze forms or the oil reaches about 350°. Add 2 teaspoons of the warm oil to the batter. Mix well. Take one shrimp and dip it into the batter, leaving the tail uncoated. Hold the shrimp by the tail with your fingers, and at the other end use the support of a spoon (to prevent the filling from sliding off). Deep fry the body first for about 10 seconds, holding the tail upright and bending the body upward slightly in the oil with the spoon. The shape of the shrimp will then resemble a sampan. Drop the shrimp into the oil and fry the whole shrimp on both sides for about 2 minutes or until golden brown and crisp. Follow the same procedure for the remaining shrimps, frying six at a time. Drain and keep warm in the oven while you fry the others.

Yield: 3 servings or up to 6 when served with other dishes.

Note: Shrimp Sampan may be reheated in a 400° oven for 5 minutes.

Kan Shao Ming Hsia
SHRIMP IN SHELLS, SZECHUAN STYLE   乾燒明蝦

Shrimps cooked in the shells have more flavor. In order to get the full flavor of shrimp, one must learn how to remove the shells in one's mouth without the help of the fingers. Bite off a section of shrimp and use the teeth and tongue to separate the shrimp from the shell. Remove the shell from the mouth with chopsticks. Removing shells in this manner is an art, but we believe the special flavor of the shrimps in the shells is worth the extra effort.

This shrimp-in-shell dish, cooked Szechuan style, uses Wine Rice as an important ingredient. The shrimps are cooked with Wine Rice for its special fragrance. Two tablespoons hot bean sauce can be added to make this a hot pepper dish, but omit salt.

1 *pound raw shrimp in their shells (about 25 to 28 shrimps)*
2 *scallions*
1 *tablespoon finely chopped gingerroot*
3 *tablespoons peanut or corn oil*
2 *tablespoons dry sherry*
1½ *teaspoons salt*
1 *tablespoon tomato catsup*
½ *cup Wine Rice (page 298) with some of its original juice*

Preparation:
Leave the shrimps whole unless large shrimps are used, in which case cut each shrimp into two or three pieces. Use scissors to cut off the shrimps' feet. Open a small section of each back and pull out the vein. Wash the shrimps. Drain and dry thoroughly with paper towels.

Split and finely chop the scallions to make about ¼ cup. Set aside on a small plate with the finely chopped ginger.

Cooking:
Heat a wok over high heat until very hot. Add the peanut oil, ginger, scallions, and shrimps. Brown both sides of the shrimps for about 3 minutes or longer if the shrimps are larger. Splash the sherry over the shrimps. Add the salt and catsup. Stir and mix for 2 more minutes. Add the Wine Rice with the juice. Stir and mix, and cook a few minutes more. Serve hot.

Yield: 4 servings or up to 8 when served with other dishes.

Variation: For Shrimps in Shells, Shanghai Style, use soy sauce and sugar instead of salt, catsup, and Wine Rice.

Mien Pao Pao Hsia Jen
DICED SHRIMP WITH CROUTONS

麵 包 爆 蝦仁

This is a famous northern dish from Tsinan in Shantung province. The fried croutons should not soak up much sauce from the dish, for the consistency of the sauce is very important.

1 *pound raw shrimp*

Marinade:
  1 *egg white*
  2 *teaspoons cornstarch*
½ *teaspoon salt*

  3 *slices firm white bread without crusts*
½ *cucumber*

Sauce:
  2 *teaspoons cornstarch*
  1 *teaspoon salt*
½ *teaspoon sugar*
⅛ *teaspoon white pepper*
  1 *tablespoon dry sherry*
½ *cup chicken broth*

1½ *cups peanut or corn oil*

Preparation:
Wash and clean the shrimps before removing their shells. Slit the back of each shrimp and carefully remove the black sand vein. (The shrimps need not to be washed again if the vein is not broken and no sand is left on shrimps.) Dice the shrimps, add the marinade ingredients and use your hand to mix well. Refrigerate for 30 minutes or longer.

Dice the bread into ⅜-inch cubes. You will have about 1½ cups croutons. Cut the cucumber lengthwise and remove seeds. Cut into ⅜-inch dice, leaving the skin on, to make about ¾ cup. Set aside with the croutons.

Combine the sauce ingredients in a small cup. Set aside near the cooking area.

Cooking:

Heat the peanut oil in a wok to about 350° and fry the croutons until golden brown. Dish out and spread on paper towels to drain.

Place a strainer over a pot near the cooking area. Heat the oil again to about 280°, add the shrimps, and quickly stir until the shrimps separate into pieces and the color changes. Then pour the shrimps and oil into the strainer. As soon as the oil drains away, remove the shrimps to a dish.

Heat the wok again. Add 2 tablespoons of the drained oil and stir-fry the diced cucumber for 1 minute. Stir the sauce well, and slowly pour into the wok, stirring until the sauce acquires a clear glaze. Add the cooked shrimps, mix with the sauce, and cook to heat through only. Add the croutons and stir once. Dish out and serve immediately.

Yield: 4 servings or up to 8 when served with other dishes.

San Hsien Kuo Pa
SEAFOOD SIZZLING RICE

三鮮鍋巴

½ *pound small raw shrimps, shelled and deveined*

Marinade:
½ *egg white, lightly beaten*
 1 *teaspoon cornstarch*
½ *teaspoon salt*

 1 *cup 1-inch pieces of cooked lobster or king crab meat*
½ *cup sliced, fresh mushrooms or ¼ cup canned,
       sliced mushrooms*
¼ *cup sliced water chestnuts*
½ *cup snow pea pods or peas*

Sauce:
 1 *cup chicken broth*
½ *tablespoon sugar*
½ *teaspoon salt*
⅛ *teaspoon pepper*
 1 *tablespoon cornstarch*
 1 *tablespoon soy sauce*

1 *tablespoon distilled white vinegar*
3 *tablespoons catsup*

3 *cups peanut or corn oil*
6 *Rice Patties (page 254), about 2 x 2 inches*

Preparation:
Clean the shrimps and split into halves lengthwise. Combine the shrimps with the marinade ingredients, and using your hand, mix well. Refrigerate for 30 minutes or longer. Put the lobster meat, mushrooms, water chestnuts, and pea pods on a plate. Combine the sauce ingredients in a small bowl.

Cooking:
Heat the oil in a wok or deep fryer until very hot, about 400°. Fry the Rice Patties 2 pieces at a time in the oil until light brown and crispy on both sides. (This takes only 10 seconds.) Drain and set aside on a heatproof platter.

Place a strainer over a pot near the cooking area. Heat the oil again to about 280°. Add the shrimps and quickly stir until the shrimps separate into pieces and the color changes. Then pour the shrimps and oil into the strainer. As soon as the oil drains away, remove the shrimps to a dish.

Before Serving:
Preheat the oven to 475°. Put the Rice Patties on the heat proof platter in the oven for 7 to 8 minutes. In the meantime heat a wok or pan with 2 tablespoons of the drained oil over moderate heat. Stir-fry the mushrooms, water chestnuts, and snow pea pods for 2 minutes. Mix the sauce ingredients and slowly pour into the wok, stirring until the sauce forms a clear light glaze. Turn the heat to high and add the cooked lobster and shrimp, mix, and cook to heat through only. Pour into a serving bowl.

Take the hot fried Rice Patties out of the oven. At the dinner table pour the cooked shrimps and vegetables over the patties to make a sizzling noise in front of the diners. Serve immediately.

Yield: 4 servings or up to 8 when served with other dishes.

Note: You may stir-fry the marinated shrimps in 3 tablespoons oil until the shrimps begin to change color. Remove and set aside.

Ch'ao Hsien Kan Pei
STIR-FRIED FRESH SCALLOPS

炒鮮干貝.

1 *pound fresh sea scallops*

Marinade:
1 *small egg white*
2 *teaspoons cornstarch*
1 *teaspoon salt*
¼ *teaspoon sugar*

2 *teaspoons finely minced fresh gingerroot*
2 *tablespoons finely chopped scallion*

Sauce:
1 *tablespoon light soy sauce*
1 *tablespoon dry sherry*
Dash of white pepper
1 *teaspoon cornstarch*
1 *tablespoon water*

1 *cup peanut or corn oil*

Preparation:
Pull off and discard the small tough outer parts of each scallop. Rinse scallops several times in cold water. Drain and dry well with paper towels. Slice the scallops into ¼-inch-thick pieces and set in a bowl. Combine the marinade ingredients and add to the scallops. Use your hand to mix well so that the scallops soak up the marinade. Set in the refrigerator at least 30 minutes or at most overnight.

Set aside the ginger and scallion on a plate. Combine the sauce ingredients in a cup.

Cooking:
Place a strainer over a pot near the cooking area. Heat a wok over high heat until it is very hot. Add the oil and heat moderately to about 280°. Add scallops and stir quickly until they separate into pieces. When most of the scallops have changed color, pour the scallops and oil into the strainer to drain. As soon as the oil has drained away, set the scallops on a dish.

Reheat the same wok, add 2 tablespoons of the drained oil, and turn heat to high. Add the ginger and scallion, stir, then add the partially cooked scallops. Stir and toss in the oil just to heat through. Mix the sauce well and pour over the scallops, stirring until the sauce thickens and coats the scallops with a light, clear glaze. Serve hot.

Yield: 3 to 4 servings or up to 6 when served with other dishes.

Variation: For Stir-Fried Fresh Scallops with Spicy Sauce use different sauce ingredients: ¼ teaspoon cayenne pepper, 1 teaspoon sugar, 1 teaspoon cornstarch, ⅛ teaspoon monosodium glutamate, 1 teaspoon distilled white vinegar, 1 tablespoon soy sauce, 1 tablespoon dry sherry.

Note: You may use 5 tablespoons oil to stir-fry the scallops instead of 1 cup oil. With a slotted spoon remove the scallops, and use the remaining oil in the wok to stir-fry the ginger and scallion.

Ha Li Cheng Tan
STEAMED CLAM-EGG CUSTARD

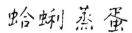

  4 *eggs*
½ *teaspoon salt*
  2 *teaspoons peanut or corn oil*
Juice of 1 *dozen clams, combined with enough
     chicken broth to make* 2 *cups*
  1 *dozen clams* (*ask fish dealer to open the clams;
     reserve their juice*)

Preparation:
Beat the eggs until whites and yolks are well-combined. Add the salt and peanut oil to the eggs. Gradually beat the warm clam juice–chicken broth liquid into the egg mixture. Combine the clams with the egg mixture. Pour this mixture into a heatproof bowl with a 2- to 3-inch rim.

Cooking:
Place the bowl on a rack in a wok or a pot containing water up to 1 inch from the rim of the bowl. Cover and bring to a boil. Let cook on low heat for about 30 minutes or until the custard is smooth and a knife inserted in the center comes out clean. Serve hot.

Yield: 6 servings as a first course.

Variation: One-half cup ground pork, beef, or chopped shrimp may be used instead of clams. If pork or beef are used, use 2 cups chicken broth (no clam juice). Adjust the seasonings. This dish may be baked in the oven instead of steamed. Combine beaten eggs, salt, oil, clams, clam juice, and broth as directed above. Pour into 6 6-ounce custard cups. Set cups in a baking pan. Add boiling water to a depth of 1 inch. Bake at 350° for about 30 minutes or until a knife inserted in center comes out clean.

Tsui Hsieh

DRUNK CRABS

In China fresh water is not free from parasites and other bacteria. Therefore, raw food must be carefully cleaned and thoroughly cooked before it is eaten. Crabs are found in both fresh water and saltwater, but only crabs fished from saltwater should be used to make Drunken Crabs.

  1 *dozen live hardshell female crabs*
 ½ *cup coarse salt*
  2 *cloves garlic*
  2 *½-inch pieces fresh gingerroot*
  1 *cup dry sherry*
 ½ *cup distilled white vinegar*
 ⅛ *teaspoon white pepper*

Open the live crabs' hard shells (you may ask the fish dealer to do this). Discard the shells but remove and reserve the roe that is attached to the shells. Remove and discard the gills and sand bags. Brush and rinse the crabs' bodies and drain well. Cut off and discard the second and third joints of the legs. Cut the bodies in sixths, each piece with a leg or two attached.

Lay one layer of cut-up crabs, including the roe, in a 1-quart wide-mouth jar. Sprinkle on some salt. Add another layer of cut-up crab and sprinkle on more salt. Continue alternating crab and salt to the top of the jar.

Crush the garlic. Crush the ginger. Put the garlic in a mixing bowl and add the sherry to soak for 5 minutes. Add vinegar, pepper, and ginger, mix, and pour into the jar of crabs. Sprinkle some more salt on top. Cover tightly and keep in the refrigerator. This will be ready to eat in 1 week and will keep for months.

The sauce may not completely cover the crabs, so tilt the jar a few times during storage. This is a small side dish to be served with plain rice. Always serve cold and raw.

Note: Drunken Crabs should be made only during the spring months, when the female crabs have plenty of roe.

Ch'ao Yu Yü Szu
SQUID WITH PRESERVED VEGETABLE

炒尤魚絲

  1 *pound fresh squid*
1½ *teaspoons salt*
  1 *cup loosely packed finely chopped canned red-in-
     snow preserved vegetable*
 ½ *cup finely shredded bamboo shoots*
  1 *teaspoon minced fresh gingerroot*
 ¼ *cup peanut or corn oil*
  1 *tablespoon dry sherry*
  1 *teaspoon sugar*

Preparation:
Under running cold water pull off the purplish black skin and re-move the internal cartilage from each squid. Remove the heads; use only the bodies, the caudal fins, and the firm arms attached to the heads of the squids. Cut the meat into julienne strips about 1½ inches long. There should be 1½ cups cut-up squid. Put the squid in a mixing bowl and add 1 teaspoon salt. Squeeze with your hand for a minute. Rinse in cold water several times and drain well.

Set aside the chopped red-in-snow, shredded bamboo shoots, and minced ginger on a plate.

Cooking:
Heat a wok and 2 tablespoons peanut oil. Stir-fry the ginger first, then add the squid and stir together for 1 minute. Splash the sherry over the squid and add ½ teaspoon sugar and ½ teaspoon salt. Mix, stir, and quickly remove the squid and sauce. Heat the same wok and add 2 tablespoons peanut oil. Stir-fry the bamboo shoots and red-in-snow for 1 minute. Add ½ teaspoon sugar and mix well. Add the cooked squid, then mix and cook together just to heat through. Serve hot, warm, or cold.

Yield: 2 to 3 servings or up to 8 when served with other dishes.

Variation: The squid may be slashed in a crisscross pattern on the inside of the body and then cut into 1 x 2-inch pieces. The meat will curl up after cooking.

Ch'ao Lung Hsia
STIR-FRIED LOBSTER WITH BLACK BEAN SAUCE

1   1½-pound live lobster (ask fish store to split the
     live lobster lengthwise and crack the big claws)
1   tablespoon salted black beans, coarsely chopped
1   scallion, finely minced
1   clove garlic, thinly sliced
½   cup ground pork
3   tablespoons peanut or corn oil
1   tablespoon dry sherry
1   teaspoon salt
½   teaspoon sugar
⅛   teaspoon black pepper
1   tablespoon soy sauce
1   cup chicken broth
1½   tablespoons cornstarch combined with 3 table-
     spoons water
1   egg

Preparation:
Using kitchen shears, cut off all the lobster's feet and claws. Save the feet from the top joints and discard the bottom hairy ones. Cut the claws into small pieces, each piece with the meat exposed. Remove the head and cut in half. Discard the gills, sand bag, and large part of the shell. Remove the vein in the back of the body and cut each half of the body into 1-inch-long sections. Set all the pieces on a dish, including the juice and roe if any.

Set the black beans, scallion, and garlic on a plate with the ground pork.

Cooking:
Heat a wok until very hot. Add 3 tablespoons peanut oil and stir-fry the garlic, scallion, black beans, and pork together until pork separates. Add the cut-up lobster and stir-fry for 2 minutes. Sprinkle sherry over lobster. Add the salt, sugar, pepper, soy sauce, and chicken broth. Mix well, cover, and bring to a boil. Let cook for 3 minutes over high heat, stirring once during this time.

Mix the cornstarch and water well. Slowly pour this into the sauce in the middle of the wok, stirring until the sauce boils and thickens. Beat the egg briefly. Slowly pour it into the wok. Immediately remove wok from the heat. Dish out and serve hot.

Yield: 2 servings or up to 6 when served with other dishes.

Variation: For Shrimps with Black Bean Sauce, substitute 1 pound medium raw shrimps for the lobster.

Shell each shrimp and split in half lengthwise. Remove the sand veins and wash well. Drain, then dry thoroughly with paper towels. Coarsely chop the black beans and set on a plate with the scallion and garlic.

Heat a wok until it is very hot. Add 2 tablespoons peanut oil, then the shrimps, and stir-fry over high heat until most of the shrimps' coloring has changed, a little less than a minute. Sprinkle the sherry over the shrimps, stir, and mix. Remove the shrimps and set aside.

Follow remaining directions for "Cooking" for Stir-Fried Lobster with Black Bean Sauce, substituting the precooked shrimps for the lobster.

Cha Sheng Hao
FRIED OYSTERS

炸 生 蠔

  1 *teaspoon salt*
  2 *dozen shucked fresh oysters*

Batter:
  1 *teaspoon salt*
½ *cup flour*
¼ *cup cornstarch*
  2 *teaspoons baking powder*
⅛ *teaspoon white pepper*
½ *cup water*

  2 *cups peanut or corn oil*
Roasted Salt and Szechuan Peppercorns (*page* 208)

Rub the salt into the oysters, then rinse with cold water several times and drain. Bring 1 quart water to a boil. Dip the oysters in the boiling water for 10 seconds; drain well.

Combine the batter ingredients and mix into a smooth batter. The consistency should be such that a thin coating clings to an oyster.

Cooking:

Heat a wok, add the oil, and heat until a haze forms above it, about 375°. Add 2 teaspoons warm oil to the batter and mix well, then add the drained oysters to the batter. Using a spoon, take one batter-coated oyster at a time and drop into hot oil. Fry 6 to 8 at a time for 30 seconds on one side. Then turn them over to the other side so that the batter will coat evenly and continue to fry for about 2 minutes or until brown and crisp on both sides. Drain on paper towels. Serve hot, with Roasted Salt and Szechuan Peppercorns as a dip.

Yield: 2 servings or up to 6 when served with other dishes; 6 servings as an appetizer.

Pao Yü Nai Yu Bai Ts'ai　　鮑魚奶油白菜
CHINESE CABBAGE WITH ABALONE IN CREAM SAUCE

Unlike most Chinese vegetable dishes, which are crisp and crunchy, this dish is soft and smooth. The flavor is delicate, and so it makes a pleasing contrast to highly seasoned dishes.

1½　*pounds celery cabbage (white part only) or*
　　　　hearts of bok choy
　3　*tablespoons chicken fat or peanut oil*
　1　*teaspoon salt*
½　*teaspoon sugar*
½　*cup chicken broth*
　1　*15-ounce can Mexican abalone*
　1　*tablespoon cornstarch combined with ¼ cup*
　　　　abalone juice

Wash and separate the cabbage leaf stalks. Cut each stalk lengthwise ½ inch wide, then cut again into 2-inch-long sections. You should have about 8 cups, packed.

Heat a large pot and add the chicken fat. Add the cut-up cabbage and stir-fry for 2 minutes. Add the salt, sugar, and chicken broth. Stir to mix well and cover. Bring to boil and cook over medium heat until the cabbage is tender and soft, stirring once or twice during this time.

Cut the canned abalone into as thin, large, and uniform slices as possible. Using a deep dish such as a soup plate as a mold, line the bottom of the dish with overlapping slices of abalone.

Using a slotted spoon, take out the cooked cabbage and place in the deep dish lined with the abalone. Save the liquid and put in a small saucepan. The dish can be made ahead of time up to this stage.

Before serving, steam the whole dish for 10 to 15 minutes just to heat it through. Take out the dish and pour the excess fluid accumulated in the dish from steaming into the liquid saved in the small saucepan. Unmold the whole dish on a platter with rim. Keep the dish warm by covering it.

Bring the liquid in the small saucepan to a boil. Mix the cornstarch with juice well and slowly add to the pan, stirring until it boils and a thin white sauce forms. Pour the hot sauce over the dish.

Yield: 4 servings or up to 8 when served with other dishes.

Variations: Thinly sliced cooked ham can be used instead of abalone. This dish becomes Chinese Cabbage with Ham in Cream Sauce.

The dish can be served without the abalone or ham. Eliminate the steaming process. Just cook the cabbage until soft and add cornstarch combined with water. This dish become Chinese Cabbage in Cream Sauce.

Ha Li Shao Lo Bo   蛤蜊燒蘿蔔
STIR-FRIED CLAMS WITH CHINESE WHITE TURNIP

1 *medium Chinese white turnip (about 1 pound)*
1 *dozen fresh clams (ask seafood dealer to open them;*
    reserve their juice)
2 *tablespoons peanut or corn oil*
2 *tablespoons finely chopped scallion*
1 *teaspoon salt*
1 *teaspoon sugar*
2 *teaspoons cornstarch combined with 2 tablespoons*
    water

Preparation:
Peel and wash the turnip. Slice into ⅛-inch-thick pieces, then cut
again into 1½-inch-long julienne strips to make about 3 cups,
packed.

Cut each clam in half and set in a bowl. Measure and set aside ½
cup clam juice.

Cooking:
Heat a wok over moderate heat until hot. Add the peanut oil, then
the scallion and turnip, and stir-fry for 2 minutes. Add salt and
sugar; mix well. Add the clam juice, cover, bring to a boil, and let
cook over low heat for 10 minutes or until the turnip is translucent
and tender. Add the clams. Stir and cook together with turnip only
long enough to heat through the clams. Mix the cornstarch and
water well and pour into the wok, stirring over high heat until the
liquid thickens and coats the ingredients with a clear glaze. Serve
hot.

Yield: 2 servings or up to 6 when served with other dishes.

Variation: Use leeks instead of turnip and reduce the cooking time
to 3 to 4 minutes. Omit the scallion and the cornstarch and water.

Note: Clams may be opened by putting them in the freezer or a hot
oven for a short while.

Pai Shao Hsiang Lo
CONCH, DIPPING METHOD

白 勺 响螺

6 *shelled large conches (about 1½ pounds)*

Sauce:
½ teaspoon salt
½ teaspoon sugar
⅛ teaspoon white pepper
1 tablespoon light soy sauce
1 tablespoon oyster sauce
1 clove garlic
4 thin slices fresh gingerroot
2 tablespoons finely shredded scallion
2 cups chicken broth
3 tablespoons peanut or corn oil

Preparation:
With a sharp knife remove the intestines and trim the outer parts of
each conch thoroughly. Wash them in cold water. Slice the conches
⅛ inch thick in as large pieces as possible to make about 1½ cups.
(For easier slicing, the conches may be semifrozen.)

Combine the sauce ingredients in a small bowl, mix well, and set
aside. Set aside the garlic, ginger, and scallion on a plate.

Cooking:
Have ready 2 woks or pots. Fill one with the chicken broth and
bring to a boil, the other with the peanut oil, heating the oil over
medium-low heat.

Brown the garlic and ginger in the oil, then remove and discard.
Put the cut-up pieces of conch in a strainer. Dip and stir the conch
with the strainer in the boiling broth for 2 seconds. Lift up the
strainer and take out quickly to drain.

Add the shredded scallion to the oil. Stir the sauce well and pour
into the oil. Stir and mix over high heat. Add the conch and quickly
blend with the sauce for 5 seconds. Remove immediately and serve
hot.

Yield: 3 to 4 servings or up to 6 when served with other dishes.

Su Cha Yuan Yang

DRIED SCALLOPS AND SEAWEED

酥炸鴛鴦

The Chinese very infrequently use seaweed in dishes because good-quality seaweed is hard to get. In this dish I improvise by using green vegetables.

    4 ounces large dried scallops
    2 tablespoons dry sherry
    ½ pound fresh spinach, washed, drained, and dried well
    2 cups peanut oil
Salt and dash of monosodium glutamate

Preparation:
Remove and discard the small tough muscle parts attached to the side of each dried scallop. Break into small pieces and soak in 1 cup warm water for 2 hours.

Add sherry to the scallops and steam for 30 minutes or until very tender. Let cool. Drain the scallops but save the liquid for soup stock. Use your fingernails to separate the scallops into the finest shreds, almost as thin as wood shavings. Set aside.

Remove the stems and veins from the spinach leaves. Use only the green leaves for this dish; shred them finely to make about 2 cups.

Cooking:
Heat the peanut oil until moderately hot. Fry the scallops until dark brown and crisp, about 3 minutes, stirring often. Scoop out with a small strainer and drain on paper towels.

Fry the spinach leaves in the same oil, stirring until the spinach turns dark green and crisp. Drain on paper towels. While the spinach is still hot, sprinkle some fine salt and a dash of monosodium glutamate on it. Mix well and set on one side of a serving platter, with the scallops on the other side. Serve as an appetizer or as part of a banquet.

Yield: 6 servings as an appetizer; 10 servings as part of a banquet.

Note: If seaweed is available, choose the green kind with no sand. Use 1 cup seaweed and stir-fry in 4 tablespoons oil until crisp. Cool and sprinkle on a little sugar.

10 Vegetables

NAME OF DISH	NATURE OF DISH
Stir-Fried Spinach	One of the basic leaf vegetable dishes
Stir-Fried Green Beans and Water Chestnuts	Also a basic dish; can be cooked with or without water chestnuts; fermented bean curd may be added
Stir-Fried Broccoli	A popular Cantonese vegetable dish, crisp and refreshing
Sweet-and-Sour Cabbage, Peking Style	This is a Chinese "hot salad"; can be precooked and served cold; for Szechuan style add hot chili pepper
Fried Bean Curd with Hot Bean Sauce	A common dish, eaten everywhere in China (Szechuan and Cantonese—with oyster sauce —versions are outstanding)
Braised Chinese White Turnips	A simple dish with sugar and soy sauce, typical of eastern cooking
Bean Curd Casserole	Slow cooking over a low fire causes the bean curd's texture to maintain its tenderness
Wheat Gluten with Vegetables	A protein and vegetable dish; one of the most popular dishes
Lady in the Cabbage	Heads of *bok choy* decorated with finely chopped shrimps; a delicate and tender dish for a party
Pork-Stuffed Cucumbers	Cucumber or zucchini stuffed with ground pork
Agar-Agar Salad with Ham	A popular vegetable salad, with shredded egg sheets and ham
White Turnip with Jellyfish Salad	Another popular salad; can be prepared ahead of time
Buddha's Delight	The most favored vegetarian dish, with 10 to 18 ingredients; fermented bean curd makes the dish a Cantonese feature
Stir-Fried Dried Shrimps with Cellophane Noodles	An unusual but simple and delicious dish from Tai Shan, in Kwungtung province
Szechuan Pickled Cabbage	The best homemade relish; can be made all year round and used as a side dish or cooked with meat

COOKING METHOD	LAST-MINUTE COOKING TIME REQUIRED	REGION OF COOKING BY ORIGIN OR POPULARITY
Quick stir-frying over high heat	5 minutes	National
Quick stir-frying	5 to 10 minutes	Southern and eastern
Quick stir-frying	5 minutes	Southern—Canton
Browning the hot pepper in the oil first, then stir-frying together with cabbage	5 minutes	Northern—Peking Western—Szechuan
Deep frying with very hot oil	5 minutes	Western—Szechuan Southern—Canton
Braising in a heavy pot	35 minutes (can be reheated)	Eastern—Shanghai
Simmering over low heat	1½ hours (can be reheated)	Eastern—Shanghai
Deep frying and stewing ahead of time; serving cold	none	Eastern—Shanghai
Steaming the vegetable while making the sauce	5 minutes	Eastern—Shanghai
Cooking in covered frying pan	20 minutes	Eastern—Shanghai
Over low heat to make egg sheets; cooking ahead of time and serving cold	none	Eastern—Shanghai
Blanching the jellyfish; cooking ahead of time and serving cold	none	Eastern—Shanghai
Stir-frying separately, then cooking together	30 minutes (can be reheated)	Southern—Canton
Stir-frying and simmering	15 minutes	Southern—Tai Shan
No cooking required	none	Western—Szechuan

NAME OF DISH	NATURE OF DISH
Fried Green Beans with Minced Meat	A typical Szechuan method of cooking
Stuffed Eggplant	With ground pork and dried shrimps; fancy and tasty
Eggplant, Szechuan Style	Eggplant cooked with hot bean sauce; fine for serving with plain rice and as an appetizer
Home Town Bean Curd	Bean curd cooked with mushrooms, bamboo shoots, fresh hot pepper, garlic, and scallion; hot and spicy
Roasted Salt and Szechuan Peppercorns	Another Szechuan homemade condiment to serve with many dishes
Hot Pepper Oil	A typical Szechuan ingredient and dip; goes well with many dishes
Cabbage with Mushrooms and Bamboo Shoots	Quickly cooked regular cabbage; goes well with rice and buns
Steamed Eggplant	Easy to cook; can be served hot or cold
Cucumber Salad Crab Meat with Cucumber Salad	A cold dish with Chinese salad dressing of soy sauce, vinegar, and sesame oil; crab meat is usually a favorite addition
Celery Cabbage Salad with Hot Pepper Oil	Simple and spicy
Marinated Radish Fans	A good decorative and contrast dish
Dried Shrimps with Celery Salad	A simple northern combination salad

COOKING METHOD	LAST-MINUTE COOKING TIME REQUIRED	REGION OF COOKING BY ORIGIN OR POPULARITY
Deep frying and stir-frying	10 minutes	Western—Szechuan
Deep frying	10 minutes	Western—Szechuan
Stir frying in the wok with oil until soft	15 minutes (can be served cold)	Western—Szechuan
Deep frying the bean curd first, then stewing together with other vegetables	20 minutes	Western—Szechuan
Dry frying; cooking ahead of time	none	Most regions
Deep frying, then straining the solids; cooking ahead of time	none	Western—Szechuan
Quick stir-frying	5 minutes	Northern—Peking
Steaming over high heat and letting cool	none	Northern—Peking
No cooking required	none	Northern—Peking
Marinating the raw vegetables, then pouring the boiling sauce over and cooling	none	Northern—Peking
Marinating in salt and sugar and cooling	none	Northern—Peking
Soaking the shrimps and serving cold with vegetables	none	Northern—Peking

Ch'ao Po Ts'ai
炒菠菜
STIR-FRIED SPINACH

1 *pound fresh spinach or romaine lettuce*
3 *tablespoons peanut or corn oil*
1 *teaspoon salt*
¾ *teaspoon sugar*

Cut the spinach leaves into 2-inch-long sections if too big. Wash and drain thoroughly.

Heat a large wok or pot over high heat until very hot. Add the peanut oil, then take as much spinach as you can hold in both hands and cover the hot oil surface of the wok so that the oil does not spatter. Stir until the spinach is slightly wilted and then add the rest. Stir-fry together until all of the spinach wilts. Add the salt and sugar and stir to mix well. Use chopsticks or a fork to remove the spinach from the wok and place on a dish. Discard the liquid in the wok. (If romaine lettuce is used, serve with the liquid.) Serve hot.

Yield: 4 servings when served with other dishes.

Note: Fresh spinach, when sold loose by weight, is left uncut with roots intact. The stem of the leaf, which is attached to the plant, is pink. This pink part of the stem is sweet and has a good flavor. When the loose fresh spinach is cooked, it tastes far better than the prewashed spinach packed in cellophane bags. The pink stems and the hearts of the spinach should be cut into 2-inch-long pieces along with the leaves and split into 2 to 4 stalks for easy washing and serving.

Variations: Chinese leeks, chrysanthemums, greens, and amaranth can be cooked in the same manner and served with their liquids.

Ch'ao Tou Chiao
炒豆角
STIR-FRIED GREEN BEANS AND WATER CHESTNUTS

1 *pound fresh green beans*
2 *tablespoons peanut or corn oil*
1 *cup sliced fresh or canned water chestnuts*

1 *teaspoon sugar*
1½ *teaspoons salt*
¼ *cup chicken broth or water*
1 *teaspoon cornstarch combined with 2 tablespoons water*

Preparation:
Snip off both the tips and the stems of the green beans. Break into 2-inch-long pieces. Wash and drain well.

Cooking:
Heat a wok over high heat until hot. Add the peanut oil and stir-fry the green beans and water chestnuts for 3 to 4 minutes (adjust the heat after the first 2 minutes). Add the sugar and salt and mix well. Add the chicken broth. Cover the wok and cook for 3 to 4 minutes (the cooking time depends on the freshness and tenderness of the beans). Mix the cornstarch and water very well and slowly add to the pan, stirring until the liquid thickens and beans and water chestnuts are coated with a light, clear glaze. Serve hot.

Yield: 6 servings when served with other dishes.

Variation: For a plain green bean dish, omit the water chestnuts and cornstarch thickening liquid. Adjust the seasoning and cook in same manner. Or to make Stir-Fried Green Beans with Fermented Bean Curd, add 2 teaspoons of a Chinese regional brand of fermented bean curd, mashing the bean curd with a little of the liquid from the jar, and adding it for the last two minutes of cooking time.

Ch'ao Chieh Lan
STIR-FRIED BROCCOLI

Broccoli will not be a delicately textured green vegetable if you do not peel the stringy skin off the small and large stems. The cooking time should be brief to eliminate the usual broccoli odors but retain the texture and color. The last-minute touch of the cornstarch and water mixture gives a shiny appearance to the dish. However, you may want to omit it for everyday meals.

1 *bunch broccoli (about 2 pounds)*
2 *tablespoons peanut or corn oil*
1 *teaspoon salt*
1 *teaspoon sugar*
2 *tablespoons (approximately) water*
1 *teaspoon cornstarch combined with 2 tablespoons cold water (optional)*

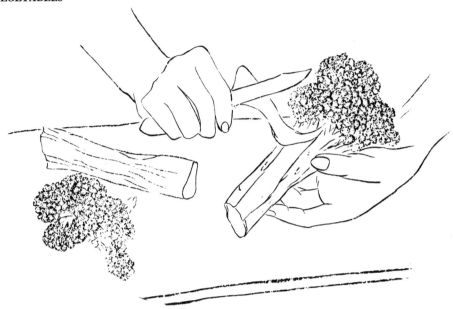

Preparation:
Using a sharp paring knife, start from the bottom of each broccoli stalk or stem and cut and peel, pulling back the tough outer layer. Jerk the knife at the base of the flowerets to detach the outer layer. Discard. Separate the flowerets with stems from the large stems and cut the large flowerets and the large stems into 1½ x ½ x ½-inch pieces to make about 6 cups. Rinse in cold water and drain.

Cooking:
Heat a wok until hot, add the peanut oil, and stir-fry the broccoli for about 2 minutes. Add salt and sugar. Mix well. Add water and cover the wok. Let cook over high heat for 2 minutes, stirring once. Serve hot. (If you are using the cornstarch and water mixture, mix well and add to the pan at the last minute of cooking.)

Yield: 4 to 8 servings when served with other dishes.

Note: For easier peeling of broccoli, let the broccoli stalks stand at room temperature for a few hours.

Variations: Asparagus, zucchini, and cauliflower may be used instead of broccoli. Peeling will not be necessary, but if zucchini are used, brush them under cold water and then cut off and discard both ends. Cut the vegetables into 1-inch pieces.

Ts'u Lu Pai Ts'ai
SWEET-AND-SOUR CABBAGE, PEKING STYLE

醋溜白菜

I call this cabbage dish a hot salad because the cabbage should be crisp and the sauce is like a hot dressing. It is also excellent when cooked a day ahead of time and served as a cold dish.

1   *small head of cabbage (about 1 pound)*
½   *teaspoon salt*
2   *tablespoons sugar*
½   *teaspoon cornstarch*
2   *tablespoons soy sauce*
2   *tablespoons distilled white vinegar*
2   *tablespoons peanut or corn oil*

Preparation:
Remove the tough outer layers of leaves from the cabbage and discard. Cut the cabbage head into quarters, cutting out and discarding the hard core from each quarter. Then cut cabbage quarters into 1½ x 1-inch chunks and separate the leaves to make about 6 cups.

Combine the salt, sugar, cornstarch, soy sauce, and vinegar in a cup. Set aside near the cooking area.

Cooking:
Sprinkle cabbage with a little water to prevent burning during cooking. Heat a wok, add peanut oil, and stir-fry the cabbage over high heat for 2 minutes. Stir the sauce in the cup making sure the sugar has dissolved. Add the sauce to the wok. Stir and mix well over high heat for another minute. Serve hot or cold.

Yield: 4 to 8 servings when served with other dishes.

Variation: Add 4 dried whole chili peppers to the oil to brown them, then add the cabbage to make Sweet-and-Sour-Cabbage, Szechuan Style.

Cha Tou Fu Chiao

炸豆腐角

FRIED BEAN CURD WITH HOT BEAN SAUCE

This is a street-corner vending-stand type of snack for people who enjoy plain hot food. Use hot bean sauce from Szechuan or oyster sauce from Canton.

1 *tablespoon salt*
2 *cups chicken broth*
4 *pieces firm bean curd*
1 *cup peanut or corn oil*
2 *tablespoons hot brown bean sauce or oyster sauce*

Preparation:
Dissolve the salt in the chicken broth. Cut each bean curd piece into 4 triangles and soak in the broth for 1 hour in the refrigerator.

Drain, and with paper towels pat dry the bean curd. Save the broth for another use.

Cooking:
Heat a wok until hot, add the peanut oil, and heat until very hot, about 385°. Deep fry the bean curd a few pieces at a time for about 2 minutes on each side or until light brown and crispy. While frying, do not move the bean curd until a crust is formed. Serve hot, with hot bean sauce or oyster sauce as dip.

Yield: 4 servings when served with other dishes.

Hung Shao Lo Po

紅燒蘿蔔

BRAISED CHINESE WHITE TURNIPS

The quality of Chinese turnips depends on the season. In the winter they are much sweeter. The amount of sugar and soy sauce should be adjusted accordingly, and one should season to taste. Proper seasoning makes this simple dish delicious.

1½ *pounds Chinese white turnips*
2 *tablespoons peanut or corn oil*
2 *teaspoons sugar*
1½ *tablespoons dark soy sauce*
¼ *cup water*

Preparation:
Peel the turnips. Wash and roll-cut into 1 x 1 x 1½-inch pieces to make about 4 cups. In a saucepan cover the turnips with water and bring to a boil. Boil for about 5 minutes. Drain and set aside.

Cooking:
Heat a heavy saucepan. Add the peanut oil and stir-fry the turnips over moderate heat for 2 minutes. Add sugar and soy sauce. Stir and mix for another minute or until the sugar and soy sauce coat the turnips. Add water, cover, bring to a boil, then turn heat down to medium-low. Let cook for about 30 minutes or until the turnips are soft and tender. Stir 2 or 3 times during cooking period. Serve hot. This dish can be cooked ahead of time and reheated.

Yield: 4 servings when served with another dish or up to 8 when served with more dishes.

Sha Kuo Lao Tou Fu
BEAN CURD CASSEROLE

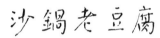

4 3 x 3 x ¾-inch pieces fresh firm bean curd
1 teaspoon salt

3 1-inch-diameter dried scallops or 15 dried shrimps
1 tablespoon dry sherry
¼ cup dried flat-tip bamboo shoots
4 dried mushrooms
8 2 x 2 x ¼-inch slices (approximately) Smithfield ham with some fat left on (¼ cup)
½ teaspoon sugar
1 cup chicken broth

Preparation:
Place bean curd in a large pot. Cover with cold water to 2 inches above the bean curd. Slowly bring to a simmer, then cook over medium heat for 20 minutes.

Remove and discard the small tough part of the muscle attached to the side of each dried scallop. Break the scallops into small pieces, then soak them in 2 tablespoons boiling water. Add the sherry and set aside for 30 minutes.

Soak bamboo shoots and mushrooms in 1 cup warm water for 30 minutes or until soft. Drain the mushrooms and bamboo shoots, saving the liquid (½ cup). Cut bamboo shoots into 2-inch-long pieces. Cut off and discard the stem of each mushroom, then cut in half. Set aside.

Cooking:
Drain the bean curd and let cool. Cut each piece into 6 pieces. Into an earthenware or heatproof casserole put the bean curd, bamboo shoots, mushrooms, ham, sugar, chicken broth, and mushroom water. Bring to a boil and let simmer for 1 hour. Add the soaked scallops with their liquid. Stir and mix, then continue simmering for 30 minutes. Serve hot, in the casserole.

Yield: 4 servings or up to 8 when served with other dishes.

K'ao Fu
WHEAT GLUTEN WITH VEGETABLES

1 *bag dried wheat gluten (about 8 pieces, each*
  2 x 1½ x ½ inches) or ½ pound frozen wheat
  gluten (2 cups, cut up)
4 *large dried mushrooms*
30 *dried tiger lily buds*
¼ *cup dried tree ears*
2 *cups peanut or corn oil*
½ *cup sliced bamboo shoots (1 x 1 x ¼ -inches)*
1 *whole star anise (optional)*
¼ *cup soy sauce, preferably 2 tablespoons each dark*
  and light
1½ *tablespoons sugar*
¼ *teaspoon monosodium glutamate*
2 *teaspoons sesame oil*
Water

Preparation:
Soak the dried wheat gluten in a pot of boiling water for 10 minutes or until soft. Drain and squeeze out some water, then break each piece into 1-inch pieces to make about 2 cups. (If frozen wheat gluten is used, completely thaw the wheat gluten and eliminate soaking in hot water.)

Wash and soak mushrooms in 1 cup warm water for 30 minutes. Remove and discard the stems but reserve the water. Cut each mushroom into 4 pieces.

Soak the tiger lily buds and tree ears in 4 cups hot water for 30 minutes. Pull off and discard the hard ends of each lily bud, if any, then pile together and cut into halves. Clean the tree ears and rinse in water several times; drain well. Set aside these 2 items with mushrooms.

Heat peanut oil in a wok until very hot. Deep fry the drained wheat gluten until brown, dry, and crispy, about 5 to 6 minutes. Remove and drain off excess oil on a few layers of paper towels (save the oil for other uses).

Cooking:
Put all ingredients and seasonings except the tree ears and sesame oil in a saucepan. Add enough water to the mushroom liquid to make 2 cups. Bring to a boil and let cook over low heat for 1 hour. There should be very little sauce left. Add the tree ears and sesame oil. Mix well, then cook 15 minutes more. Serve hot or cold.

Yield: 4 servings or up to 10 when served with other dishes.

Note: This dish can be cooked ahead of time; it will keep unspoiled for 1 week in the refrigerator. It is usually served cold and is excellent for a first course cold dish.

Mei Nü Ts'ai Hsin
LADY IN THE CABBAGE

美女菜心

6 *small heads* bok choy
1 *cup chicken broth*
1 *tablespoon cornstarch*

Filling:
½ *pound raw shrimps, shelled, deveined, and finely*
      chopped to a pulp
2 *tablespoons finely chopped pork fat*
½ *egg white, lightly beaten*
1 *teaspoon cornstarch*
1 *teaspoon salt*
1 *teaspoon dry sherry*

1 *teaspoon fine strips and 2 tablespoons minced*
      cooked Smithfield ham
1 *teaspoon black sesame seeds*
2 *tablespoons soaked hair seaweed*
2 *tablespoons peanut or corn oil*
Salt to taste
1 *tablespoon cornstarch combined with 3 tablespoons*
      water

Preparation:
Remove the outer leaves of each *bok choy* and cut into 3-inch-long
sections (hearts) from the stems up, saving the tops and outer parts
of leaves for another use. Wash and drain well.

Parboil the 6 *bok choy* hearts in chicken broth until just tender.
Drain, saving the broth. Split each *bok choy* heart lengthwise and
arrange on a platter. Sprinkle a little flour on the cut side of each
half of the bottom stalks. Set aside.

Combine the filling ingredients and mix them thoroughly. Divide
into 12 portions. Put 1 portion of shrimp mixture at the bottom end
of each half *bok choy* heart. Use a sandwich spreader dipped in
cold water to smooth the shrimp mixture and press on the black
sesame seeds, ham strips, and hair seaweed to make the features of
a face: i.e., for hair, eyes, eyebrows, and mouth.

Cooking:
Steam the whole dish over high heat for five minutes. Meanwhile,
heat a wok, add the peanut oil, then the reserved chicken broth.

Add salt to taste. Mix the cornstarch and water well. *Slowly* pour
it into the broth, stirring until it boils and thickens into a thin sauce.
Keep hot over low heat.

Remove the lady-in-cabbage platter from the steamer. Pour off
excess liquid, then pour the sauce over the cabbage. Sprinkle the
minced ham on the top part of each *bok choy* stalk only. Serve hot.

Yield: 2 servings or up to 6 when served with other dishes.

Huang Kua Ch'ien Jou　　　　黄 瓜 嵌 肉
PORK-STUFFED CUCUMBERS

　3　*cucumbers, peeled and cut into 1½-inch-long*
　　　sections (about 15 sections)

Filling:
½　*pound ground pork (about 1 cup)*
1　*tablespoon water*
2　*teaspoons cornstarch*
1　*teaspoon salt*
¼　*teaspoon sugar*
2　*teaspoons dry sherry*

15　*pieces cooked Smithfield ham, 1/16 inch thick and*
　　　1 inch round or square (optional)
2　*tablespoons peanut or corn oil*
1　*cup chicken broth*
½　*teaspoon salt*

Preparation:
Use a teaspoon to dig out the seeds of each cucumber section, but
do not dig through to other end. The cucumber sections should be
cuplike.

Combine the filling ingredients, stirring in one direction to mix well. Divide into 15 portions. Stuff each cucumber section with a portion of the filling and cover the openings of each "cup" with a slice of ham.

Cooking:
Heat a large frying pan over moderate heat. Add the oil and place the filled cucumbers meat side up in the pan. Fry for 2 minutes. Add the chicken broth and salt. Cover, bring to a boil, and cook over medium-low heat for about 20 minutes or until the cucumbers are tender. Baste with the liquid twice during this time. There will be about ¼ cup liquid left when the dish is done. Transfer the stuffed cucumbers to a dish. Pour the sauce on top. (You may thicken the sauce with cornstarch and water and then pour it over the cucumbers.) Serve hot.

Yield: 3 servings or up to 8 when served with other dishes.

Note: The stuffed cucumbers may be steamed in a deep dish (reduce the broth to ¼ cup).

Variation: Zucchini may be used in place of cucumbers.

Yang Ts'ai Pan Huo T'ui
AGAR-AGAR SALAD WITH HAM

洋菜拌火腿

  1 *egg*
  1 *teaspoon dry sherry*
  1 *ounce agar-agar*
  4 *cups finely shredded lettuce*
½ *cup finely shredded boiled ham*

Sauce:
  2 *teaspoons sugar*
½ *teaspoon salt*
¼ *teaspoon monosodium glutamate*
  1 *tablespoon light soy sauce*
  1 *tablespoon wine vinegar*
  1 *tablespoon sesame oil*

Preparation:
Beat the egg thoroughly with sherry. Set aside for 30 minutes. Cut the agar-agar into 2-inch-long sections. Soak in cold water for 10

minutes. Drain and squeeze out the water. You should have about 2 cups. Set agar-agar in a mixing bowl with the shredded lettuce and mix well. Set the shredded ham on a small plate.

Combine the sauce ingredients. Just before serving, combine the sauce with the agar-agar and lettuce in the mixing bowl. Transfer onto a serving platter and top with ham.

Cooking:
Heat an 8-inch skillet until very hot. Turn the heat down to low, allowing the pan to cool for 2 minutes. With a piece of paper towel, wipe the pan with a little oil. Pour in half of the beaten egg with sherry and tip the pan from side to side until a thin, round egg sheet forms. Flip or turn the sheet over and fry for 30 seconds more. Transfer to a plate and cool. Repeat with the other half of the egg. Cut the egg sheet into 2-inch-wide pieces, then cut into julienne strips and garnish the top of the Agar-Agar Salad. The salad can be made ahead of time and refrigerated, but add the sauce before serving.

Yield: 2 to 3 servings or up to 8 when served with other dishes.

Note: Canned abalone and cooked chicken may be added to the salad.

Hai Che Pan Lo Po Szu　　海蜇拌蘿蔔絲
WHITE TURNIP WITH JELLYFISH SALAD

¼ *pound salted shredded jellyfish* (*about 1½ cups*)
 2 *cups* (*packed*) *peeled and shredded Chinese
     white turnips*
 1 *teaspoon salt*
½ *teaspoon sugar*
⅛ *teaspoon monosodium glutamate*
½ *tablespoon light soy sauce*
 2 *teaspoons sesame oil*

Preparation:
Wash the salt and sand from the jellyfish and cover with water to soak. Let stand at least 4 hours, changing the water several times until the salt is washed off. Drain the jellyfish and put in a bowl. Add hot water to cover, immediately drain, rinse, and soak in cold water. Drain and squeeze dry before serving.

Put the shredded turnip in a mixing bowl, sprinkle it with the salt, mix well, and set aside for 30 minutes.

Pour off the excess liquid from the turnip. Add the jellyfish, sugar, monosodium glutamate, soy sauce, and sesame oil. Toss to mix and serve cold.

Yield: 6 servings when served with other dishes.

Note: This dish can be prepared ahead of time, but add the dressing just before serving. If jellyfish comes in sheets, cut them into fine strips and soak longer.

Lo Han Chai
BUDDHA'S DELIGHT

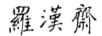

Buddha's Delight is one of the most popular vegetarian dishes in China. It usually consists of more than 10 outstanding ingredients, and it varies from region to region. The eastern region's version has as many as 18 ingredients, some of which involve extensive preparation. For practical purposes, some canned ingredients and locally available vegetables are used. Using fermented bean curd in this dish is a Cantonese custom.

   1 *tablespoon dried hair seaweed*
   1 *teaspoon oil*
   4 *dried mushrooms*
  ¼ *cup dried tree ears*
   2 *ounces cellophane noodles*
   2 *ounces* erh chu (*dried soybean milk skin*)
  ½ *cup sliced carrots*
  ½ *cup sliced bamboo shoots*
  ½ *pound celery cabbage, cut into 2 x 1-inch pieces*
       (*about 3 cups*)
  ½ *cup canned mock abalone or canned seasoned*
       vegetable steak
  30 *canned gingko nuts or 10 cooked chestnuts*
   5 *tablespoons peanut or corn oil*
   1 *teaspoon salt*
   2 *teaspoons sugar*
  ¼ *teaspoon monosodium glutamate*
   2 *tablespoons light soy sauce*
   2 *tablespoons fermented bean curd*
   1 *tablespoon sesame oil*

Preparation:

In separate bowls of hot water soak the hair seaweed (to make it easier to separate, add the oil), mushrooms (use warm water, not hot), tree ears, cellophane noodles, and dried bean milk skin for 20 minutes or until soft.

Cut off and discard the mushroom stems, then cut each mushroom into halves, reserving the mushroom water for later use. Set the carrots, bamboo shoots, and celery cabbage on a large plate with the mushrooms.

Rinse the tree ears several times after soaking. Drain well. Cut soaked cellophane noodles into 4-inch-long sections. Rinse and cut the soaked bean milk skin into 2 x 1-inch pieces. Set out the abalone (if vegetable steak is used instead of mock abalone, cut into 1-inch chunks) and drained hair seaweed. Set on a large plate.

Boil the gingko nuts in salted water for 5 minutes. Drain and set aside with abalone.

Cooking:

Heat a wok or pot over moderate heat until very hot. Add 3 tablespoons peanut oil and stir-fry the cabbage, bamboo shoots, carrots, and mushrooms for 2 to 3 minutes. Remove and set aside. Heat 2 tablespoons peanut oil in the same wok over medium heat. Stir-fry the gingko nuts, cellophane noodles, tree ears, bean milk skin, and hair seaweed for 2 minutes. Add mock abalone and cooked vegetables. Stir and mix well. Add the salt, sugar, monosodium glutamate, and light soy sauce, and also the reserved mushroom water, together with enough additional water to make 1½ cups. Mix well. Cover and cook for 20 minutes over medium-low heat.

Add the fermented bean curd and sesame oil to the Buddha's Delight, then mix to blend well. Serve hot.

Yield: 6 servings or up to 10 when served with other dishes.

Note: This dish can be cooked ahead of time. Just heat it up before serving and serve hot.

Hsia Mi Chu Fen Szu
STIR-FRIED DRIED SHRIMPS WITH CELLOPHANE NOODLES

蝦米煮粉絲

This is a good summer dish from Tai Shan, in Kwuntung province. The secret of this dish is that instead of first softening the dry cellophane noodles in water, they are put directly into the pot to soak up the tasty sauce.

20 *dried shrimps, about ½ inch in diameter*
1 *½-inch piece fresh gingerroot*
⅛ *teaspoon white pepper*
2 *ounces cellophane noodles*
2 *cucumbers*
3 *tablespoons peanut or corn oil*
1½ *teaspoons salt*
1 *cup chicken broth or ⅛ teaspoon monosodium glutamate combined with 1 cup water*

Preparation:
Use ¼ cup boiling water to soak the dried shrimps for 1 hour or until they are very soft. Drain, saving the water. Press the ginger in a garlic press and add the juice along with the pepper to the drained shrimps. Set aside.

Use kitchen shears to cut the dried cellophane noodles into 4-inch-long pieces. Set aside.

Peel the cucumbers; cut diagonally first into ¼-inch-thick slices, then cut again into 2-inch-long julienne strips until you have about 3 cups. Set aside.

Cooking:
Heat a wok over moderate heat. Add the peanut oil and the drained shrimps and stir-fry for about 2 minutes. Add the cucumber strips; stir-fry together for 1 minute. Add the shrimp water, stir, and mix well. Add the salt and broth, then add the cut-up noodles to the sauce. Cover and cook over low heat for about 10 minutes. Stir twice during this time so the cellophane noodles soften and absorb the sauce. If the dish begins to get too dry and the noodles remain hard, the dish needs more water and cooking. Serve hot or at room temperature.

Yield: 2 servings or up to 6 when served with other dishes.

Szechuan P'ao Ts'ai

四 川 泡 菜

SZECHUAN PICKLED CABBAGE

Szechuan Pickled Cabbage is a delicious homemade relish, and it can be made all year round. It can be used as a side dish or cooked with meat. If you keep it in aged brine for a long time, it will become a very tasty sauerkraut. The gin in the recipe keeps the vegetable crisp, enhances the taste, and slows fermentation.

1 1-*pound head cabbage*
4 *fresh or dried hot chili peppers*
2 *tablespoons salt*
1 *cup hot water*
3 *cups cold water*
¼ *teaspoon Szechuan peppercorns (optional)*
2 *tablespoons gin*

Remove and discard the tough layers of leaves from the cabbage. Cut the cabbage into 1½ x 1-inch pieces and separate the leaves. You should have about 8 cups. Wipe the chili peppers clean. Set aside with the cabbage.

In a 1½- to 2-quart wide-mouth jar, dissolve the salt in the hot water. Add the cold water, peppercorns, and chili peppers. Mix well. When the liquid cools, add the gin and cabbage. Cover and keep the jar in the refrigerator for about 4 to 5 days. Remove the cabbage from the liquid and serve cold.

Keep the liquid in the refrigerator all the time. The longer it sits, the better it tastes. Add about 2 teaspoons salt each time you add 6 to 8 cups cut-up fresh cabbage. Cabbage soaked in aged brine will be pickled in 2 to 3 days. After adding fresh cabbage 2 times, replace the chili peppers and add 1 tablespoon gin. *Use only clean, dry chopsticks or forks to take out the cabbage.*

Variations: Other vegetables, like cut-up cauliflower, broccoli stems, white turnips (do not remove the skins), young green beans, carrots, or young gingerroots, can be combined with or used instead of cabbage in the same jar.

Note: When the liquid gets too sour, it is time to strain the aged brine with a paper towel–lined strainer and add more freshly made liquid.

Kan Shao Tou Chiao
FRIED GREEN BEANS WITH MINCED MEAT

乾燒豆角

1 *pound fresh green beans*
2 *tablespoons rinsed and chopped Szechuan preserved*
    vegetable
½ *pound ground or hand-chopped fresh pork*
    (about ¼ cup)
2 *cups peanut or corn oil*
1 *tablespoon soy sauce*
½ *teaspoon sugar*

Preparation:
Snip off both the tips and the stems of the green beans, leaving them whole. Rinse and drain well. Set aside.

Set Szechuan preserved vegetable on a small plate with the chopped pork.

Cooking:
Place a strainer over a pot near the cooking area. Heat a wok until very hot, and add the peanut oil. When the oil is hot, about 375°, add the green beans and fry for about 3 minutes or until the beans become slightly wrinkled. Stir for even frying. Pour the beans and oil into the strainer (save the oil for another use). Keep the drained beans warm in a heated oven.

Heat the same wok and add 1 tablespoon of the drained oil. Stir-fry the chopped pork until the meat separates into bits. Add soy sauce and mix and stir. Add the chopped preserved vegetable and sugar. Stir together with the meat. This will be a dry meat mixture. Pour on top of the fried green beans. Serve hot.

Yield: 2 servings or up to 8 when served with other dishes.

Variation: Tientsin preserved vegetable may be used instead of Szechuan preserved vegetable.

Ch'ieh Tzu Ping
STUFFED EGGPLANT

茄 子 餅

Filling:
½ pound ground pork (about 1 cup)
6 large dried shrimps, soaked in 2 tablespoons hot
    water for 30 minutes, then drained and finely
    chopped
1 scallion, finely chopped
1 tablespoon cornstarch
½ teaspoon salt
½ teaspoon sugar
¼ teaspoon pepper
1 tablespoon soy sauce

1 medium or 3 to 4 small eggplants (about 1 pound)
1 egg, beaten
1 cup bread crumbs
2 cups peanut or corn oil

Preparation:
Combine the filling ingredients in a mixing bowl, mixing in one
direction until the meat holds together. Set aside.

Peel the eggplant and cut into ⅕-inch-thick slices. They may be
too big for easy handling, so cut again to smaller slices but not less
than 1½ inches on the sides (1½ x 1½ x ⅕-inch slices). Spread
about 1 tablespoon of the filling mixture on one slice of eggplant and
cover with another. Dip each stuffed eggplant sandwich in the
beaten egg, then roll in the bread crumbs. Set aside on a plate.

Cooking:
Heat the oil in a wok or deep fryer to 350°. Deep fry a few coated
eggplant pieces at a time for 2 minutes on each side or until brown.
Serve hot.

Yield: 4 servings or up to 8 when served with other dishes.

Variation: Beef may be used instead of pork.

Yü Hsiang Ch'ieh Tzu

EGGPLANT, SZECHUAN STYLE

魚 香 茄 子

Sauce:

½ teaspoon salt
2 teaspoons sugar
1 tablespoon hot brown bean sauce
1 tablespoon soy sauce
¼ cup chicken broth

1 clove garlic, thinly sliced
1 tablespoon minced gingerroot
1½ pounds fresh eggplant (firm, shiny, and light)
1 cup peanut or corn oil
2 teaspoons distilled white vinegar
1 teaspoon sesame oil

Preparation:

Combine the sauce ingredients in a small bowl and mix well. Set the sliced garlic and minced ginger on a small plate.

Wash the eggplant and remove the stem but do not peel. Cut the eggplant into 2 x ½ x ½-inch fingerlike strips to make about 8 cups.

Cooking:

Heat a wok over high heat until very hot. Add the peanut oil and heat again. Add the cut-up eggplant, stir, and turn the pieces for about 5 minutes (depending upon the tenderness of the eggplant). The eggplant will soak up most of the oil in the beginning. When the pieces start to wilt and soften, some oil will come out again. Pour the contents of the wok into a strainer over a pot and drain, reserving the oil for later use.

Heat the same wok with 1 tablespoon of the drained oil. Add the garlic and ginger and stir for 1 minute. Stir the sauce ingredients, mixing well, and add to the wok. Add the cooked eggplant and mix well with the sauce. Cook over high heat for about 2 minutes or until the sauce coats the eggplant. Add the vinegar and sesame oil. Stir a few more times. Serve hot or cold.

Yield: 4 servings or up to 8 when served with other dishes; 10 servings as an appetizer, spread on toasted thin bread or crackers.

Chia Ch'ang Tou Fu

HOME TOWN BEAN CURD

家常豆腐

  6 *medium dried mushrooms*
  ½ *cup sliced bamboo shoots (1 x 1½ x ⅛ inches)*
  2 *tablespoons finely shredded gingerroot*
  2 *tablespoons finely shredded fresh hot pepper or*
      ½ *teaspoon crushed dried hot chili pepper*
  2 *cloves garlic, thinly sliced*
  1 *scallion, cut into 2-inch-long sections*
  4 *3 x 3 x ¾ -inch squares fresh firm bean curd*
  ½ *teaspoon salt*
  ¼ *cup peanut or corn oil*
  1 *teaspoon sugar*
  ¼ *teaspoon monosodium glutamate*
2½ *tablespoons soy sauce*

Preparation:
Wash and soak the mushrooms in ½ cup warm water for 30 minutes. Drain but save the water (¼ cup). Cut mushrooms into halves. Set on a large plate.

Set the bamboo shoots, ginger, hot pepper, garlic, and scallion on the same plate as mushrooms.

Cut each bean curd piece into 8 pieces and sprinkle on salt. Set aside for 10 minutes. Drain the bean curd. Heat a wok to very hot and add the peanut oil. Fry the bean curd over medium-high heat until light brown on one side, about 2 minutes, then turn and fry until light brown on the other side. Remove and set aside, but leave the oil in the wok.

Cooking:
Heat the same wok, and with the remaining oil, stir-fry the ginger, garlic, hot pepper, and scallion for 1 minute. Add the bamboo shoots and mushrooms and stir-fry for 2 minutes. Add the fried bean curd, sugar, soy sauce, monosodium glutamate, and ¼ cup mushroom water. Cover and bring to a boil. Cook for 10 minutes over medium heat, stirring once. When the sauce is almost gone, dish out. Serve hot.

Yield: 4 servings or up to 8 when served with other dishes.

Hua Chiao Fen
ROASTED SZECHUAN PEPPERCORNS

花椒粉

1 *tablespoon Szechuan peppercorns*

Roast the Szechuan peppercorns over medium heat in a dry frying pan for about 5 minutes or until they are fragrant. Cool, then finely grind the peppercorns with a mortar and pestle or in a blender or crush with a rolling pin. Store in a tightly capped jar.

Hua Chiao Yen
ROASTED SALT AND SZECHUAN PEPPERCORNS

花椒鹽

¼ *cup coarse salt*
 2 *tablespoons Szechuan peppercorns*
 1 *teaspoon whole black peppercorns*

Heat salt with Szechuan peppercorns and whole black peppercorns in a dry pan. Stir the spices or shake the pan a few times while roasting until the peppercorns are fragrant, about 5 minutes. Cool, then crush with a rolling pin or in a blender.

Strain through a fine sieve. Use the salt and peppercorn mixture sparingly as a dip for dishes that call for it. Store the rest in a jar for other uses, such as for scrambled eggs.

Yield: Approximately ¼ cup.

La Yu
HOT PEPPER OIL

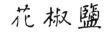

½ *teaspoon ground Roasted Szechuan Peppercorns
      (above)*
½ *cup corn oil*
 2 *tablespoons cayenne pepper*
 1 *teaspoon paprika*

Heat a wok and add the corn oil. Heat the oil until it just starts to smoke. Turn off the heat, wait for 30 seconds (for a heavy pan wait a little longer), then add the cayenne pepper, Roasted Szechuan Peppercorns, and paprika. Stir well and let sit until the solids settle.

Strain the oil through a paper towel–lined strainer. Discard the solids. Store the oil in a jar without refrigerating. Use 1 to 2 teaspoons for a dish or as a dip according to taste.

Yield: Approximately ½ cup.

Tung Ku Ch'ao Pai Ts'ai 冬菇炒白菜
CABBAGE WITH MUSHROOMS AND BAMBOO SHOOTS

  6 *dried mushrooms*
  1 *1-pound head cabbage*
 ½ *cup sliced bamboo shoots* (1 x 1½ x ⅛ *inches*)
  3 *tablespoons peanut or corn oil*
1¼ *teaspoons salt*
 ½ *teaspoon sugar*

Preparation:
Wash and soak the dried mushrooms in ½ cup warm water for 30 minutes. Drain the mushrooms, but reserve the water (¼ cup). Remove and discard the mushroom stems and cut the mushrooms into halves. Set aside.

Remove and discard the first layers of leaves from cabbage. Core the cabbage and cut into 1 x 1½-inch pieces. Separate the pieces if they stick together to make about 8 cups. If the cabbage is very dry, sprinkle some water on it to prevent burning during the high heat of stir-frying.

Cooking:
Heat a wok over high heat, add the peanut oil and then the bamboo shoots and cabbage. Stir constantly for 2 minutes. Add the mushrooms and stir-fry together for 1 more minute. If the heat is too high and the cabbage starts to brown, lower the heat to medium. Add the salt and sugar and mix well. Add the ¼ cup reserved mushroom water. Cover. Let cook together over high heat for about 2 minutes. Stir once during cooking. Serve hot.

Yield: 4 to 6 servings when served with another dish.

Variation: *Bok choy* or Chinese cabbage can be used instead of American cabbage.

Cheng Ch'ieh Tzu
STEAMED EGGPLANT

蒸 茄 子

During the summertime eggplants are especially good. There is no need to peel the skin off because it is tender and has a chewy texture. This dish can be prepared ahead of time and served cold. It is perfect to serve with hot dishes at the same meal.

1 *medium eggplant (about 1 pound)*

Sauce:
  1 *teaspoon sugar*
⅛ *teaspoon cayenne pepper*
  1 *tablespoon soy sauce*
  2 *teaspoons cider vinegar*
  1 *tablespoon sesame oil*

Preparation and cooking:
Wash the eggplant and remove and discard the stem. Cut into eight pieces. Lay eggplant in a deep dish or a heatproof glass pie plate and steam for 20 minutes over high heat or until soft.

Turn the heat off under the steamer. Let stand for 10 minutes. Remove the eggplant dish and pour off the liquid that has accumulated during the steaming. Use chopsticks or fork to separate the eggplant into 1 x 3-inch-long strips. Remove any seeds and tough pith. Mix the sauce ingredients well and pour over the eggplant. Serve hot or cold.

Yield: 4 to 6 servings when served with other dishes.

Pan Huang Kua
CUCUMBER SALAD

拌 黄 瓜

  2 *medium cucumbers*
½ *teaspoon salt*
  1 *teaspoon sugar*
  1 *tablespoon light soy sauce*
  1 *tablespoon wine vinegar*
  2 *teaspoons sesame oil*

Peel the cucumbers and cut lengthwise in two. Remove and discard any seeds from each cucumber half, then cut crosswise into ¼-inch pieces. You should have about 3 cups.

Combine the remaining ingredients and mix well. Pour over the cucumbers before serving. Toss and mix well. Serve cold.

Yield: 4 servings when served with other dishes.

Variations: Sesame oil is quite fragrant and has a nutty flavor. You may use salad oil instead.

Hsia Jou Pan Huang Kua
CRAB MEAT WITH CUCUMBER SALAD

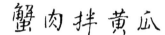

    2 *medium cucumbers*
    1 *cup cooked fresh, frozen, or canned crab meat*
    2 *tablespoons cider vinegar*
 1½ *tablespoons light soy sauce*
   ⅛ *teaspoon pepper*
    1 *tablespoon sesame oil*

Peel the cucumbers and cut lengthwise in two. Remove and discard seeds from each cucumber half, then slice crosswise into ⅛-inch pieces. Place the cut-up cucumber in a salad bowl.

Break the crab meat into small pieces if large and discard all bits of shell and cartilage. Mix with cucumber.

Combine the remaining ingredients and mix well. Pour over the crab meat and cucumber mixture before serving. Toss and mix well. Serve cold.

Yield: 4 servings or up to 8 when served as an appetizer or with other dishes.

La Pai Ts'ai

CELERY CABBAGE SALAD WITH HOT PEPPER OIL

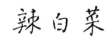

1½ *pounds celery cabbage (white part only, and preferably*
    the more tender stems)
 2 *teaspoons salt*
 1 *teaspoon grated fresh gingerroot*
 1 *tablespoon peanut or corn oil*
 ¼ *cup distilled white vinegar*
 5 *tablespoons sugar*
 ¼ *teaspoon monosodium glutamate*
 1 *teaspoon Hot Pepper Oil (page 208) (to taste)*

Preparation:
Cut the cabbage stalks into 2-inch sections. Shred lengthwise into
¼ x 2-inch strips. You should have about 8 cups. Put the cabbage
strips in a container and sprinkle the salt all over them. Mix well
and pack down tightly. Let stand for about 1 hour.

Squeeze and discard the liquid from the cabbage. Put the cabbage
strips back into the container. Distribute the grated ginger evenly
throughout the cabbage. Pack down again.

Cooking:
In a saucepan bring the peanut oil, vinegar, sugar, and monosodium
glutamate to a boil. Pour over the cabbage and cover for ½ hour.
Then use a small plate to hold back the cabbage, and pour the
liquid into the saucepan. Bring to a boil and pour over the cabbage
again; cover and chill. The cabbage and liquid can be covered and
kept in the refrigerator for several weeks.

Take out the cabbage and pour off the excess juice. Add the hot
pepper oil to taste to the cabbage. Mix well and place on a plate.
Serve cold.

Yield: 1½ cups cabbage salad; 8 to 12 servings when served with
other dishes.

Variation: To add some color and texture to the salad, add ¼ cup
very finely shredded carrot and marinate with the cabbage.

T'ang Yen Hung Lo Po

MARINATED RADISH FANS

糖醃紅蘿葡

24 *1-inch-diameter fresh crisp, tender red radishes*
 1 *teaspoon salt*
 1 *tablespoon sugar*

Cut off and discard the roots and green tops of each radish. Wash the radishes and drain well. Slash each radish crosswise into thin slices, about 1/16 inch, but do not cut through the radish; the slices should all still be connected at the base.

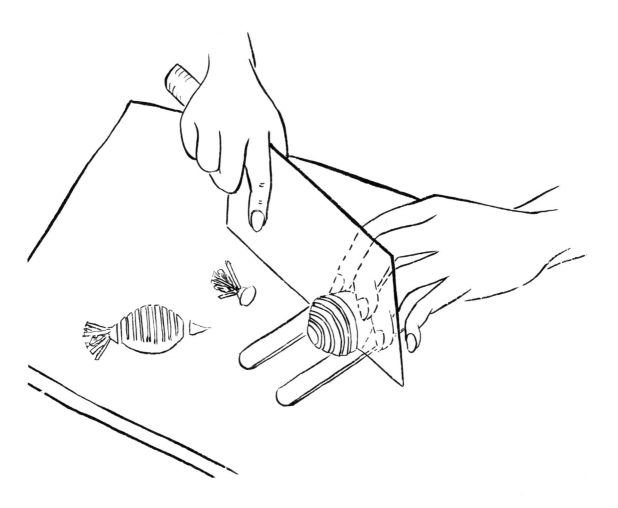

Add the radishes, salt, and sugar to a 1-quart glass jar. Cover the jar and shake well so that each radish is coated with the seasonings. Let the radishes stand for at least 1 hour or as long as overnight.

Pour off all the accumulated liquid from the jar and discard. The radishes will have become soft and pliable. When pressed, the slashed slices of the radishes will spread out into a decorative fan-like shape. The radish fans can be used as a good-tasting garnish for a salad.

Note: To avoid cutting through the radish, put the radish in between 2 sticks and then slice.

Hsia Mi Pan Ch'in Ts'ai
DRIED SHRIMPS WITH CELERY SALAD

蝦米拌芹菜

15 *dried shrimps, about ½ inch in diameter*
 1 *small bunch celery or 1 to 2 celery hearts*
½ *teaspoon salt*
 2 *teaspoons sugar*
 1 *tablespoon light soy sauce*
 1 *tablespoon wine vinegar*
 2 *teaspoons sesame oil*

Break the dried shrimps into halves and soak them in 2 tablespoons hot water for 30 minutes.

Scrape off the outer layer of each stalk of celery. Break into halves and pull off any stringy parts. Wash, drain, and dry well. Cut each stalk of celery lengthwise into ½-inch pieces, then cut again crosswise into 1½-inch-long sections. You should have 3 cups. Put them in a mixing bowl.

Combine the remaining ingredients and the soaked shrimps with their soaking liquid. Mix well to dissolve the sugar and add to the celery. Toss to mix well. Let set in the refrigerator for 30 minutes. Serve cold.

Yield: 4 to 6 servings when served with other dishes.

採蓮圖
甲寅始夏
琪作

11 Soups

NAME OF DISH	NATURE OF DISH
Clear Chicken Stock	A pure chicken stock
Rich Meat Stock	Opaque meat and chicken stock
Egg Drop Soup	A basic recipe that can lead to many other exotic and delicate soups; seaweed variation
Vegetarian Vegetable Soup	A colorful and tasty soup; by adding beef, this dish becomes Beef with Vegetable Soup
Meatball with Spinach Soup	A meat and vegetable soup; can be served as a one-dish meal with rice or buns
Chicken Velvet with Bird's Nest Soup	Bird's nests are expensive and are considered a delicacy
Fish Maw Soup	Fish maw, also considered a delicacy, is less expensive than bird's nests; it is already deep fried and takes 30 minutes to develop
Fish Balls: Basic Recipe	Not difficult to make, but requires a special technique
Fish Ball Soup	Once fish balls are made, an easy-to-make soup; delicate and delicious
Ningpo Fish Chowder	Fillet of gray sole or whiting used; tasty and easy to cook
Ten Varieties Hot Pot	An eastern specialty; good for formal or informal dinners, especially in wintertime; also a good one-course meal because of all the variety
Chinese Mustard Green Soup	A simple and popular soup, to serve with or at the end of meal; bean curd variation
Winter Melon Soup	A typical Cantonese specialty, subtle and delicate; crab and chicken are added for a deluxe version
Shrimp Ball Soup	With poached shrimp balls made ahead of time, this is easy to cook
Shark's Fin Soup	A banquet soup, especially good in the Cantonese version
Chrysanthemum Fire Pot	Another typical Cantonese dish; good for a one-course meal

COOKING METHOD	LAST-MINUTE COOKING TIME REQUIRED	REGION OF COOKING BY ORIGIN OR POPULARITY
Slow simmering	none	Northern—Shantung Southern—Canton
Stir-frying and cooking over low heat	none	Northern—Shantung Southern—Canton
Boiling	5 minutes	National
Stir-frying and simmering	none (can be reheated)	National
Simmering	10 minutes	Eastern—Shanghai Western—Szechuan
Boiling and simmering	5 minutes	Northern—Shantung
Boiling and simmering	20 minutes	Eastern and southern
Bringing slowly to a boil	10 minutes	Eastern—Foochow
Slowly heating the ready-made fish balls	10 minutes	Eastern—Foochow
Boiling	5 minutes	Eastern—Ningpo
Reheating in a traditional fire pot or chafing dish	15 minutes	Eastern—Shanghai
Boiling	10 minutes	Southern—Canton
Boiling and simmering	5 minutes	Southern—Canton
Bringing slowly to a boil	10 minutes	Southern—Canton
Boiling and simmering	45 minutes	Southern—Canton
Cooking at dining table	10 minutes	Southern—Canton

NAME OF DISH	NATURE OF DISH
Pork with Szechuan Preserved Vegetable Soup	A hot and spicy Szechuan soup, well received by other regions; very easy to cook
Sizzling Rice Soup	A dish popular all over China and abroad (the rice patties may take time to make)
Yunnan Chicken	A fancy, special way of cooking
Hot-and-Sour Soup	A popular northern soup; easy to make and inexpensive
Dried Shrimp with Cellophane Noodle Soup	A delicately flavored thin soup that goes well with a heavy main dish
Hot-and-Sour Tripe Soup	More of a special soup with the tripe, especially for those who love tripe
Mongolian Fire Pot	A fire pot using only lamb as the only meat; the self-mixed sauce is also interesting

COOKING METHOD	LAST-MINUTE COOKING TIME REQUIRED	REGION OF COOKING BY ORIGIN OR POPULARITY
Boiling	10 minutes	Western—Szechuan
Baking and boiling	10 minutes	Western—Szechuan
Steaming in advance and reheating		Western—Yunnan
Boiling	10 minutes	Northern—Peking
Stir-frying and boiling	10 minutes	Northern—Tsinan
Cooking over low heat and reheating before serving		Northern—Peking
Cooking at dining table	10 minutes	Northern—Mongolian

HOMEMADE STOCK

Meats like chicken and ham and the more economical parts of meats, such as chicken backs and necks and pork bones, are used to make rich stocks to add to soups and gravies instead of water. Sometimes when a light, delicate flavor is desired, water with a pinch of monosodium glutamate can be used, as in vegetarian cooking. Homemade stock will certainly improve a dish's flavor.

There are two types of soups and gravy bases: clear stock and opaque stock.

Shang T'ang
CLEAR CHICKEN STOCK   上 湯

1 5-pound (approximately) fowl, cut into quarters
3 quarts cold water

Into a large pot put the cut-up chicken with enough water to cover it. Bring to a boil and boil for 2 minutes. Discard the water and rinse the chicken and pot with water. Add the 3 quarts cold water and the blanched chicken. Bring to a boil again, cover, turn down the heat to very low, and simmer for about 3 to 4 hours.

Let cool. Slowly and gently pour out the stock, then discard the chicken. Skim most of the chicken fat off the top of the stock, but leave some to give the stock flavor.

Yield: About 3 quarts clear chicken stock.

Note: To clear a cloudy broth, drop a few tough outer leaves of celery cabbage or any bland-tasting leafy vegetable into the soup for the last few minutes of cooking. Let them cook until soft, then discard when the stock is ready. Instead of discarding the chicken, one can cook the chicken just until it is tender, rather than for 3 or 4 hours, and serve it. Then, boil the stock down to 3 to 4 cups.

Nung Shang T'ang
RICH MEAT STOCK

濃上湯

1 *tablespoon peanut or corn oil*
1 *about 5-pound (approximately) fowl, cut into quarters*
2 *pig's knuckles, split lengthwise, then cut in two*
3 *quarts water*

Heat a large pot and add the peanut oil, then the chicken and pork. Stir and mix to sear the meat. Add the water and bring to a boil. Skim off the scum. Turn down heat to medium-low and let cook for about 3 to 4 hours. Using a large spoon, mash the chicken meat and bones thoroughly in the pot. The stock will now be milky white. Let cool.

Use a strainer to strain the stock. Discard the solids. Remove some fat and store the stock in the refrigerator for up to 4 days or in the freezer for up to 1 month. Rich Meat Stock can be used to make heavier soup stock or as a gravy base.

Yield: About 2½ quarts.

CANNED CHICKEN BROTH

For a quick and less expensive stock, canned chicken broth or stock can be used. In order not to change the taste of a dish, canned chicken broth made without any vegetables should be used for making sauces. For making chicken soup, dilute each cup of canned broth with ½ cup of water.

Tan Hua T'ang
EGG DROP SOUP

蛋花湯

This basic recipe for egg drop soup can lead to many other exotic and delicate soups. Two important points: First, the right consistency and thickness of the cornstarch mixture must be attained, and second, it is essential that the egg is only barely cooked.

3 cups Clear Chicken Stock (page 220) or 1 13¾-ounce
  canned chicken broth with enough water added
  to make 3 cups
1 teaspoon salt
1½ tablespoons cornstarch combined with ½ cup water
1 egg
1 teaspoon finely chopped scallion
2 teaspoons sesame oil

In a saucepan bring the stock to a boil. Add the salt. Stir the cornstarch and water and slowly add it to the pan, stirring until the
soup thickens and boils again. In a bowl beat the egg thoroughly.
Remove the soup from the heat and slowly pour the egg into the
soup. Stir once. Pour the soup into a tureen or individual bowls and
garnish with the chopped scallion and sesame oil. Serve at once.

Yield: 4 servings as a first course.

Variation: For Seaweed Egg Drop Soup place a few pieces of black
seaweed in the soup bowls. Then pour the hot soup over.

Su Ts'ai T'ang
VEGETARIAN VEGETABLE SOUP

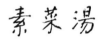

Vegetarian vegetable soup can be very tasty, and is especially good
during the summer months. The slow cooking keeps the soup clear
and the vegetables intact. The tomatoes color the oil red and make
the soup attractive.

¼ pound cabbage
1 carrot
2 ribs celery
2 small potatoes
4 cups water
2 medium tomatoes
2 tablespoons peanut or corn oil
1½ teaspoons salt
½ teaspoon sugar

Preparation:
Cut the cabbage into 1 x 1½-inch pieces to make about 2 cups.
Peel the carrot and diagonally slice it into ¼-inch pieces. Cut the
celery into 1-inch-square pieces. Peel the potatoes and cut into

1-inch chunks. Place all the cut-up vegetables in a heavy saucepan with the water.

Cut the tomatoes into wedges. Heat the peanut oil in a small saucepan and stir-fry the tomatoes for 2 minutes. Set aside.

Cooking:
Bring the pot of vegetables to a boil. Partially cover with the lid, turn down the heat, and simmer for about 1 hour.

When the vegetables are soft, add the cooked tomatoes, salt, and sugar to the soup. Gently stir to blend well. Serve hot or slightly cooled.

Yield: 6 servings with other dishes.

Variation: For Beef with Vegetable Soup cook 1 pound soup beef with bone for 1 hour. Remove bone, then combine the beef with the vegetable soup.

Bo Ts'ai Jou Yüan T'ang
MEATBALL WITH SPINACH SOUP

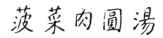

2 *ounces cellophane noodles*
½ *pound finely ground pork (about 1 cup)*
1 *tablespoon cornstarch*
½ *teaspoon salt*
1 *tablespoon soy sauce*
½ *egg, lightly beaten*
2 *tablespoons water*
2 *cups canned chicken broth diluted with 2 cups water*
Salt and pepper to taste
2 *cups tender spinach or watercress leaves*

Preparation:
Soak the cellophane noodles in hot water for about 15 minutes. Drain, and cut the noodles into 4-inch-long pieces. Set aside.

Combine the pork with the cornstarch, salt, soy sauce, egg, and 2 tablespoons water. Use a spoon to mix and stir in one direction until meat holds together. Set aside.

Cooking:

Bring the chicken broth with water to a simmer. Dip a teaspoon in cold water and with it scoop up some meat. Shape meat into a 1-inch ball in the palm of your hand. Drop into the simmering soup. Let cook for 2 minutes. Remove the scum. Add soaked noodles and cook for 2 more minutes. Add salt and pepper to taste. Add spinach, stir, and cook some more. Serve hot.

Yield: 6 to 8 servings as a first course or 2 servings as a one-dish meal with rice or buns.

Variations: If you like hot, peppery soup, add 2 tablespoons shredded Szechuan preserved vegetable. Ground beef may be used instead of pork.

Chi Jung Yen Wo T'ang
CHICKEN VELVET WITH BIRD'S NEST SOUP 雞茸燕窩湯

Bird's nests are made from seaweed and chewed by swiftlets living in the South Pacific. They are built prior to egg-laying. In their original form, some down is still embedded in the nest. The nests are found adhering to walls of caves and cliffs. Bird's nest soup can be either salty or sweet. For a sweet bird's nest soup see Bird's Nests with Rock Sugar Soup (page 299).

   2 *ounces bird's nests (about 6 whole ones or*
      ⅔ cup of the loose kind)
   1 *½-inch chunk fresh gingerroot, crushed*
   1 *cup Clear Chicken Stock (page 220)*
   1 *tablespoon dry sherry*
  ⅛ *teaspoon white pepper*
  ½ *teaspoon sugar*
   1 *tablespoon peanut or corn oil*

Chicken Velvet:
   1 *small whole chicken breast, skinned and boned*
  ¼ *cup cold water*
  ½ *tablespoon cornstarch*
  ½ *teaspoon salt*
   1 *tablespoon dry sherry*
  ⅛ *teaspoon monosodium glutamate*
   2 *egg whites*

3 *cups Clear Chicken Stock* (*page* 220)
Salt and white pepper to taste
2 *tablespoons minced cooked Smithfield ham*
1½ *tablespoons cornstarch combined with* ¼ *cup water*

Preparation:
Soak the bird's nests in 2 cups warm water for at least 4 hours. Rinse very well with water and pick out the down. Drain and place the bird's nests in a small saucepan with the crushed ginger. Cover with 2 cups warm water and bring to a boil for 2 minutes. Rinse, drain, and squeeze the nests dry (you will have about 1½ cups). Discard the water and ginger. Return the nests to the saucepan. Add 1 cup chicken stock and bring to a boil. Add the sherry, pepper, sugar, and peanut oil and simmer for 30 minutes for the loose bird's nests and 15 minutes for the whole bird's nests. They are now ready to be combined with the soup.

Remove and discard as much of the membrane and tendons from the chicken breast as possible. Cut the chicken into small strips. Use a fine-holed plate in a meat-grinder to grind the chicken twice into a mixing bowl; grind until the chicken is a smooth paste. (It is fine enough when the paste feels smooth when rubbed between your fingers.) Gradually add the cold water about ½ tablespoon at a time while mixing the chicken paste in one direction. Add the cornstarch, salt, sherry, and monosodium glutamate. Continue mixing. The chicken mixture should be light and creamy-smooth. Beat the egg whites until slightly foamy. Mix the egg whites into the chicken mixture until well combined. Chicken Velvet can be made ahead of time and kept in the refrigerator as long as overnight.

Cooking:
Pour 3 cups chicken stock into a pot. Add the cooked bird's nests and their liquid. Bring to a boil and add salt and white pepper to taste. Mix the cornstarch with water and slowly pour into the soup, stirring until it thickens and boils. Keep the soup on low heat, just warm enough for it to simmer slowly. Ladle 2 cups of thickened hot soup into the Chicken Velvet, gently but thoroughly mixing it. Pour the Chicken Velvet and soup mixture back into the remaining soup in the simmering pot. Let it cook to almost a boil, stirring to disperse the nests evenly in the soup. Do not overcook. Remove the pot from the heat. Pour the soup into a heated tureen or individual bowls, sprinkle with the minced ham and serve at once.

Yield: 8 servings as a first course.

Yü Tu T'ang
FISH MAW SOUP

魚肚湯

Fish maw is actually the air bladder of a fish. It has a puffed, spongy texture and is always cooked with Rich Meat Stock so that the dish is spongy, juicy, and delicate to the taste. Fish maw can be purchased already deep-fried in Chinese food stores.

    4 *medium dried mushrooms*
    2 *ounces fried fish maw*
    1 *½-inch piece fresh gingerroot*
    1 *tablespoon dry sherry*
    ¼ *teaspoon white pepper*
    4 *cups Rich Meat Stock (page 221)*
    ½ *cup sliced bamboo shoots (1 x 2 x ⅛-inch pieces)*
   10 *fresh snow pea pods, ends and strings removed,*
        cut in half
    ½ *cup sliced cooked Smithfield ham*
        (1 x 2 x ⅛-inch pieces)
    1 *teaspoon salt (to taste)*

Preparation:
Wash and soak the mushrooms in ½ cup warm water for 30 minutes. Drain. Remove and discard the mushroom stems and cut each mushroom into 4 pieces. Set aside on a plate.

Soak the fish maw in cold water for 30 minutes; use a plate to weigh down the fish maw when soaking.

In a pot bring the fish maw and soaking water to a boil. Add the ginger, sherry, and pepper. Remove from the heat, and using a large spoon, stir maw around several times. Allow it to cool, and then with your hand, squeeze the maw in the warm water 2 or 3 times to rinse out the oil. Squeeze out all the water and cut into ½ x 1½-inch strips. You should have about 2 cups.

Cooking:
Heat the Rich Meat Stock in a saucepan and add the fish maw, bamboo shoots, and mushrooms. Bring to a boil, then simmer for 15 minutes. Add the snow pea pods and ham, then add salt. Mix well and serve hot.

Yield: 8 servings as a first course.

Yü Yüan Jung

FISH BALLS: BASIC RECIPE

魚 圓 茸

¾ pound fillet of pike, sea bass, or gray sole

Seasonings:
⅓ cup cold water
Juice of 1 ½ -inch piece gingeroot (extract juice with
     garlic press; discard pulp)
1½ teaspoons salt
¼ teaspoon sugar
¼ teaspoon monosodium glutamate
1 tablespoon cornstarch
1 tablespoon peanut or corn oil

2 egg whites

Preparation:
Cut the fish into small cubes. Use a meat-grinder with a fine-holed
plate to grind the fish twice. Or with a cleaver, chop the fish into
a fine paste. Put the fish paste in a mixing bowl.

Combine the seasoning ingredients in a cup and mix well. Beat the
fish paste with an electric mixer and slowly add the seasoning mixture 1 teaspoon at a time. The fish paste will become stiffer and
resistant. Add egg whites one at time, continuing to beat the mixture. The fish paste will become lighter and smoother.

Cooking:
Pour 2 quarts cold water into a pot. Turn the heat to medium-low.
Use a round measuring tablespoon dipped in cold water to scoop
up some fish paste. Wet your other hand. Flip the fish paste from
the spoon into your wet palm and shape into a ball 1 inch in diameter. Drop the shaped Fish Balls into the water while it is still cool
as the balls are made. If the water begins to boil, lower the heat.
When the balls float to the surface of the water, let them simmer
for about 2 minutes. They are then ready to be removed from the
pot.

Gently rinse the Fish Balls with cold water. Transfer to a container
with enough cold water to cover until ready to use. They can be
kept in the refrigerator for up to 1 week. Fish Balls are used in
Fish Ball Soup (page 228) or Ten Varieties Hot Pot (page 229).

Yield: 20 1-inch-diameter fish balls.

Yü Yüan T'ang
FISH BALL SOUP

魚圓湯

4 cups cold Clear Chicken Stock (page 220)
1 recipe Fish Balls (page 227)
1 teaspoon chopped scallion
1 tablespoon fish sauce
Salt and white pepper to taste

Preparation and cooking:
Pour the chicken stock into a pot. Add the Fish Balls to the cold stock. *Slowly* bring to a boil, turn heat to low, and simmer for 5 minutes. Add chopped scallion, fish sauce, and salt and white pepper to taste. Serve hot.

Yield: 6 servings as a first course.

Variation: Sliced cooked Smithfield ham, bamboo shoots, and mushrooms may be added to the soup. Adjust the seasonings accordingly.

Huang Yü Keng
NINGPO FISH CHOWDER

  2 egg whites
½ pound fillet of gray sole or whiting
  1 teaspoon salt
⅛ teaspoon white pepper
¼ cup finely shredded bamboo shoots
½ cup finely shredded red-in-snow preserved vegetable
  2 tablespoons finely chopped coriander leaves
      (optional)
  1 13¾-ounce can chicken broth, diluted with enough
      water to make 3 cups
1½ tablespoons cornstarch combined with 3 tablespoons
      water
  2 teaspoons sesame oil

Preparation:
Place 1½ egg whites in a mixing bowl (reserve ½ egg white for marinating the fillet). Cut the fillet into ¼-inch cubes and use your hand to mix it well with ½ egg white, ½ teaspoon salt, and the white pepper. Set aside.

Set the shredded bamboo shoots, chopped preserved vegetable, and chopped coriander leaves on the same plate.

Cooking:
Pour the diluted chicken broth into a cook-and-serve pot. Bring to a boil and add the bamboo shoots, preserved vegetable, and ½ teaspoon salt. Cook for 2 minutes. Add the fillet. Stir the cornstarch and water well and slowly add to the soup. Bring to a boil again, then lower the heat. Beat the egg whites until foamy. Slowly add to the soup. Gently stir once. Remove pot from the heat. Add the coriander and sesame oil. Serve hot.

Yield: 6 servings as a first course; up to 8 to 10 servings when served with other dishes.

Shih Ching Nuan Kuo
TEN VARIETIES HOT POT

十景暖鍋

Ten Varieties Hot Pot is a specialty dish of the eastern region of China. It is usually served in the wintertime, toward the end of a formal or informal dinner. It makes a good buffet dish for a big party, and it can also be served as a one-course dinner for a small family. Ten Varieties Hot Pot is usually served with a bowl of plain rice for each person, along with a small dish of soy sauce as a dip.

½ *pound heart of celery cabbage, cut lengthwise into*
    3 x ½ -inch pieces and parboiled
 2 *ounces cellophane noodles, soaked in hot water for*
    20 minutes and cut into 4-inch-long pieces
12 *Fish Balls (page 227)*
12 *cooked meatballs (see Meatball with*
    Spinach Soup, page 223)
12 *Fried Shrimp Balls (page 160)*
 8 *dried mushrooms, soaked until soft, stems removed,*
    and cut into halves
½ *cup sliced bamboo shoots (1 x 2 x ⅛ -inch pieces)*
½ *cup sliced cooked Smithfield ham*
    (1 x 2 x ⅛ -inch pieces)
12 *1 x 2 x ⅛ -inch slices cooked Star Anise Beef (page 128)*
 1 *cooked Egg and Pork Roll (page 91) cut diagonally*
    into 12 pieces
 6 *cups chicken broth*

In a traditional fire pot or chafing dish place first the cabbage, then the cellophane noodles, then the fish, meat, and shrimp balls on top. Next arrange all the remaining ingredients except for the chicken broth, overlapping in the desired pattern. Pour the chicken broth over them (more hot chicken broth may be added when serving). Cover, bring to a boil, and simmer for 10 minutes before serving.

Yield: 6 servings or up to 12 when served with other dishes.

Chieh Ts'ai T'ang
CHINESE MUSTARD GREEN SOUP

芥菜湯

½ pound Chinese mustard green
 1 13¾-ounce can chicken broth, diluted with enough
      water to make 3 cups
 1 teaspoon salt

Wash and cut the mustard green into 1-inch-square pieces. Set aside.

Bring diluted chicken broth to a boil. Add the salt and mustard green and boil over moderate heat for about 5 to 8 minutes or until the vegetable is bright green and just soft. Serve hot.

Yield: 4 servings with or at the end of a meal.

Note: Any vegetable soup made with greens should be cooked without being covered so that the greens will retain their color.

Variation: For Mustard Green Soup with Bean Curd, add 1 sliced fresh bean curd cake and slowly bring to a boil.

Tung Kua T'ang
WINTER MELON SOUP

 4 medium dried mushrooms
 1 pound winter melon
 3 cups Clear Chicken Stock (page 220)
¼ cup diced bamboo shoots (about ¼-inch dice)
¼ cup diced cooked Smithfield ham (about ¼-inch dice)
 1 teaspoon salt (to taste)

Preparation:
Wash and soak the mushrooms in ½ cup warm water for 30 minutes. Drain. Remove and discard the stems. Dice the mushrooms into ¼-inch cubes. Set aside on a plate.

Cut off the skin and remove the seeds and pith from the winter melon. Dice into ¼-inch pieces.

Cooking:
Bring the chicken stock to a boil in a saucepan. Add the winter melon, mushrooms, and bamboo shoots. Simmer for 10 minutes. The soup can be set aside at this stage and reheated later.

When ready to eat, heat the soup and add the ham. Cook for 1 minute, then add salt. Serve hot.

Yield: 6 serving as a first course.

Variations: If winter melon is not available, cucumber may be used instead. For Deluxe Winter Melon Soup add ¼ cup each of cooked king crab meat and chicken meat to the soup at the last minute.

Shang T'ang Hsia Wan
SHRIMP BALL SOUP

上 湯 蝦丸

 3 *cups chicken broth*
12 *Poached Shrimp Balls (page 161)*
 1 *teaspoon finely chopped scallion*
 1 *tablespoon fish sauce*
Salt and white pepper to taste

Preparation and cooking:
Pour the chicken broth into a pot. Add the drained shrimp balls to the chicken broth. Slowly bring to a boil, turn heat to low, and simmer for 5 minutes. Add the chopped scallion, fish sauce, and salt and pepper to taste. Serve hot.

Yield: 4 servings as a first course.

Yü Ch'ih T'ang

SHARK'S FIN SOUP

魚翅湯

4 *ounces precooked cleaned dried shark's fin*
   (with bone and skin removed)
1 *½-inch piece fresh gingerroot, crushed*
1 *whole chicken breast, skinned and boned*

Marinade:
½ *egg white*
1 *teaspoon cornstarch*
½ *teaspoon salt*

4 *dried mushrooms*
4 *cups Clear Chicken Stock (page 220)*
1 *tablespoon dry sherry*
⅛ *teaspoon white pepper*
1 *teaspoon salt*
1 *tablespoon light soy sauce*
2 *tablespoons cornstarch combined with ¼ cup water*
2 *tablespoons finely shredded cooked Smithfield ham*

Preparation:

In a saucepan cover the shark's fin with 4 cups cold water and soak for at least 8 hours. Drain off the water, add 4 cups fresh warm water to the pan, and bring to a boil. Add the crushed ginger. Reduce the heat to low and cook for 1 hour. Drain off the water again, discarding the ginger. Rinse the shark's fin well under cold running water. Set aside.

Cut the chicken breast into ⅛-inch-thick slices; cut again into 1½-inch-long julienne strips. Place the chicken strips in a mixing bowl and add the marinade ingredients. Use your hand to mix well. Place in the refrigerator.

Wash and soak the mushrooms in ½ cup hot water for 30 minutes. Drain. Remove and discard the stems. Cut the mushroom caps into julienne strips and set aside.

Cooking:

In a 2-quart saucepan bring the chicken stock and shark's fin to a boil. Add the sherry and pepper and simmer for 30 minutes. Add the mushrooms, salt, and soy sauce, then the chicken. Stir to separate the shreds. Remove the scum that accumulates on top. Mix the cornstarch and water well and slowly pour in, stirring until the soup thickens and boils again. Remove from heat and transfer to a tureen. Garnish with the ham. Serve hot.

Yield: 6 to 8 servings as a first course.

Chü Hua Kuo
CHRYSANTHEMUM FIRE POT

菊花锅

1 *whole chicken breast, skinned and boned, then cut into 1 x 2 x ⅛ -inch slices*
1 *pound tender beef, cut into 1 x 2 x ⅛ -inch slices*
½ *pound raw shrimps, shelled, deveined, and split laterally in halves*
½ *pound fillet of gray sole or yellow pike, sliced into 1 x 2 x ¼ -inch pieces*
1 *dozen shucked clams or oysters*
¼ *pound chicken livers, sliced into 1 x 2 x ⅛ -inch pieces*
1 *teaspoon salt*
¼ *teaspoon white pepper*
2 *teaspoons dry sherry*
2 *teaspoons peanut or corn oil*
1 *large chrysanthemum flower*
½ *cup coriander leaves and tender stems*
2 *ounces cellophane noodles, boiled in water for 5 minutes, left soaking until cool, and cut into 4-inch-long pieces*
½ *pound fresh spinach or romaine lettuce, washed and drained*
2 *pieces fresh tender bean curd, sliced into 2 x 1 x ½ -inch pieces*
8 *cups chicken broth*

Sauce:
2 *eggs*
½ *teaspoon sugar*
3 *tablespoons light soy sauce*
2 *tablespoons dry sherry*
2 *tablespoons sesame oil*

Preparation:
On two platters or four plates arrange the chicken, beef, shrimps, sole, clams, and chicken livers in one layer with pieces partially overlapping. Sprinkle the salt, white pepper, sherry, and oil on top

and decorate with chrysanthemum petals and coriander. Cover with clear plastic wrap and refrigerate until ready to serve.

Put drained cellophane noodles, spinach, and bean curd in 2 serving bowls.

Sauce:
Beat the eggs thoroughly, then add the sugar, soy sauce, sherry, and sesame oil.

Pour the chicken broth into either a traditional fire pot or an electric casserole or skillet on the dining table. Bring the broth to a boil. The broth must continue to simmer during the time the dish is served and eaten.

Place 2 to 3 tablespoons mixed sauce in each of 6 individual rice bowls. Put the meat, fish, and vegetables on the table and allow each person to serve himself, holding chopsticks in one hand and the sauce bowl in the other.

Cooking at dining table:
The method of cooking is for each person to use the chopsticks to dip a thin slice of meat, fish, or vegetable into the boiling broth and let it cook to the desired degree. It is then dipped into one's own sauce bowl and eaten while hot. You may serve steamed or baked rolls with the meal. The sauce should be used a little at a time as you eat. The vegetables may be added at any time.

Yield: 6 servings

Cha Ts'ai Jou Pien T'ang   榨菜肉片湯
PORK WITH SZECHUAN PRESERVED VEGETABLE SOUP

- 1 1-*inch center-cut pork chop, with bone and fat removed*
- 3 *cups water*
- 1 *teaspoon chopped scallion*
- 1 *teaspoon dry sherry*
- ½ *teaspoon salt*
- 1 *teaspoon light soy sauce*
- ⅛ *teaspoon monosodium glutamate*
- 2 *tablespoons sliced washed Szechuan preserved vegetable (1 x 2 x ⅛-inch pieces)*

Preparation:
Slice the pork into 1 x 2 x ⅛-inch pieces and slap with the side of a cleaver to tenderize. Set aside.

Cooking:
Bring the water to a boil. Add the pork, scallion, and sherry and cook for 5 minutes. Remove the scum and add the salt, soy sauce, and monosodium glutamate. Add the preserved vegetable. Cook for 1 more minute. Serve hot.

Yield: 4 servings as part of a meal.

Kuo Pa T'ang
SIZZLING RICE SOUP

锅 巴 湯

½ *pound small raw shrimps, shelled and deveined*

Marinade:
  1 *teaspoon cornstarch*
½ *teaspoon salt*

  2 *tablespoons peanut or corn oil*
  2 *teaspoons dry sherry*
  6 *deep-fried Rice Patties (page 254)*
  4 *cups chicken broth*
¼ *cup fresh or thawed frozen peas*
¼ *cup diced canned bamboo shoots (¼-inch dice)*
¼ *cup diced canned mushrooms*
¼ *cup diced fresh or canned water chestnuts*
Salt and white pepper to taste

Preparation:
Dice the cleaned shrimps into ¼-inch pieces. Add the cornstarch and salt, and using your hand, mix well. Set the marinade and shrimps in the refrigerator for at least 30 minutes.

Heat a wok until very hot. Add the peanut oil and stir-fry the shrimps to separate them into pieces. Splash on the sherry. Mix well, remove, and set aside.

Cooking:
Preheat the oven to 475°. Set the Rice Patties on a heatproof plate and heat in the hot oven for about 7 to 8 minutes just before serving.

In a cook-and-serve pot bring the chicken broth to a boil and add the peas, bamboo shoots, mushrooms, and water chestnuts. Bring to a boil again and cook over medium heat for 5 minutes. Season with salt and white pepper to taste. Add the cooked shrimps and cook just to heat through.

Take the hot soup and hot Rice Patties from the oven to the dinner table. Pour the Rice Patties into the hot soup. If the Rice Patties and soup are hot, there should be a sizzling noise. Serve immediately.

Yield: 6 servings as a first course.

Yunnan Ch'i Kuo Chi
YUNNAN CHICKEN

雲南汽鍋雞

A round earthenware pot with a cone in the center is the secret of this recipe. It is called a Yunnan pot. The cone tapers to a small hole at the top on the same level as the top rim. A heavy lid fits over all and the pot is placed over a large saucepan of boiling water. As the steam rises, it is forced through the small opening of the cone and disperses on the underside of the lid, dropping gently onto the chicken in the pot. The result: a superbly flavored chicken broth and chicken meat that is tender, moist, and flavorful.

Yunnan chicken is nice for company meals as it requires no last-minute attention. It can be cooked in advance and reheated for about 15 minutes. Serve it from the cooker: The chicken can be served first, with soy sauce as a dip, and with other meat and vegetable dishes as an entrée. Then ladle the clear broth into soup bowls and serve later.

1 *3- to 4-pound chicken, preferably freshly killed*
6 *dried mushrooms*
6 *2 x 1 x ¼ -inch slices Smithfield ham*
1 *scallion, cut into 2-inch-long sections*
2 *cups chicken broth*

Preparation:
Wash the chicken. Pat dry. Cut each leg and thigh into 3 uniform pieces. Then cut remainder of carcass into similar-size pieces. (Remove backbone, neck, and wing tips to use for broth.)

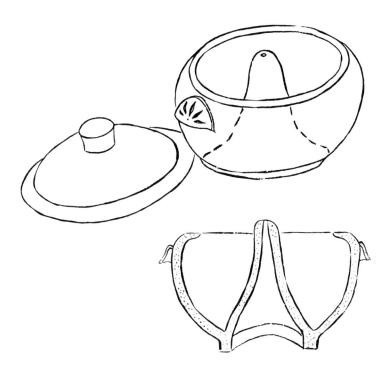

Wash and soak the mushrooms in ½ cup warm water for 30 minutes. Remove and discard the stems. Reserve the mushroom water to add to the soup instead of water. Set aside on a plate with the ham and scallion.

Cooking:
Arrange the chicken evenly around the cone of a Yunnan pot. Add mushrooms, ham, scallion, chicken broth, the reserved mushroom water, and enough additional water to make 1 cup. Cover the pot and place it over a large saucepan (so that it rests on the saucepan's rim) of boiling water over medium-high heat. Check the water level every half hour. Have a kettle of hot water on low heat so the water can be replenished if necessary.

The cooking time may be 1 to 2 hours, depending on the maturity of the chicken and the flow of steam. Test the chicken after 1 hour. It should be tender but firm. It should not fall off the bones.

Yield: 4 servings or up to 8 when served with other dishes.

Note: As a substitute for a Yunnan pot use a deep bowl. Fit the bowl into a large pot with a rack. The water level should be 1½ inches below the bowl's rim. Cover the pot and steam the chicken over medium-low heat for about 2 hours.

Variation: ½ cup dried flat-tip bamboo shoots can be used instead of chicken and ham; just wash and soak them with the mushrooms until soft. Save the soaking water to use in the soup and cook in the same manner.

Suan La T'ang
HOT-AND-SOUR SOUP

酸辣湯

 20 *tiger lily buds*
  2 *tablespoons dried tree ears*
  1 *4 x 4 x 1½-inch piece fresh tender bean curd*
1¼ *teaspoons salt*
  3 *cups canned chicken broth plus 1 cup water*
  1 *tablespoon soy sauce*
 ½ *cup julienne strips of pork or ground pork*
 ¼ *teaspoon pepper*
  2 *tablespoons cider vinegar*
  2 *tablespoons cornstarch combined with ¼ cup water*
  1 *egg*
  1 *teaspoon sesame oil*
  2 *teaspoons minced scallion*

Preparation:
Soak the tiger lily buds and tree ears in hot water in separate bowls for ½ hour or until soft. Pick off and discard the hard ends, if any, of the lily buds. Pile buds together, then cut in half. Wash the tree ears several times, drain, squeeze dry, and break into smaller pieces. You should have about 1 cup. Set aside with the lily buds.

Handle the bean curd gently. Slice it ¼ inch thick, then cut again into 2-inch-long julienne strips. Sprinkle with ¼ teaspoon salt and set aside for 10 minutes.

Cooking:
Combine in a 2-quart saucepan the chicken broth and water, 1 teaspoon salt, and soy sauce. Bring to a boil over moderate heat, then add the pork. Stir around to separate the pork strips. Remove the scum. Add the lily buds and tree ears. Cook together over low heat for 2 to 3 minutes.

Pour off excess water from the bean curd and drop into the soup. Add the pepper and vinegar and *slowly* bring to a boil. Mix the cornstarch and water well and pour into the soup, stirring gently until it thickens and boils again. In a bowl beat the egg thoroughly. Remove the soup from the heat and slowly pour in the beaten egg. Let it stand for a few seconds to allow the hot soup to partially cook the egg. Stir in the sesame oil and sprinkle the top with the scallion. Serve at once.

Yield: 6 to 8 servings as a first course.

Variation: For those who dislike hot, peppery soup, omit the vinegar and pepper; this soup then becomes Mandarin Soup.

Fen Szu Hsia Mi T'ang   粉絲蝦未湯
DRIED SHRIMP WITH CELLOPHANE NOODLE SOUP

This delicately flavored thin soup goes well with a heavy main dish.

15 *dried shrimps, about ½ inch in diameter*
 2 *tablespoons dry sherry*
 2 *ounces cellophane noodles*
 2 *teaspoons finely chopped scallion*
 1 *tablespoon peanut or corn oil*
 1 *teaspoon salt*
 2 *cups canned chicken broth, diluted with 1 cup water*
 2 *teaspoons sesame oil*

Preparation:
Soak the shrimps in the sherry for at least 30 minutes. Drain and set on a small plate, but reserve the sherry.

Soak the noodles in hot water for about 10 minutes. Drain. Using kitchen shears, cut into 4-inch-long pieces. Set the scallion aside on the same plate as the shrimps.

Cooking:
Heat the peanut oil in a pot over moderate heat. Add the drained shrimps and scallion and stir-fry for 1 minute. Splash in the reserved sherry. Add the soaked noodles and salt, then mix well. Add the diluted chicken broth and bring to a boil. Reduce the heat, cover, and simmer for 5 minutes. Add the sesame oil, mix, and serve hot.

Yield: 4 to 6 servings as a first course.

Variation: This soup can be given a hot-and-sour flavor by adding 1 tablespoon cider vinegar and ⅛ teaspoon white pepper.

Suan La Niu Tu T'ang
HOT-AND-SOUR TRIPE SOUP

酸辣牛肚湯

Tripe is the muscular lining of a cow's stomach. Use the light-colored honeycomb tripe, which is already partially cooked and is available almost anywhere.

  1 *pound partially cooked tripe*
  1 *13¾-ounce can beef broth, diluted with 2 cups*
     water
  1 *½-inch piece gingerroot, crushed*
  1 *scallion, cut in half*
  1 *tablespoon dry sherry*
  1 *teaspoon salt*
 ⅛ *teaspoon white pepper*
1½ *tablespoons cider vinegar*
  1 *tablespoon cornstarch combined with 3 tablespoons*
     water
  2 *teaspoons sesame oil*
 ¼ *cup coarsely chopped coriander leaves*

Preparation:
Trim the fat off the tripe and cut into 1 x 2-inch strips. Wash and squeeze in a pot of hot water several times. Blanch the tripe in a pot of boiling water for 1 minute. Drain and rinse.

Squeeze the tripe dry and put in a heavy pot. Add the diluted beef broth, ginger, and scallion. Bring to a boil and add the sherry. Cover and turn the heat to low. Simmer for about 3 to 4 hours or until tripe is tender but crisp. Discard the ginger and scallion. The soup may be cooked ahead of time up to this point and reheated later.

Cooking:
Before serving, reheat the soup. Add the salt, pepper, and vinegar. Mix the cornstarch and water well and slowly stir it into the soup

until the soup thickens. Add the sesame oil. Pour the soup into a
soup tureen or individual bowls and garnish with chopped coriander. Serve hot.

Yield: 6 servings as a first course.

Shuan Yang Jou
MONGOLIAN FIRE POT   涮羊肉

   3 *pounds partially frozen leg of lamb, with bones,*
        tendons, and gristle removed
   2 *ounces cellophane noodles, soaked in boiling water*
        for 20 minutes, then drained and cut into 4-inch-
        long pieces
 ½ *pound fresh spinach (tender parts only), well*
        washed
 ½ *pound celery cabbage, cut into 2 x 1-inch pieces and*
        parboiled
   2 *pieces fresh tender bean curd, cut into 2 x 1-inch*
        pieces
   6 *to 8 cups lamb broth, made from scraps and bone*
        from the leg of lamb

Sauce:
   2 *tablespoons sesame paste, diluted with 4 tablespoons*
        warm water
   1 *tablespoon red fermented bean curd*
 ¼ *cup light soy sauce*
   2 *tablespoons sesame oil*
   2 *tablespoons dry sherry*
   2 *tablespoons wine vinegar*
   1 *tablespoon sugar*
   2 *teaspoons Hot Pepper Oil (page 208)*
   1 *scallion, finely chopped*
   1 *teaspoon finely minced garlic*
   1 *teaspoon fresh ginger juice (use garlic press)*
 ¼ *cup finely chopped coriander leaves*
 ¼ *cup water*

 12 *baked Sesame Seed Pings (page 275), heated in the*
        oven before serving

Preparation:
Have the lamb partially frozen so that it is easy to slice. Slice the meat into 2 x 4 x ⅛-inch pieces and arrange in 1 layer with pieces partly overlapping on 6 plates. Put soaked cellophane noodles, spinach, celery cabbage, and bean curd in 2 serving bowls.

Pour the broth into either a traditional fire pot or an electric casserole or skillet on the dining table. Bring the broth to a boil. The broth must continue to simmer during the time the dish is served and eaten.

In a bowl mix the sauce ingredients well. Place 2 to 3 tablespoons mixed sauce in each of 6 individual rice bowls. Put the lamb plates, vegetables, and buns on the table and allow each person to serve himself, holding chopsticks in one hand and the sauce bowl in the other.

Cooking at dining table:
The method of cooking is for each person to use the chopsticks to dip a thin slice of lamb into the boiling broth and let the lamb cook to the desired degree. The cooked meat is then dipped into one's own sauce bowl and eaten while hot. Serve the baked Sesame Seed Buns during the meal. After all the lamb has been eaten, drop the vegetables, noodles, and bean curd into the broth, cook briefly, and eat while hot. This ends the meal with a tasty hot soup with vegetables.

It is more comfortable if not more than 6 persons share a pot at one table.

Yield: 6 servings.

Note: For easy slicing, have the butcher remove the lamb bone, tendons, and gristle. Tie the meat with strings as for a roast. Freeze it until it is firm enough to cut with a electric slicer. Remove the strings and cut into paper-thin slices. One half pound of lamb is a good-size portion for each serving.

南浦
秋光

12 Rice, Noodles, Dumplings, and Other Tien Hsin

NAME OF DISH	NATURE OF DISH

Plain Rice:
  Boiled Rice
  Steamed Rice
	Only water and rice are used
	  Recipes for long-grain and oval-grain rice
	  Hunan and Hupeh style and Cantonese style

Steamed Rice with Preserved Meat	A special cooking method from Canton used to cook rice and preserved meat
Rice Patties	A basic recipe; used for dishes and as snacks

Fried Rice:
  Ham and Egg Fried Rice
  Beef and Egg Fried Rice
	Use leftover rice for a delicious quick meal
	  A basic recipe, lends itself to other variations
	  Chopped beef and vegetables with fried rice

Plain Rice Congee	For breakfast, a light meal, or a snack; usually served with special "small dishes" or leftovers

Seasoned Rice Congees:
  Chicken Rice Congee
 	
  Beef Rice Congee
 	
  Fish Rice Congee
 	
  Vegetable Rice Congee
  Millet Congee
	For snacks or light meals
	  Use leftover chicken, broth cooks with rice
	
	  Marinated sliced beef barely cooked in congee
	  Sliced raw fish cooked in the hot congee
	
	  Uses *bok choy* for a special fragrance
	  Wonderful beverage to accompany a *chiao-tzu* meal

Stir-Fried Rice Cake	Best rice cake from Ningpo in Chekiang; good for a quick meal or snack

Noodles:
  Roast Pork Lao Mien
 	
  Stir-Fried Rice Noodles with
    Shrimps and Vegetables
  Egg Noodles with Meat Sauce
 	
  Noodle Salad
	For a quick meal or snack
	  A typical Cantonese-style soft noodle dish with oyster-flavored sauce
	  An Amoy specialty, but also served in other areas
	  Meat with brown bean sauce
	
	  Egg noodles served cold, with finely shredded meat, vegetables, and two kinds of sauce

COOKING METHOD	LAST-MINUTE COOKING TIME REQUIRED	REGION OF COOKING BY ORIGIN OR POPULARITY
Boiling and simmering	35 minutes	All regions
Steaming in water	35 minutes	Hunan, Hupeh, and Canton
Steaming the rice and meat at the same time	40 minutes	Southern—Canton
Baking and air drying; last-minute deep frying or baking	10 minutes	Western—Szechuan
Stir-frying	5 minutes	Most regions
Stir-frying	10 minutes	Southern—Canton
Slow simmering (can be reheated)	10 minutes	All regions
Boiling and simmering (can be cooked ahead of time)	10 minutes	Southern—Canton
Boiling and simmering (can be cooked ahead of time)	10 minutes	Southern—Canton
Boiling and simmering (can be cooked ahead of time)	10 minutes	Southern—Canton
Simmering partially covered	1½ hours	Eastern—Shanghai
Boiling and simmering	30 minutes	Northern—Peking
Quick stir-frying	10 minutes	Eastern—Ningpo
Tossing over high heat	5 minutes	Southern—Canton
Stir-frying	10 minutes	Eastern—Amoy
Boiling the noodles and stir-frying the meat	15 minutes	Northern—Peking
Boiling the noodles and serving cold	none	Eastern—Shanghai Western—Szechuan

NAME OF DISH	NATURE OF DISH
Yeast Dough:	A basic recipe for yeast dough with which to make plain or stuffed buns, particularly good for a light meal or snack
Plain Steamed Buns	A basic recipe for buns to be served with various dishes
Lotus Leaf Buns	Fancy and delicate-looking buns
Roast Pork Steamed Buns	Roast pork is a Cantonese specialty, as is this
Ground Meat Steamed Buns	Ground meat is used in all regions
Meat and Vegetable Steamed Buns	A typical Shanghai-style dish, with little meat and a lot of vegetable
Panfried Meat Buns	Panfrying gives crispiness to the bun and adds extra flavor too
Deep-Fried Devils	A popular morning snack that goes well with congee or other *tien hsin* (*dim sim*)
Scallion Pancakes	Salty layered pancakes
Sesame Seed Pings	An interesting Chinese pastry, particularly good for Mongolian Fire Pot
Dough for Boiled and Fried Meat Dumplings:	Cold water dough; mixing and kneading is the key
Fillings for Boiled and Fried Meat Dumplings Boiled Meat Dumplings Fried Meat Dumplings	Three different varieties of filling to choose from
Steamed Meat Dumplings	More delicate in filling and in shape
Curry Puffs	Improvise the dough; similar to pie crust; with meat or shrimp filling, adding mashed potato to maintain the moisture is the secret; can be made ahead of time and kept in freezer; easy to cook, needs little attention at the last minute; versatile for all occasions as an appetizer or snack, or with coffee, tea, or drinks
Spring Rolls:	There are two kinds of spring rolls, called egg rolls in the United States; the wrappers and fillings are very different
Shanghai Spring Roll Wrappers	A cooked wrapper, using high-gluten flour
Canton Spring Roll, Won Ton, or *Shao Mai* Wrappers	An uncooked skin made with a dough of flour, egg, and water
Shanghai Spring Rolls	The filling is moist and soft and the wrapper is very crispy
Canton Spring Rolls	The filling is dry but tasty and the skin is crispy

COOKING METHOD	LAST-MINUTE COOKING TIME REQUIRED	REGION OF COOKING BY ORIGIN OR POPULARITY
		The main staple in the northern region; other regions use as a light meal or snack
Steaming over high heat (can be reheated in the steamer)	10 minutes	Northern—Peking
Steaming	5 minutes	All regions
Stir-frying the filling and steaming the buns	5 minutes	Southern—Canton
Steaming over high heat	15 minutes	All regions
Stir-frying the filling and steaming the buns over high heat (can be reheated)	10 minutes	Eastern—Shanghai
Panfrying	15 minutes	Eastern—Shanghai Northern—Peking
Deep fat frying	5 minutes	All regions
Panfrying	10 minutes	Northern—Peking
Panfrying and steaming (can be reheated in the oven)	15 minutes	Northern—Mongolian
		The filled dumpling cooked in boiling water is the staple food of the northern region
Boiling	10 minutes	
Frying	15 minutes	
Steaming over moderate heat	10 minutes	Northern—Peking
Stir-frying the filling and baking the puff in the oven (can be reheated in the oven)	10 minutes	Northern—Peking
Stir-frying the filling and deep frying the finished roll; can be reheated in hot oil or in the oven	10 minutes	Southern—Canton Eastern—Shanghai
Quickly cooking paper-thin pancakes; can be made ahead of time	5 minutes	Eastern—Shanghai
No cooking is needed; can be made ahead of time	5 minutes	Southern—Canton
Deep frying the finished roll; can be reheated in hot oil or in the oven	10 minutes	Eastern—Shanghai
Deep frying the finished roll; can be reheated in hot oil or in the oven	10 minutes	Southern—Canton

NAME OF DISH	NATURE OF DISH
Amoy Pancakes with Filling and Condiments	Use Shanghai Spring Roll Wrapper to wrap the hot filling and the side dishes; a finger food
Won Tons	Similar to meat dumplings. Good for snacks, light meals, or appetizers, including won ton soup, plain won ton, panfried and fried won ton
Steamed Meat Dumplings	Cantonese steamed dumplings
Steamed *Har Gow* and *Fun Gor*	Both *har gow* and *fun gor* use the same dough, which has a translucent appearance and delicate texture, but they have different kinds of filling and shapes
White Turnip Cakes	Similar to cornmeal-mush scrapple, but made with different ingredients
Desserts (Sweet *Tien Hsin*):	The Chinese very often prefer these sweet dessert dishes served as a snack (*tien hsin*)
Wine Rice	Rice made into Wine Rice through fermentation; has the same flavor and effect as wine; interesting and refreshing, homemade Wine Rice can be served as a snack or dessert and is also used as an ingredient in cooking
Sesame Seed Balls	Made of glutinous flour with Red Bean Paste; deep-fried puffed-up balls with sesame seeds outside
Bird's Nests with Rock Sugar Soup	Bird's nests are considered a delicacy; a delicate and nourishing soup, served hot as a banquet dessert or special snack soup
Red Bean Paste	Puree of red beans; can be used in Red Bean Paste Steamed Buns, Eight Precious Rice Pudding, and Honey Bananas
Red Bean Paste Steamed Buns	A sweet version of steamed buns, served as a snack or dessert
Almond Curd	Made of almond-flavored gelatin, delicate and refreshing; lychee or mandarin oranges add extra flavor
Eight Precious Rice Pudding	A classical banquet dessert
Cantonese Steamed Cake	A Cantonese specialty, usually served hot as a snack with tea
Water Chestnut Cake	Translucent appearance, good for a snack or dessert; can be served cold or broiled and served hot

COOKING METHOD	LAST-MINUTE COOKING TIME REQUIRED	REGION OF COOKING BY ORIGIN OR POPULARITY
Stir-frying the filling and side dishes; the plastic-wrapped wrapper may be reheated in steamer	20 minutes	Eastern—Amoy
Boiling, deep frying, or panfrying	10 to 20 minutes	Eastern and southern
Steaming over high heat	20 minutes	Southern—Canton
Stir-frying the filling and steaming the finished dumpling	5 minutes	Southern—Canton
Boiling and stir-frying, then steaming the whole cake; panfrying slices before serving	5 minutes	Southern—Canton
Steaming the rice, then letting it ferment; can be kept in refrigerator for a long time	none	Eastern and western
Deep frying; can be reheated in the oven	none	Eastern, western, and southern
Slow simmering; can be reheated	5 minutes	Eastern and southern
Simmering and stir-frying; can be cooked ahead of time	none	All regions
Steaming over high heat; can be reheated in the steamer	10 minutes	Eastern, western, and southern
Dissolving gelatin in boiling water; serving cold	none	Eastern—Shanghai
Steaming; can be reheated	15 minutes	Eastern—Shanghai
Steaming over very high heat; can be reheated in the steamer	10 minutes	Southern—Canton
Broiling	5 minutes	Southern—Canton

NAME OF DISH	NATURE OF DISH
Candied Pecans	For nibbling and appetizers
Spun Apples	A candied apple cooked at the last minute
Honey Bananas	In northern and western China there are two ways to make deep-fried Red Bean Paste with a coating; Honey Bananas is a new version, using bananas as a base, with a batter coating and a red bean paste filling
Walnut Cream	Puree of red jujube dates and walnuts, nourishing and tasty; a typical northern dish

COOKING METHOD	LAST-MINUTE COOKING TIME REQUIRED	REGION OF COOKING BY ORIGIN OR POPULARITY
Boiling and deep frying; can be cooked ahead of time	none	Western—Hunan
Deep-fat frying the apple while caramelizing the sugar at the same time	15 minutes	Northern—Peking
Deep-fat frying with batter; can be reheated	10 minutes	Northern and western
Slowly bringing to a simmer; can be reheated	5 minutes	Northern—Peking

RICE (*Mi*)

There are many ways of cooking the various types of rice. The proportion of rice and water varies, depending on the dryness of the rice and on personal tastes. The manner in which the rice is cooked varies from region to region.

Three kinds of rice are commonly used in Chinese cooking. Glutinous rice is used for stuffing, and when it is ground into flour, it is used to make sweet pastries. Long- and oval-grain rices are used for cooking plain rice for daily meals. Long-grain rice is more popular because it takes more water when cooking; hence it yields more cooked rice per cup of raw rice. Oval-grain rice, when cooked, has a softer texture and stickier consistency. Many people prefer this type of rice to the fluffier long-grain rice.

Chinese cooks always wash rice before cooking it. Very often talc is added when the rice is being polished. That is why a rice such as California pearl has a shiny look and a slippery feeling when handled. It is important that all talc be removed from the rice. Wash it until the water comes out clear before cooking.

Pai Fan
PLAIN RICE   白 飯

Following are the different methods of cooking plain Chinese rice. For cooking plain rice, only water and rice are used.

Chu Fan
BOILED RICE   煮 飯

Long-grain rice: With 1 cup rice, use 1¾ cups water; with 2 cups rice, use 3 cups water; and with 3 cups rice, use 4 cups water. Thereafter, use an additional ⅞ cup water for each cup rice. (1 cup raw rice yields 3 cups cooked rice.)

Oval-grain rice: With 1 cup rice, use 1½ cups water; with 2 cups rice, use 2½ cups water. Thereafter, use an additional ⅞ cup water for each cup rice. (1 cup raw rice yields 2½ cups cooked rice.)

In a heavy saucepan with a tightly fitting lid wash and drain the rice several times. Add fresh water (the amount of water for the rice). Place the saucepan over moderate heat and bring the rice to a boil. Boil for 3 to 4 minutes or until all water is absorbed by the rice. Cover with the lid and turn heat down to a slow simmer. Cook for 20 minutes. Turn off the heat but do not remove the pot from the stove or lift the cover; let the rice steam for 10 minutes.

Fluff the rice with wet chopsticks. Serve in warm bowls. Rice can be kept hot in a covered casserole in the oven at 140° to 170° for up to 30 minutes without drying up.

Cheng Fan
STEAMED RICE, HUNAN AND HUPEH STYLE

The proportion of water to rice in cooking by steaming in the following manner need not be as accurate as that needed for the boiling method, since the excess water is drained off. If more than 2 cups rice (6 cups when cooked) are needed, just add rice and water in the same proportion.

2 cups long-grain rice
5 cups water

In a saucepan, wash and drain the rice several times. Add the water and bring it to a boil. Boil for 5 minutes. Stir to loosen the grains of rice stuck to the bottom of the pot. Drain off water from the rice. (The water from the partially cooked rice can be used as a soothing hot beverage or to starch clothes.)

Transfer the drained rice into the tier of a steamer lined with wet cheesecloth. Cover the steamer and let it steam over high heat for about 30 minutes or until the rice is soft.

Cheng Chung Fan
STEAMED RICE, CANTONESE STYLE

Steaming rice in bowls is a popular way of cooking rice in the southern part of China. In some restaurants the rice is cooked ahead of serving time by steaming in individual bowls and then heated up as it is needed.

1 *cup oval- or long-grain rice*
1 *cup water for oval-grain rice, 1¼ cups water for*
long-grain rice

Wash and drain the rice several times. Put the washed rice in a 4-cup heatproof bowl and add the water. Let the rice soak in the water for 30 minutes.

Place the bowl with rice and water on a rack in a pot containing several inches of water. The water level should be about 1½ inches below the bowl's rim. Cover the pot. Bring it to a boil and cook over moderate heat for about 30 minutes or until the rice is soft. Fluff the rice with wet chopsticks and serve in the same bowl. If the bowl has a cover, cover the rice between servings. (You may steam more rice than this at one time, using, of course, several bowls and a large pot.)

La Wei Fan
STEAMED RICE WITH PRESERVED MEAT

臘味飯

Follow the recipe for Steamed Rice, Cantonese Style (page 000). After the rice has steamed for 10 minutes, place on top of the rice either 3 or 4 pieces of Chinese sausage, ¼ preserved pressed duck, or 1 strip of preserved belly of pork. When the rice is done, so is the meat. Cut up the meat and serve with the rice.

Yield: 4 to 6 servings when served with another dish.

Kuo Pa
RICE PATTIES

鍋巴

1½ *cups long-grain rice*
2 *cups cold water*
Oil
Fine salt to taste

Preparation:
Rinse the rice with water. Put the rice and cold water on a 10 x 15-inch jelly-roll pan and spread the rice evenly to make a thin layer. (The grains should touch each other. If you must use a smaller pan, adjust the quantities of rice and water accordingly.) Let stand for 30 minutes.

Cooking:

Cover the pan with aluminum foil and bake in a preheated 350° oven for 30 minutes. Remove the foil, wet the back of a spatula, and press the rice down firmly. Reduce the heat to 300° and continue baking the rice, uncovered, for about 1 hour. The rice will be dry at the sides of the pan, but the center will still be damp.

Take the rice out of the oven and break it into 2 x 2-inch pieces. Leave them out overnight. Make sure the Rice Patties have thoroughly dried.

Fry the dried Rice Patties in very hot oil (about 400°) 2 pieces at a time for about 10 seconds on each side. Drain. The patties will be light brown and crispy. Sprinkle on some fine salt while the patties are still hot. Break into desired-size pieces for snacks or appetizers.

Unsalted fried Rice Patties can be kept in tins and reheated just before serving in a very hot oven (475°) and used in the recipes for Seafood Sizzling Rice (page 170) and Sizzling Rice Soup (page 235).

Thoroughly dried Rice Patties can be kept in tins for a long time. They can be fried when needed.

Huo Tui Tan Ch'ao Fan
HAM AND EGG FRIED RICE

火腿蛋炒飯

Our making a bowl of fried rice is just like your making a peanut butter sandwich for a quick meal. This is because we always have leftover rice, which is just the kind of rice that is required (it must be cooked and cold). Stir-fry the leftover rice with chopped scallions in a little oil and season it with salt or soy sauce. This is the very basic version. You can add eggs and any leftover cooked meat with gravy, seafood, or vegetables. The dish may be kept warm in a covered bowl in a warm oven (140° to 200°) for up to ½ hour.

    3 *tablespoons peanut or corn oil*
    2 *tablespoons chopped scallion*
    3 *cups cold cooked rice, with the rice grains separated*
    1 *egg*
    1 *teaspoon salt*
    ½ *cup cooked ham*
    ½ *cup cooked fresh or frozen peas, or chopped lettuce*

Heat a wok or pan over high heat until very hot. Add 2 tablespoons peanut oil and swirl to coat the pan. Turn the heat down to moderate. Add the scallion and cook for few seconds, then add the rice and stir-fry until the rice is hot, about 2 minutes. Make a well in the center of the rice and add 1 tablespoon oil. Break the egg into the center and scramble it with the oil until it has a soft consistency. Then mix it in with the rice. Add salt, mix well, then add ham and peas, stirring to cook some more. Serve hot.

Yield: 2 servings.

Variations: For Yang Chow Fried Rice (Chicken, Turkey, Roast Pork, Shrimp, or Lobster Egg Fried Rice). Use 1 cup diced cooked chicken, turkey, roast pork, shrimps, or lobtser in addition to the ham. Increase the salt to 1½ teaspoons.

Niu Jou Tan Ch'ao Fan
BEEF AND EGG FRIED RICE

牛肉蛋炒飯

  5 *tablespoons peanut or corn oil*
  2 *eggs*
  ½ *cup ground beef*
  2 *teaspoons cornstarch*
  2 *tablespoons water*
  4 *cups cold cooked rice, with the rice grains separated*
  1 *teaspoon salt*
  1 *tablespoon soy sauce*
  ¼ *teaspoon monosodium glutamate*
  2 *cups finely shredded lettuce*

Cooking:
Heat a wok or pan over high heat until very hot. Turn heat down to moderate and add 1 tablespoon peanut oil. Beat the eggs and scramble them in the hot oil to a soft consistency. Dish out and set aside. Use chopsticks to mix the ground beef in one direction with cornstarch and water, a little at a time, and continue mixing until the meat holds together. Heat the same wok until very hot and add 2 tablespoons peanut oil. Stir-fry the beef over moderate heat until the meat separates into bits. Remove and set aside. Heat the same wok with 2 tablespoons peanut oil. Add the rice and stir-fry until the rice is hot, about 2 minutes. Add the cooked beef, salt, soy sauce, and monosodium glutamate, and mix well with the rice. Add

the scrambled eggs and lettuce, stirring to mix well, and cook some more. Serve hot.

Yield: 3 or 4 servings.

Pai Chou
PLAIN RICE CONGEE

白 粥

Rice Congee is made by boiling water with a few grains of rice. In most parts of China it is eaten for breakfast instead of coffee and toast. It may be served at any time to someone who wishes to have a light meal and to a person who is not feeling well enough to have a regular meal.

There are two ways to cook congee: One is plain, and the other is flavored by adding either meat, seafood, or vegetables. The plain congee is always accompanied by one or more small dishes of meat or highly seasoned food, such as fermented bean curd, salted fish, or preserved vegetables. Roasted peanuts or beans, fresh or preserved eggs, or any leftover dishes also go well with the hot congee. A few different recipes for congee follow.

In a 3- to 4-quart saucepan place ¾ cup oval-grain rice (or ½ cup long-grain and ¼ cup glutinous rice) and wash several times. Drain. Add 8 cups water and bring to a boil. Cook gently over medium heat, partially covered, for 30 minutes. Turn heat down to low. Cover the saucepan and simmer for about 1½ hours or until the contents look like gruel. (The water thickens and the rice grains become very soft.) Congee is best served when very hot, accompanied by small portions of salty and highly seasoned dishes.

Yield: 4 servings.

Chi Chou
CHICKEN RICE CONGEE

雞粥

    1 *recipe Plain Rice Congee (page 257)*
    1 *cup finely shredded lettuce*
   ¼ *cup finely shredded Canton or Szechuan preserved*
        vegetable
    1 *cup cooked chicken (either 1 5-ounce can boneless*
        chicken or leftover White Cut Chicken, page 50)
 1½ *teaspoons salt*

Follow the recipe for Plain Rice Congee. Use 4 cups chicken broth with 4 cups water instead of 8 cups water to cook the congee. The congee may be cooked ahead of time and the chicken and lettuce garnish added at serving time.

Before serving, prepare the lettuce and preserved vegetable and set on a plate. Cut the chicken into bite-size pieces and set aside, including the chicken liquid from the can.

Bring the congee to a boil. Add salt and chicken pieces and liquid. Mix well, then turn off the heat. Serve hot, in individual rice bowls. Garnish each bowl with 2 tablespoons lettuce and 1 teaspoon preserved vegetable. Use remaining lettuce and preserved vegetable for additional helpings.

Yield: 4 servings.

Niu Jou Chou
BEEF RICE CONGEE

牛肉粥

Follow the recipe for Plain Rice Congee (page 257). Use 4 cups chicken broth with 4 cups water instead of 8 cups water to cook the congee. The congee may be cooked ahead of time.

Slice ½ pound tender beef into 1 x 1½ x ⅛-inch pieces. Using your hand, mix well with 1 teaspoon cornstarch, 1½ tablespoons soy sauce, and 1 tablespoon water. Add the seasoned beef to the boiling plain congee and gently stir once to separate the slices. Cover and turn off the heat. Let sit for 2 minutes. Add salt to taste and serve hot.

Yield: 4 servings.

Yü Sheng Chou
FISH RICE CONGEE

魚 生 粥

Follow the recipe for Plain Rice Congee (page 257). Use 4 cups chicken broth with 4 cups water instead of 8 cups water to cook the congee. The congee may be cooked ahead of time.

Slice ½ pound fillet of yellow pike, gray sole, or sea bass into 1 x 1½ x ⅛-inch pieces. Mix slices with 1 teaspoon salt, ⅛ teaspoon white pepper, and 1 teaspoon sesame oil. Spread out 8 to 10 slices of the marinated fish in a large soup bowl. Bring congee to boil and add salt to taste. Ladle the boiling congee over the fish slices in the bowl and serve hot with Chicken Rice Congee (page 258) recipe's garnish plus chopped fresh coriander leaves.

Yield: 4 servings.

Ts'ai Chou
VEGETABLE RICE CONGEE

菜 粥

Wash and drain 1 pound *bok choy*. Cut stalk and leaves into ½-inch pieces. Set aside.

Follow recipe for Plain Rice Congee (page 257). After the rice cooks gently over medium heat for 30 minutes, add the cut-up *bok choy*, 2 teaspoons salt, and 3 tablespoons peanut or corn oil. Stir well and bring to a boil again. Turn heat to medium-low, partially cover the pan, and let cook for about 1 hour or until the vegetable is very soft and the rice becomes a gruel.

Yield: 4 servings.

Hsiao Mi Chou
MILLET CONGEE

小米粥, 小米稀飯

Bring 4 cups water to a boil in a 2-quart saucepan. Add ½ cup millet, washed, and stir well. Bring to a boil again. Turn heat down to medium-low. Partially cover the pan and cook for ½ hour or until the millet is very soft. Serve hot, without any seasoning.

Millet congee is a northern specialty. It is usually served during or after a Chiao-tzu meal.

Ch'ao Nian Kao
STIR-FRIED RICE CAKE

炒年糕

4 *or 5 pieces fresh rice cake, each about 5 x 1⅛ x ½*
  inches (1 pound)
4 *dried mushrooms, soaked in warm water until soft,*
  and finely shredded
1 *cup shredded pork (about ½ pound)*
½ *cup shredded bamboo shoots*
3 *cups shredded celery cabbage*
¼ *cup red-in-snow preserved vegetable, chopped*
4 *tablespoons peanut or corn oil*
1 *tablespoon dry sherry*
1½ *tablespoons soy sauce*
½ *teaspoon sugar*
1 *teaspoon salt*
⅛ *teaspoon monosodium glutamate*

Preparation:
Cut the rice cake pieces into ⅛-inch-thick slices and soak in cold water. You should have about 3 cups. Drain before cooking.

Set aside the mushrooms, pork, bamboo shoots, celery cabbage, and chopped red-in-snow on a large plate.

Cooking:
Heat a wok until very hot. Add 2 tablespoons peanut oil and stir-fry the pork over moderate heat until the pieces separate. Splash on the sherry, then add 1 tablespoon soy sauce and the sugar. Stir, and add the mushrooms. Cook together a few more minutes. Remove and set aside.

In the same wok heat 2 tablespoons peanut oil. Stir-fry the bamboo shoots and celery cabbage for about 2 minutes or until the cabbage starts to wilt. Add salt and monosodium glutamate and mix well. Put back the pork mixture. Add the chopped red-in-snow and cook together with vegetables for 1 minute. Add the drained rice cakes and sprinkle ½ tablespoon soy sauce on the sliced rice cakes. Stir with the meat mixture until the cake slices are limp. Do not overcook. Serve hot.

Yield: 4 servings as a light meal.

Variation: Sliced beef, shrimp, or chicken and other vegetables may be used instead of pork and celery cabbage.

NOODLES

Lao Mien (*lo mein* in Cantonese) is a method of cooking in which cooked noodles are mixed with other ingredients. The noodles should be soft, no crust should form, and there should not be any gravy in the dish. To make a good *lao mien* dish, always use fresh egg noodles.

Ch'a Shao Lao Mien

ROAST PORK LAO MIEN

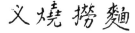

¼ pound Chinese Roast Pork (*page* 115) *or ready-made
    Chinese roast pork*
 1 *scallion*
½ *pound fresh egg noodles*
 3 *tablespoons peanut or corn oil*
½ *pound fresh bean sprouts (about* 3 *cups)*
 1 *tablespoon soy sauce*
½ *teaspoon salt*
1½ *tablespoons oyster sauce*

Preparation:
Cut the roast pork into ⅛-inch-thick slices, then cut again into 2-inch-long julienne strips to make about 1 cup. Split the scallion and cut into 2-inch-long sections. Set aside with the roast pork.

Boil the noodles in 2 quarts boiling water for 3 to 4 minutes or until the noodles are just soft. Drain and rinse with cold water. Drain well (you will have about 4 cups of noodles) and add 1 tablespoon peanut oil. Toss well and set aside.

Cooking:
Heat a wok and add 2 tablespoons peanut oil. Stir-fry the scallion and roast pork over high heat for 1 minute. Add the bean sprouts. Stir and mix with the roast pork. Spread the noodles on top of this mixture. Sprinkle the soy sauce, salt, and oyster sauce on the noodles. Now mix and toss thoroughly over high heat for 3 to 4 minutes. Make sure the noodles are thoroughly cooked and mixed with the other ingredients. Dish out onto a warm platter and serve hot.

Yield: 2 servings as a light meal.

Hsia Jen Ch'ao Mi Fen
STIR-FRIED RICE NOODLES WITH
SHRIMPS AND VEGETABLES

蝦仁炒米粉

½ *pound raw shrimps*
½ *pound dried rice noodles*
2 *cups shredded celery cabbage or fresh bean sprouts*
2 *tablespoons shredded scallion*
4 *tablepsoons peanut or corn oil*
1 *tablespoon dry sherry*
1 *teaspoon salt*
½ *teaspoon sugar*
1½ *tablespoons light soy sauce*
½ *cup chicken broth*

Preparation:
Shell and split each shrimp lengthwise into halves. Remove the sand veins and wash well. Drain, then dry thoroughly with paper towels.

Soak the dried rice noodles in cold water for 5 minutes; drain well. Set the celery cabbage and scallion on a plate.

Cooking:
Heat a wok over high heat until hot. Add 2 tablespoons peanut oil and stir-fry the shrimps for 1 minute. Splash on the sherry, mix, and dish out.

Heat the same wok with 2 tablespoons peanut oil. Stir-fry the scallion and cabbage for 2 minutes, then add the salt, sugar, and soaked rice noodles. Fry, stirring, for 2 more minutes. Add the soy sauce and broth. Turn the heat to high and stir-fry until all the liquid is absorbed. Add the cooked shrimps and mix well until heated through. Serve hot.

Yield: 3 to 4 servings as a light meal.

Cha Chiang Mien

EGG NOODLES WITH MEAT SAUCE

炸醬麵

1 *medium cucumber*
2 *cloves garlic*
2 *cups fresh bean sprouts, parboiled for 30 seconds*
2 *scallions*
3 *tablespoons peanut or corn oil*
1 *pound ground pork*
1 *tablespoon dry sherry*
⅓ *cup ground brown bean sauce*
2 *teaspoons sugar*
½ *cup chicken broth*
1 *pound fresh or dried egg noodles*

Preparation:

Peel cucumber and slice as thin as possible, then cut again into 1½-inch-long julienne strips. Crush the garlic with the side of a cleaver and finely slice. Assemble both items on a serving plate with the parboiled bean sprouts for use as a garnish.

Finely chop the scallion to make about ½ cup. Set aside near the cooking area.

Cooking:

Heat a wok over moderate heat until very hot. Add 2 tablespoons peanut oil and stir-fry the pork for about 2 minutes or until it separates into bits. Splash on the sherry and add the chopped scallion. Stir-fry together for 1 more minute. Add the bean sauce and sugar and stir some more. Pour in the broth and bring to a boil. Cook over medium-low heat for about 10 minutes, stirring most of the time. When the liquid has evaporated and the meat sauce starts to separate from the oil, the sauce is cooked.

Fill a 4- to 5-quart kettle half full of water. Bring to a rolling boil. Add the noodles. Stir with chopsticks or fork, bring to a boil, then turn the heat down to medium. Cook for 3 to 5 minutes. Drain. Add 1 tablespoon peanut oil to the drained noodles and toss well to keep them from sticking together. Serve the noodles in individual soup plates. Each person helps himself to about 2 tablespoons of the meat sauce and the 3 garnishes to taste. Mix well with the noodles.

Yield: 6 servings.

Liang Pan Mien
NOODLE SALAD

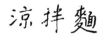

This is a one-dish meal that offers an opportunity to use interesting serving accessories. It lends itself to picnics as well as home luncheons. It consists of cold egg noodles, finely shredded meat, and mixed vegetables, with a tasty vinegar and soy sauce or peanut butter and pepper sauce. The meat and vegetables may be arranged on a platter or tray and the noodles in a salad bowl. Each person receives a soup or salad bowl with about a cupful of noodles. He mixes his own sauce and adds other ingredients himself. Chinese cooks prefer to buy fresh egg noodles at Oriental food stores, but very thin egg noodles or spaghetti may be used instead.

1 *pound fresh egg noodles*
2 *tablespoons sesame oil*
1 *tablespoon soy sauce*

Drop the noodles into 3 to 4 quarts of boiling water and stir to separate them. Boil for about 4 to 5 minutes or until just the desired tenderness. Rinse under cold water and drain thoroughly. Add the oil and soy sauce to the noodles and toss well. Cover and chill in the refrigerator for no more than 2 hours.

Suggested cooked meat and vegetables: shredded roast pork or boiled chicken, turkey, duck, or ham; shredded Egg Sheets (below); shredded cucumbers, radishes, lettuce, or blanched fresh bean sprouts.

EGG SHEETS

Beat thoroughly 2 eggs with a pinch of salt and set aside for 10 minutes. Remove the foam on top of the eggs. Heat an 8-inch skillet until very hot. Turn heat down to low and let the pan cool off. Lightly grease the pan. Pour in ¼ of the beaten egg and tip the pan around so the egg spreads into a thin, even layer in the pan. Cook over low heat until the egg coagulates. Lift up and flip over and let cook briefly on the other side. Repeat procedure to make 3 more sheets. Let cool, then shred into very fine 2-inch-long strips.

Following are two different sauces to serve with the noodle salad. You may use either of them or both in the same meal. Different seasoning ingredients may be set on the table, and each person makes his own sauce.

VINEGAR AND SOY SAUCE

¼ *cup light soy sauce*
¼ *cup wine vinegar*
 2 *tablespoons sesame oil*
 2 *teaspoons sugar*
¼ *teaspoon monosodium glutamate*

Mix all ingredients together and serve in a sauce boat.

PEANUT BUTTER AND PEPPER SAUCE

 2 *tablespoons peanut butter or sesame paste, diluted*
      with 3 tablespoons warm water to make a smooth,
      thin sauce
½ *teaspoon salt*
 2 *teaspoons sugar*
¼ *teaspoon monosodium glutamate*
 2 *tablespoons soy sauce*
 1 *tablespoon wine vinegar*
 2 *tablespoons sesame or corn oil*
 2 *teaspoons Hot Pepper Oil (page 208) or 1 teaspoon*
      cayenne pepper
 2 *cloves garlic, finely chopped*
 2 *tablespoons finely chopped scallion*

Mix all ingredients except the garlic and scallion together into a
very smooth sauce. Add the finely chopped garlic and scallion before serving. Serve in a sauce boat.

YEAST DOUGH

Making an attractive as well as tasty steamed bun is not easy. So
much depends upon the quality of the flour, the yeast, the temperature of the liquid mixed into the dough, and even the weather,
which affects the rising of yeast dough. A dough rises best and
fastest when the weather is humid and warm. Texture depends on
the gluten content of the flour. The rising time depends on the
room's temperature and the amount and the freshness of the yeast.
Kneading is very important; too little kneading produces coarse
buns with low volume. Repeated kneading, replenishing the dough
by sprinkling it with flour, is a necessity. Find a warm, cozy place
for dough to rise (85°), perhaps in an unheated oven with a pan of

hot water beneath the dough, or in a deep pan of warm water or near a range or radiator.

The taste of steamed buns depends on the quality and proportion of the ingredients. The technique of handling a raised yeast dough is just as important. However, if the recipes are followed correctly, there is no reason a batch of steamed buns should fail. Making steamed buns is a challenging procedure and if the results are good, it is most satisfying.

Following is a recipe for yeast dough that can be made into buns, with or without filling. Fillings may consist of meat, vegetables, or red bean paste. Without filling, the dough can be made into Plain Steamed Buns (page 267) or Lotus Leaf Buns (page 267).

If the filling is made ahead of time and refrigerated, it should be taken out and left at room temperature before using. Once the buns are cooked, they can be stored in the freezer. Buns are always eaten hot, and the best way to reheat them is to put them in the steamer and resteam.

Fa Mien

YEAST DOUGH

3½ *cups all-purpose flour*
½ *package active dry yeast (about 1 teaspoon)*
¼ *cup lukewarm water*
1 *cup milk*
2 *tablespoons sugar*
½ *teaspoon baking powder*

Place the flour in a large mixing bowl. Sprinkle yeast over lukewarm water and soak for 2 minutes. Heat the milk to warm, add the sugar, and dissolve. Mix the yeast mixture well and combine it with the milk, then slowly stir into the flour, forming a soft, firm dough. Knead until smooth and leave in the bowl. Cover the bowl with a damp towel and let rise in a warm place for about 1½ to 2 hours or until doubled in bulk.

Punch the risen dough down and turn it out onto a lightly floured surface. Add the baking powder and knead for 10 minutes or until dough is smooth, sprinkling flour onto the dough from time to time while kneading. (With an electric mixer with a dough hook, use speed number 2 for 10 minutes. Also add flour during kneading, but only if the recipe is doubled.)

Note: When doubling this recipe, let the dough rise for an extra hour.

Man Tou
PLAIN STEAMED BUNS

饅頭

1 *recipe Yeast Dough* (*page* 266)

Set up a steamer with 2 steamer tiers. Arrange on each tier 10 2-inch-square pieces of waxed paper 2 inches apart. Roll the dough into a long sausagelike roll about 1 inch in diameter. Cut the roll into 20 1½-inch-long buns. Set the buns on the waxed paper in the steamer. Cover and let rise for about 45 minutes.

Bring the steamer water to a boil. Put the steamer tiers over the boiling water and steam the buns over high heat for 20 minutes. (Steam both tiers at one time.)

Yield: 20 3 x 2-inch buns.

Ho Yeh Chüan
LOTUS LEAF BUNS

荷葉捲

1 *recipe Yeast Dough* (*page* 266)
2 *teaspoons peanut or corn oil*

Cut 40 pieces of waxed paper, each 2 inches square. Set aside. Follow the recipe for Yeast Dough (page 266), but after kneading, divide the dough into 2 halves and keep 1 half in the covered bowl. Roll the first half into a sausage-shaped roll. Break or cut into 20 pieces and roll into balls. With the palm of the hand, flatten each into a circle, then roll each piece with rolling pin into a 2½-inch disk. Brush halfway around the edge of each disk with peanut oil and fold over to make a half-moon shape. Make line impressions with a knife to look like the veins of a leaf, then use a chopstick and fingers to form a leaf shape. Set each bun on a square of waxed

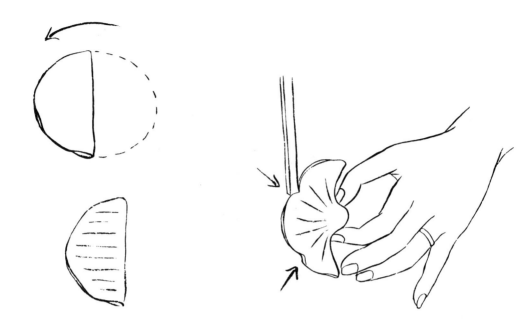

paper and place them 1 inch apart in 2 steamer tiers. Cover and let rise for about 20 minutes.

Repeat with the second half of the dough, but knead the dough again so that the air bubbles knead out, and sprinkle with some flour while kneading before shaping into buns. Keep the buns on a tray and cover with a dry towel; let rise for 20 minutes.

Bring the steamer water to a boil. Put the first batch of buns on the 2 steamer tiers over the boiling water and steam over high heat for 10 minutes. Remove the steamed Lotus Leaf Buns to cool. Transfer the second batch to the steamer tiers and steam for 10 minutes.

Yield: 40 buns.

Ch'a Shao Pao
ROAST PORK STEAMED BUNS

叉燒飽

Filling:
½ *pound Chinese Roast Pork (page 115) or ready-made*
    Chinese roast pork (with some fat)
½ *cup water*
1½ *tablespoons flour*
½ *tablespoon cornstarch*

1½ *tablespoons sugar*
  2 *tablespoons soy sauce*
 ½ *tablespoon oyster sauce*
 ½ *tablespoon sesame oil*

  1 *recipe Yeast Dough (page 266)*

Preparation:
Cut the roast pork into very thin slices, then cut into ¼ x ¼ -inch pieces. You should have about 2 cups. In a saucepan combine the water, flour, and cornstarch. Mix and stir to dissolve. Add the sugar, soy sauce, oyster sauce, and sesame oil. Heat and stir the mixture until it thickens. Add the cut-up roast pork. Mix and blend well. Let the filling cool.

Set up a steamer with 2 steamer tiers. Arrange on each tier 10 2-inch-square pieces of waxed paper, 2 inches apart. Follow the Yeast Dough recipe. Roll the dough into a sausage-shape roll. Break or cut into 20 pieces and roll into balls, each about 1½ -inches in diameter. With the palm of the hand, flatten each into a circle, then roll each with a small rolling pin into a 3-inch disk. The center of each disk should be thicker than the edge.

Put about 1 heaping tablespoon of filling in the center of each disk. Flute the edges of the disk and gather them together to form a pouch by making pleats and pinching with the thumb and fore-finger. Set each finished bun on a square of waxed paper. Cover them as they are made and let rise for about 30 minutes.

Cooking:
Bring the water in the steamer to a boil. Put the steamer tiers over the boiling water and steam the buns over high heat for about 15 minutes. (Steam both tiers at one time.)

Yield: 20 3-inch buns.

Jou Pao
GROUND MEAT STEAMED BUNS

肉飽

1 *recipe Yeast Dough (page 266)*

Filling:
1 *recipe filling for Panfried Meat Buns (page 271)*

Follow the recipe for Roast Pork Steamed Buns (page 268) except put 2 tablespoons of the filling in each bun and steam for 20 minutes.

Yield: 20 3-inch buns.

Ts'ai Jou Pao
MEAT AND VEGETABLE STEAMED BUNS

菜肉飽

Filling:
½   *pound (about 1 cup) ground pork*
 1 *teaspoon cornstarch*
 2 *tablespoons light soy sauce*
 4 *tablespoons peanut or corn oil*
 2 *teaspoons finely minced fresh gingerroot or*
      ¼ teaspoon black pepper
 1 *10-ounce package frozen chopped collard greens,*
      thawed and squeezed dry
 1 *cup finely chopped bamboo shoots*
¼   *cup finely chopped soaked dried mushrooms or*
      ½ cup finely chopped fresh mushrooms
 1 *cup coarsely chopped soaked dried tree ears*
 2 *teaspoons salt*
 1 *teaspoon sugar*
¼   *teaspoon monosodium glutamate*
 2 *teaspoons sesame oil*

 1 *recipe Yeast Dough (page 266)*

Combine the pork with the cornstarch and soy sauce, stirring until the meat soaks up the liquid. Set aside.

Heat a wok over moderate heat until very hot. Add 2 tablespoons peanut oil and stir-fry the pork and ginger until the pork separates into bits. Dish out. Heat the same wok and add 2 tablespoons peanut oil. Stir-fry the collard greens, bamboo shoots, mushrooms, and tree ears for about 2 minutes. Add the salt, sugar, monosodium glutamate, and sesame oil and mix well. Add the cooked pork and blend with the vegetables. Let cool and use as the filling for the buns.

Follow the recipe for Roast Pork Steamed Buns (page 268) except put 2 heaping tablespoons filling in each bun.

Yield: 20 3-inch buns.

Note: The filling should not have any liquid.

Sheng Chien Pao Tzu
PANFRIED MEAT BUNS
生 煎 飽 子

This is a delicious bun of yeast dough stuffed with a savory meat filling. The cooking method, a combination of frying and steaming, may be unfamiliar to most Western cooks. Oil and steam are capable of reaching quite high temperatures, so the pork cooks thoroughly in a short time.

Filling:
    1 *pound ground pork (about 2 cups)*
    2 *teaspoons finely minced fresh gingerroot*
    ½ *cup finely chopped scallions*
    ½ *teaspoon salt*
    2 *tablespoons soy sauce*
    1 *tablespoons sesame or corn oil*
    ¼ *cup chicken broth*

    1 *recipe Yeast Dough (page 266)*
    2 *tablespoons peanut or corn oil*
    2 *tablespoons minced scallion or sesame seeds*

Preparation:
Combine the filling ingredients in a mixing bowl, using a spoon to mix them in one direction until the meat holds together.

Let the dough rise for 1 hour. Knead the dough on a lightly floured surface for 10 minutes. Shape the dough into a long roll, then cut it into 20 pieces. Sprinkle flour on the pieces to prevent sticking. With the palm of your hand flatten each piece, then roll each piece into a

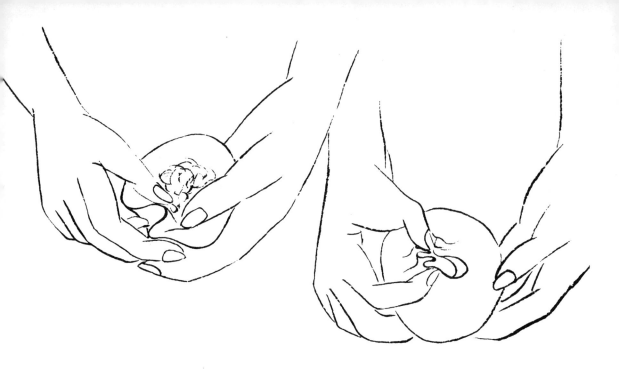

2½-inch circle. Put about 1½ tablespoons of the filling in center of each circle. Flute the edges of the circle and gather them together to form a pouch by pinching with the thumb and forefinger. Set the finished buns on a lightly floured tray. As soon as all the buns are made, set 2 large skillets on burners.

Cooking:
Bring 1 cup water to a boil in each pan over medium heat. Arrange the finished buns 1 inch apart in the pans while the water is boiling. Cover the pans and let the buns cook in the boiling water for about 8 to 10 minutes or until the water has evaporated. Now add 1 table-spoon peanut oil to cover the bottom of each pan (do not get any on the buns). Press the chopped scallion onto the top of each bun. Cook until a crust forms on the bottoms of the buns, then carefully separate each bun. Turn them upside down to brown the tops for just 1 minute (no need to turn if you don't want to brown the scallion or sesame seeds). Serve hot.

Yield: 20 2½-inch buns.

Note: Leftover buns may be reheated in a covered frying pan without oil, but sprinkle them with 1 tablespoon water. After the water evaporates, continue cooking for 2 more minutes.

Variation: Beef, lamb, chicken, or shrimps may be used instead of pork; add 1 tablespoon oil to the filling in addition to the other ingredients.

272

Yu T'iao
DEEP-FRIED DEVILS

油條

Toward the end of the Sung Dynasty there was a great general by the name of Yoh Fei who was very faithful and loyal to the emperor. At that time a group of barbarians had just invaded northern China and overrun the whole area. Yoh Fei was the only one who was able to hold the line while trying to recover the lost territories.

In the meantime, an evil minister named Chin Kwei had made a deal with the northern barbarians. He had sent out twelve Imperial orders to get General Yoh Fei back and place him in jail in the name of the emperor.

Later on people realized that Yoh Fei was a loyal general and that it was Chin Kwei who was the traitor. So they made Yu-Cha Kwei (or Yu T'iao) represent Chin Kwei, and twisted and deep fried them.

1½ *teaspoons salt*
1½ *teaspoons alum*
  1 *teaspoon baking soda*
1½ *teaspoons baking powder*
  ⅞ *cup room temperature water*
  2 *cups all-purpose flour*
  6 *cups peanut or corn oil*

Place salt, alum, baking soda, and baking powder in a mixing bowl. Add water. Using a pair of chopsticks, stir in the flour. This will be a very soft dough, so wet your hands with water to push and pat to a fairly smooth dough. Do not overwork it. Cover well and leave at room temperature for at least 4 hours.

Transfer half of the dough at a time to a flat surface near a stove. Use flour on the surface of the dough and hands to prevent the dough from sticking. Shape the dough into an oblong form ⅓-inch thick and 2 inches wide. Cover with a damp cloth. It is easier to use a dough scraper to shape the dough and to cut dough.

Meanwhile, set a large wok on the stove. Pour in the oil and heat to about 385°. Prepare a tray lined with paper towels and place 3 chopsticks alongside.

Sprinkle some flour on top of dough. Use the scraper to cut the dough crosswise into ¾-inch strips. Take two strips and lay one on top of the other. Lay a chopstick directly over the strips and press down. Hold the two ends of the dough strips and pull until it is 8 inches long. Then, holding one end, swirl it a few times to twist the dough. Lift both ends of the dough and gently lower into the oil. Use chopsticks to turn the dough around until it becomes golden brown. This should take a little less than a minute. Drain on paper towels. Deep fry 2 to 3 pieces at a time.

Yield: 20 pieces (6 inches long)

Note: The fried dough can be reheated in a 400° oven for about 5 to 6 minutes. This is a complicated recipe; the success of the fried dough depends on the cook's technique.

Ts'ung Yu Ping
SCALLION PANCAKES

葱油餅

   2 *cups all-purpose flour*
⅔ *cup water*
   2 *teaspoons salt*
¼ *cup lard*
   4 *teaspoons finely chopped scallion*
   8 *teaspoons oil*

Put the flour into a large bowl and make a well in the center of the flour. Gradually add the water, and with your fingers stir to combine to make a soft but not sticky dough (if it is too dry, add more water). Knead it until it feels smooth. Put the dough back into the bowl and cover with a damp cloth. Let the dough stand for about 15 minutes.

Turn dough onto a lightly floured surface and knead again for 2 minutes. Divide the dough into 4 parts. Roll out one at a time into a rectangle about 10 x 6 x ⅛-inch thick. Sprinkle ½ teaspoon salt on the dough, and with a rolling pin, roll over the salted dough once. Spread 1 tablespoon lard and sprinkle 1 teaspoon scallion evenly on the dough. From the long end roll the dough loosely into a 10-inch sausagelike shape and pinch the dough to seal the open edge. Coil it into a patty and tuck the ends underneath. Gently press with your hand and roll flat with a rolling pin into a pancake, about ¼ inch thick and 6 inches in diameter. Cover with a dry cloth. Repeat procedure with the other 3 pieces of dough.

Heat a frying pan. Add 2 teaspoons oil and fry 1 pancake at a time. If a large frying pan is used, add more oil and fry 4 pancakes at a time. Fry each side over medium heat for about 5 minutes with cover on or until both sides are browned and crisp. Shake the pan several times during cooking. Cut each pancake into 4 pieces and serve hot.

Yield: 4 pancakes.

Note: The pancakes can be reheated in 450° oven for about 5 minutes.

Chih Ma Shao Ping
SESAME SEED PINGS

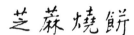

Sesame Seed Pings traditionally accompany Mongolian fire pots. However, they are also excellent with other dishes and soups.

1 *teaspoon active dry yeast*
1 *cup lukewarm water*
2 *teaspoons sugar*
3 *cups all-purpose flour*
3 *tablespoons peanut butter*
2 *teaspoons sesame oil*
1 *teaspoon salt*
1 *tablespoon corn syrup combined with 2 tablespoons*
    warm water
½ *cup white sesame seeds*

Preparation:
Dissolve the yeast in lukewarm water for 2 minutes. Add sugar, mix, and let stand for 2 more minutes.

Put the flour in a large mixing bowl. Add the dissolved yeast to the flour. Knead and gather into a ball. Add more water a little at a time if the dough seems too dry. The dough should be pliable, soft, and smooth. Cover with a damp cloth and let rise in warm place for about 30 minutes.

Mix the peanut butter with sesame oil and set aside.

Knead the dough on a lightly floured surface for 5 minutes (sprinkle the dough with a little flour from time to time during kneading).

Roll out into a large rectangular sheet about ¼ inch thick, 20 inches long, and 8 inches wide. Sprinkle the salt on it and spread the peanut butter mixture evenly over the dough. Roll as a jelly roll lengthwise to make a 1-inch-diameter cylinder and cut into 1½-inch-long sections. You should have about 14 pieces. Seal each section at both ends by pulling and pinching toward the center. With your hands shape dough into a 3-inch-diameter round, ½-inch thick *ping*.

Brush the top of each *ping* with the diluted corn syrup and dip the top into the sesame seeds. Lightly roll with the rolling pin so that the seeds are pressed in.

Cooking:
Place the *pings* in 2 large skillets. Cover and let set for 20 minutes, while you clean up the working area. Now turn the heat on to medium-low for about 10 minutes. Shake the pans several times with the covers on. By now the bottom of each *ping* will be lightly browned. Turn over, cover, and brown the sesame seed sides for 10 minutes. Serve hot.

Yield: 14 2½-inch *pings*.

Note: These *pings* may be wrapped in foil and reheated in a 350° oven for 15 minutes.

BOILED AND FRIED MEAT DUMPLINGS

This dough and filling are used to make such northern specialties as boiled and fried meat dumplings, or in Chinese, *chiao-tzu* and *kuo-t'ieh*, respectively. The dough calls for only two ingredients— flour and water—so it is deceptively simple. Mixing and kneading is, however, an important step. It develops the gluten in the flour, which gives stretch to the dough. This holding quality prevents the breaking of the wrappers.

Chiao-tzu P'i
DOUGH FOR BOILED AND FRIED MEAT DUMPLINGS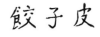

2 *cups all-purpose flour*
⅔ *cup cold water* (*warm water for fried dumplings*)

Put the flour into a large bowl and make a well in the center. Gradually add the water, and with your fingers, stir to make a firm dough (it is important to start with a firm dough; if it is too dry, add more water). Knead it until it feels smooth. Put the dough in the bowl and cover with a damp cloth. Let stand for about 15 minutes. The dough can be made ahead of time and kept in a tightly covered container in the refrigerator for up to 2 days.

Prepare any of the fillings below and set aside.

Chiao-tzu Haien   餃子餡
FILLINGS FOR BOILED AND FRIED MEAT DUMPLINGS

Ground Pork with Vegetable Filling

1½ teaspoons salt
  1 cup finely chopped celery cabbage
½ pound ground pork (about 1 cup)
  1 tablespoon soy sauce
  1 tablespoon sesame or vegetable oil
  2 tablespoons chicken broth
  1 tablespoon finely chopped scallion

Sprinkle ½ teaspoon salt on the chopped celery cabbage. Mix, pack it down, and set aside for 10 minutes. Place cabbage in a towel and squeeze out the excess water. Set the cabbage aside.

Combine the ground pork with 1 teaspoon salt and the soy sauce and stir the mixture with chopsticks or a spoon in one direction. Slowly add the sesame oil and broth one tablespoon at a time while mixing. Add the chopped scallion and cabbage and mix some more until the meat holds together.

Note: ½ cup chopped cooked green beans or ¼ cup grated carrot may be used instead of the celery cabbage.

Ground Beef with Scallion Filling

½ pound ground beef or lamb (about 1 cup)
½ teaspoon minced fresh gingerroot
  1 teaspoon salt
⅛ teaspoon monosodium glutamate
½ tablespoon soy sauce
  2 tablespoons sesame or vegetable oil
  2 tablespoons beef or chicken broth
½ cup finely chopped scallions

Shrimp and Pork with Bamboo Shoots Filling

½ pound ground pork with fat (about 1 cup)
1½ teaspoons salt
1 tablespoon soy sauce
1 tablespoon peanut or corn oil
2 tablespoons chicken broth
¼ cup finely minced bamboo shoots
1 teaspoon minced gingerroot
½ pound raw shrimps, shelled, deveined, and finely
   chopped

Combine the ingredients for either one of the above fillings and mix, using the same directions as in the Ground Pork with Vegetable Filling recipe.

Wrapping Boiled and Fried Meat Dumplings:
Turn dough onto a lightly floured surface and knead for 5 minutes. Divide it into 2 parts: keep one half covered in a bowl and shape the other half into a sausagelike cylinder about 10 inches long and 1 inch in diameter. Cut into 15 pieces. Lay the pieces cut sides down on surface and dust lightly with flour. Press each piece with the palm of your hand to flatten it to a ¼-inch thickness. Use a small rolling pin to roll each piece into a 2½-inch-diameter disk about ⅛ inch thick. Turn clockwise a quarter turn as you roll to keep the shape round and the edges thinner than the center. Cover the finished disks with a dry cloth to prevent drying up.

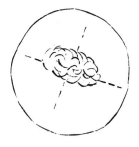

Put about 1 tablespoon filling in the center of each wrapper. Fold the dough in half to cover the filling. Starting from one end pinch the edge of the dough, and with the fingers of the other hand, push the extra dough around to the front so that pleats form on the center front. Use your thumb and forefinger to press and seal the openings. Arrange the meat dumplings on a floured tray and cover with a dry cloth. Repeat procedure with the remaining dough. The meat dumplings can be frozen on the tray, then transferred to a plastic bag or container. They will keep in the freezer for several weeks.

Yield: 30 dumplings.

Cooking Boiled Meat Dumplings (chiao-tzu):
Bring 2 quarts water to a boil in a large pot. Add about 30 meat dumplings and stir once. Cover and bring to boil. Add 1 cup cold water, cover, and wait until the water boils again. Repeat the cold water treatment twice more. When the meat dumplings float to the top, remove with a strainer. Serve hot, with a dip of 1 part vinegar to 2 parts light soy sauce and a bowl of hot Millet Congee (page 259) or the dumpling cooking water as a beverage.

Cooking Fried Meat Dumplings (kuo-t'ieh):
Heat 1 large or 2 small, heavy frying pans until very hot over moderate heat. Remove the frying pans from the heat and add ½ tablespoon oil to coat each pan. Arrange 30 uncooked dumplings in a winding circle. Return the frying pans to the heat and fry dumplings until bottoms turn light brown. Add ½ cup hot water, cover, and cook over medium-high heat until the water has evaporated. Repeat twice. This takes about 10 minutes. Uncover, add 1½ tablespoons oil around the sides, and let the dumpling bottoms fry some more or until a dark brown crust forms on the bottom. Carefully free the sides and bottom of the dumplings from the pan. Serve hot, brown sides up. Use rice or wine vinegar and Hot Pepper Oil (page 208) as a dip.

Note: A large electric skillet is very good for frying these dumplings.

Cheng Chiao Tzu
STEAMED MEAT DUMPLINGS   蒸餃子

Preparation:
Follow the instructions for making a filling and wrapping for Boiled and Fried Meat Dumplings (pages 277–279). To the filling add 1 envelope unflavored gelatin in addition to the other ingredients. For

the dough use the hot water dough as described in the recipe for Mandarin Pancakes (page 87).

Cooking:
Use a steamer tier lined with lightly dampened cheesecloth. Place the dumplings directly on the cloth, ½ inch apart. Cover and steam over medium-high heat for 15 minutes. Serve in the steamer.

Steamed meat dumplings, when made properly, have a large amount of juice. The best way to eat them is to use your fingers to lift one by the top and immediately transfer it to a spoon so that when one bites into the delicious steamed dumpling, no sauce is lost.

Yield: 30 dumplings.

Chia Li Chiao
CURRY PUFFS

咖哩餃

Make either one of the following fillings:

Meat Filling

>   2 *tablespoons peanut or corn oil*
>   1 *pound ground pork or beef (about 2 cups)*
>   1½ *tablespoons soy sauce*
>   2 *teaspoons salt*
>   1½ *teaspoons sugar*
>   1 *cup minced onion*
>   2 *teaspoons imported Madras curry powder*
>   ½ *cup packed, mashed potatoes*

Heat a wok over moderate heat until hot. Add 1 tablespoon peanut oil and the pork (if beef is used, add 2 tablespoons more oil). Stir-fry the pork until it separates into bits and add soy sauce, salt, and sugar. Stir and mix well, then remove and set aside. Heat the same wok with 1 tablespoon peanut oil. Stir-fry the onion until it wilts and add the curry powder. Stir and cook the onion for 1 minute. Add the cooked meat and mashed potatoes. Stir and mix thoroughly. Let cool, then put in the refrigerator to chill.

Shrimp Filling

1 *pound fresh or frozen shrimps (any size), thoroughly*
   thawed
1 *cup finely minced onion*
3 *tablespoons lard or vegetable shortening*
2 *teaspoons imported Madras curry powder*
1 *tablespoon salt*
1 *teaspoon sugar*
¼ *teaspoon monosodium glutamate*
½ *cup mashed potatoes*

Cover the shrimps with water and bring just to the boiling point (for baby shrimps). Drain, then grind or chop them finely. Set in a mixing bowl. Stir-fry the onion with the lard until it wilts, add the curry powder, and stir together for 1 minute. Pour the onion mixture onto the shrimps and add the remaining ingredients. Mix and stir thoroughly. Let cool, then put in the refrigerator to chill.

Dough for Curry Puffs

2 *level cups all-purpose flour*
⅔ *cup shortening or lard*
⅓ *cup ice water*

In a large mixing bowl combine the flour with the shortening and work with your fingertips until the shortening is evenly mixed in and has the grain of cornmeal. Stir in the ice water and mix and pat into 2 balls.

Wrapping and Cooking:
Roll out the dough one ball at a time on a lightly floured surface into a circle about 1/16 inch thick. Using a cookie-cutter, cut out circles about 3 inches in diameter. Knead the scraps into the remaining dough to roll out to make more circles.

Place about 1 heaping teaspoon of filling in the center of each round, fold over into a half-moon shape, and seal the edges tightly, making a scalloped edge. Place the puffs on an ungreased baking sheet and prick each puff with a fork. Brush the tops with beaten egg. Bake in a 400° oven for about 20 minutes.

Yield: Makes about 60 puffs.

Note: The Curry Puffs can be frozen before or after baking. They can be reheated in a 350° oven for 10 minutes.

Shanghai Chun Chüan P'i 上海春捲皮
SHANGHAI SPRING ROLL (EGG ROLL) WRAPPERS

Spring rolls are called egg rolls in the United States. In China they are served especially on Chinese New Year's Day. Spring rolls are symbols of prosperity because they resemble Chinese gold bars of the old days. Following are two kinds of spring rolls. The wrappers and fillings are very different.

> 2 *pounds unbleached flour (about 6 cups)*
> 1 *teaspoon salt*
> 3½ *cups water*

Mix the flour with salt in a large mixing bowl. Add 2 cups water, mix, knead, and gradually add 1½ cups water while kneading and mixing. An electric mixer with a dough hook can be used. The kneading will take 20 minutes by hand and 10 minutes by machine. Knead until a very soft, smooth, and elastic dough is formed. Leave in a tightly covered bowl for at least 2 to 3 hours in the refrigerator.

Heat a large ungreased electric skillet or a large griddle to 375°. The temperature is very important, for if the pan is too cold, a thick layer will stick to the pan, and if the pan is too hot, it will not stick at all. Place a large plate and a piece of paper towel alongside the pan.

Take up a good handful of dough in one hand at a time and keep the rest in the refrigerator. The dough is very soft and will drip, so rotate your wrist in a constant slow motion, keeping the dough up and working it with your fingers and palm. Press the dough onto the bottom of the pan in a circular motion, then quickly pull it back, leaving a very thin film of dough on the hot surface. The dough will start to dry at the edges in about 10 seconds. With your other hand, peel the whole spring roll wrapper off the pan and put on a large plate. Continue the procedure with the remaining dough. Pile the wrappers in one stack. After making about 10 wrappers, the dough may get too warm and hence lose its elasticity, so let chill in the refrigerator. There may be some dry dough remaining on the hot pan; just wipe it off periodically with the paper towel. Cover the wrappers with a slightly damp towel until ready for use. If served the same day, there is no need for refrigerating or reheating in the steamer. Leftover wrappers can be divided up, covered with plastic wrap, and stored in the refrigerator for weeks or in the freezer for months. This recipe for spring roll wrappers is also used for Amoy Popia (page 287).

Yield: 50 7-inch wrappers.

Canton Chun Chüan, Hun Tun, Shai Mai P'i 廣東春捲皮
CANTON SPRING ROLL (EGG ROLL), WON TON, 餛飩皮
OR SHAO MAI WRAPPERS 燒賣皮

½ *teaspoon salt*
2 *level cups all-purpose flour*
1 *egg*
½ *cup water (approximately)*

Mix the salt and flour in a mixing bowl. Make a well in the center of the flour and pour the egg and water into it. With your fingers, stir to combine all the ingredients (add more water if the dough is too dry), then mix and knead until the dough is smooth and soft. Cover with a dry cloth and let set for 15 minutes.

Divide the dough in half. On a floured surface roll out the halves one at a time into a paper-thin sheet, about 24 x 12 inches. With a sharp knife, pastry wheel or cookie-cutter, cut 6-inch squares for Canton spring roll wrappers, 3-inch squares for won ton wrappers, or 3-inch rounds for *shao mai* wrappers. Sprinkle a little flour in between the pieces and stack them. Cover with a dry towel. They are now ready for use.

Yield: 16 Canton spring roll wrappers, 64 won ton wrappers, or 64 *shao mai* wrappers.

Shanghai Chun Chüan
SHANGHAI SPRING ROLLS (EGG ROLLS)

上 海 春 捲

½ *pound pork*
 1 *tablespoon soy sauce*
½ *teaspoon sugar*
 2 *tablespoons cornstarch*
 6 *dried mushrooms*
 1 *pound celery cabbage*
½ *cup shredded bamboo shoots*
 2 *cups peanut or corn oil*
 1 *tablespoon dry sherry*
 1 *teaspoon salt*
¼ *teaspoon monosodium glutamate*
 3 *tablespoons water*
 1 *egg*
20 *Shanghai Spring Roll Wrappers* (*page* 282), *round
     or square, about 7 inches in diameter* (*ready-made
     wrappers can be used*)

Preparation of the filling:
Slice the pork and cut again into 2-inch-long julienne strips. You
should have about 1 cup. Mix well with the soy sauce, sugar, and
½ tablespoon cornstarch. Set aside.

Wash and soak the mushrooms in ½ cup warm water for 30 minutes. Drain, cut off, and discard the stems, and cut mushrooms into
julienne strips. Finely shred the celery cabbage to make about 6
cups. Set these 2 items on a large plate with the bamboo shoots.

Heat a wok until very hot. Add 1½ tablespoons peanut oil and
pork. Stir-fry the pork over high heat until it separates into shreds,
splash on the sherry, stir, and mix well. Add the mushrooms and
cook together for 1 minute. Remove and set aside.

Heat the same wok and add 1½ tablespoons peanut oil. Add the
bamboo shoots and cabbage. Stir-fry until the cabbage wilts. Add
the salt and monosodium glutamate. Mix well. Put the meat mixture
back into the wok, mix, and cook together with the vegetables for
1 more minute. Combine 1½ tablespoons cornstarch with the
water, mix well, and add to the liquid in the wok. There should be
about 3 to 4 tablespoons liquid left in the center of the wok (take
some out if there is too much). Stir until the liquid boils and thickens and coats the meat and vegetables. Remove and let cool.

How to wrap the spring rolls:

Beat the egg in a bowl and set aside with a pastry brush. While wrapping, keep the unused spring roll wrappers in one stack, covered with a damp cloth. If the wrappers get too stiff due to long storage, carefully separate them. Wrap a warm damp cloth around them until soft, or just steam them over low heat for a few minutes. Then stack and cover with a damp cloth.

Take one spring roll wrapper at a time and place rough side down on the table. Take about 2 tablespoons of filling and put at the lower corner of the wrapper. With your hands, roll into a cylinder about 4 inches long. Lift the flap over the filling and roll a little to tuck the edge or point under the filling. Brush the exposed edges of the wrapper with beaten egg. Now roll the cylinder to the center. Bring the two end flaps up over the top of the enclosed filling and gently press. Continue rolling into a neat 5-inch-long spring roll. The beaten egg will seal the edges and keep the wrapper intact. Cover with a kitchen towel until ready to cook. For storing one day, cover with plastic wrap and place in the refrigerator until ready to fry.

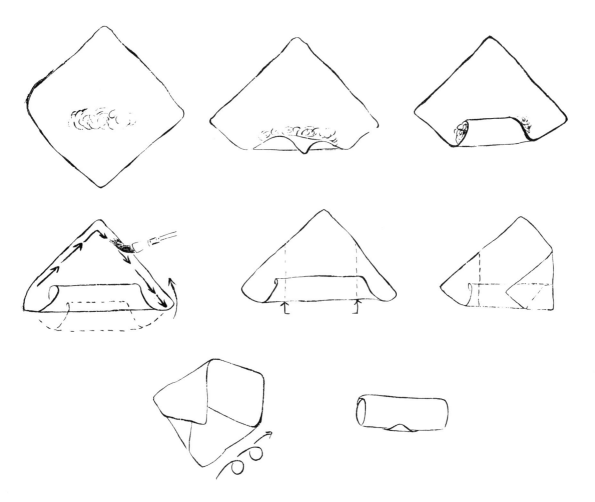

Cooking:

Heat 1 cup plus 13 tablespoons peanut oil in a wok, frying pan, or deep fryer to about 350°. Place 6 spring rolls in the oil and deep fry for 5 to 6 minutes or until golden brown and crispy, turning them for even frying. Transfer the spring rolls to paper towels to drain. Keep warm in the oven while the rest of the spring rolls are being fried. Serve hot, with wine vinegar and Hot Pepper Oil (page 208) as a dip.

Yield: 20 spring rolls.

Note: Spring rolls can be frozen after frying. They can be reheated in a 450° oven for about 10 minutes (on a rack, not in a pan).

Canton Chun Chüan
CANTON SPRING ROLLS

廣東春捲

½ pound fresh bean sprouts (*about 3 cups*)
 4 cups finely chopped celery
½ cup finely chopped fresh mushrooms
 3 tablespoons peanut or corn oil
½ pound ground pork
 1 tablespoon dry sherry
 1 tablespoon soy sauce
½ teaspoon sugar
½ pound raw shrimps, shelled, deveined, and diced
 2 teaspoons salt
¼ teaspoon monosodium glutamate
 1 pound Canton Spring Roll Wrappers (*page 283*),
        about 16 to 18 pieces (*ready-made wrappers can
        be used*)
 2 cups peanut or corn oil

Preparation for the filling:

Rinse the bean sprouts in a pot of cold water and discard any husks that float to the surface. Drain to dry well. Set aside the bean sprouts with the chopped celery and mushrooms.

Heat a wok over high heat until very hot. Add 1 tablespoon peanut oil and pork, stir-fry the pork until it loses its reddish color, then splash in the sherry, soy sauce, and sugar. Stir to mix well with pork. Add the shrimps and stir-fry together for 2 minutes. Remove and set aside.

Heat the same wok with 2 tablespoons peanut oil over medium heat. Add the celery and stir-fry for 5 minutes or until the celery is very dry. Add the mushrooms and bean sprouts and stir together for 2 to 3 minutes more. Add the salt and monosodium glutamate and stir to mix well. Return the pork and shrimp mixture to the wok and stir until all the ingredients are well-combined. There should not be any liquid. (Drain them if there is some.) Remove to cool and use as filling.

How to wrap and cook the spring rolls:
Follow the recipe for Shanghai Spring Rolls (page 282) except use Canton Spring Roll Wrappers instead of Shanghai Spring Roll Wrappers.

Yield: 16 spring rolls.

Variations: Cabbage may be used instead of bean sprouts. Beef may be used instead of pork.

Amoy Popia 厦門薄餅
AMOY PANCAKES WITH FILLING AND CONDIMENTS

Popia is an Amoy (a city in southern Fukien) specialty, eaten only on special occasions. The *popia*, meaning "thin pancake," is actually the same as the Shanghai spring roll wrapper without being fried, but the manner in which it is eaten is different. The *popia* is used to wrap cooked food; it is a finger food. A hot filling with a variety of flavorings and condiments is served at the dining table and the diners wrap whatever they choose. *Popia* are a lot of fun to eat.

24 *steamed Shanghai Spring Roll Wrappers (page 282)*
    (ready-made wrappers can be used)

Filling:
   8 *tablespoons peanut or corn oil*
   2 *cups finely shredded pork*
   2 *tablespoons dry sherry*
   4 *tablespoons light soy sauce*
   1 *teaspoon sugar*
   1 *scallion, finely shredded*
   1 *pound raw shrimps, shelled, deveined, and*
       coarsely chopped
1½ *teaspoons salt*
   1 *cup finely shredded winter bamboo shoots or carrots*
   4 *pieces plain pressed bean curd, finely shredded*
   1 *pound fresh snow pea pods, strings removed*
       and finely shredded

Side dishes to accompany the filling:
   ½ *pound fresh bean sprouts, heads and roots removed,*
       blanched in boiling water for 30 seconds, rinsed
       in running cold water, and drained well
   2 *eggs, beaten, made into 4 very thin omelets and*
       cut into slivers
   ½ *cup roasted peanuts, finely ground*
   1 *cup coarsely chopped tender coriander leaves*
   ¼ *cup finely shredded scallion (white part only)*
   2 *tablespoons hot bean sauce combined with 2 table-*
       spoons hoisin *sauce*
   ½ *cup dried green seaweed, stir-fried in 2 tablespoons*
       oil until dark green and crispy
   ½ *cup dried flat fish fillets (no salt added), cut with*
       scissors into very small bits and stir-fried in 2
       tablespoons oil until crispy

Cooking the filling:
Place a large heavy pot near the cooking area. Heat a wok over high
heat until hot. Add 3 tablespoons peanut oil, then the pork, and
stir-fry for 2 minutes. Splash on 1 tablespoon sherry and 2 tablespoons soy sauce and add ½ teaspoon sugar. Stir and mix, then
add shredded scallion. Stir-fry together for 1 minute. Remove and
place in the large pot.

Heat the same wok and add 2 tablespoons peanut oil. Stir-fry the
shrimps for 2 minutes. Splash on 1 tablespoon sherry and add 1 tea-

spoon salt. Mix well and remove to the same large pot. Heat the
wok again. Add 3 tablespoons peanut oil and stir-fry the bamboo
shoots and pressed bean curd, mix, and cook together for 2 minutes.
Add ½ teaspoon salt, 2 tablespoons soy sauce, and ½ teaspoon
sugar and cook for another 2 minutes. Remove and place in the
large pot with the pork and shrimps.

Heat the large pot with all the partially cooked ingredients over
low heat and bring it to the boiling point. Add the shredded snow
pea pods. Stir and mix well. Partly cover the pot and slowly simmer
for about 2 hours. Check and stir once every 15 minutes. Make sure
the heat is low enough so that it does not burn the ingredients.
When the dish is done, it should be moist but with very little sauce.
It can be reheated, using low heat. It takes about ½ hour to thoroughly heat up. Serve filling piping hot.

Serving:
A lazy Susan is the perfect serving implement for such a meal. Put
the large bowl of hot filling in the center and the side dishes and
wrappers around the edges. Each person takes a wrapper and places
it on his own plate. Then he takes a few strips of scallion, dips them
in the sauce, and places them in the center of the wrapper. He adds
a little of each of the side dishes, then takes 3 to 4 tablespoons hot
filling. He wraps the *popia* with filling, egg roll fashion, with one
end tucked in and eats it with his fingers.

Yield: 6 to 8 servings.

Hun Tun
WON TONS

餛飩

½ 10-*ounce package frozen chopped spinach or ½ cup finely
   chopped blanched vegetables (celery cabbage or
   green beans)*
1 *pound ground pork (about 2 cups)*
1 *teaspoon salt*
1 *tablespoon soy sauce*
1 *tablespoon cornstarch*
1 *egg*
1 *tablespoon peanut or corn oil*
75 *Won Ton Wrappers (page 283), each 3 x 3 inches
   (ready-made wrappers may be used)*

Thaw out and drain the spinach or blanched vegetables. Combine
the pork, salt, soy sauce, cornstarch, egg, and oil. Stir the mixture in

one direction until the meat holds together, then add spinach and mix some more.

Have ½ cup cold water in a cup ready. Cover the stack of won ton wrappers with a damp cloth while wrapping to prevent them from drying out.

How to wrap a won ton:
Place 1 teaspoon filling just below the center at a corner of a wrapper. Fold the corner over the filling and roll toward the center, leaving 1 inch of the opposite corner unrolled. Dip a finger in the water and moisten one end of the rolled wrapper. Take the two rolled ends in the fingers of both hands and pull them toward each other until the ends meet and overlap. Pinch the ends firmly together to seal. As each won ton is finished, place it on a tray and cover with a dry towel until ready to cook. At this stage the won tons can also be frozen on a tray, then transferred to a plastic bag or container. They will keep in the freezer for several weeks. When ready to serve, cook in boiling water for 2 minutes longer without defrosting.

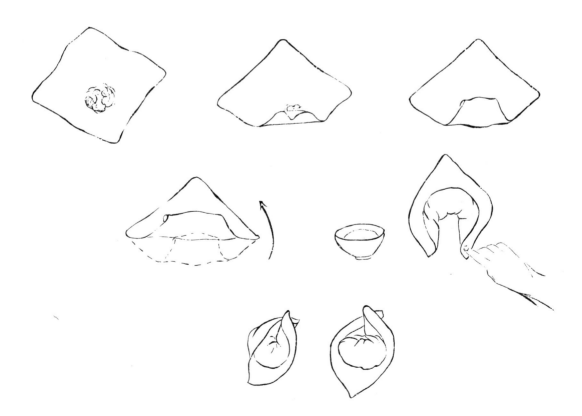

How to cook a won ton:
In a large pot bring 2 quarts water to a boil and drop in the desired number of won tons. Bring to a boil again and add ½ cup cold water. Bring to boil. Repeat adding cold water once more. When the won tons are done, they will float to the top. Drain. Following are different ways to serve the cooked and uncooked won tons:

To serve as won ton soup:
3 *cups chicken broth*
2 *teaspoons minced scallion*
4 *teaspoons sesame oil*
8 *teaspoons soy sauce*
Pepper to taste

Bring the chicken broth to a boil. Divide the scallion, sesame oil, soy sauce, and pepper at the bottom of 4 individual soup bowls. Pour the hot broth over these. As a soup course, add 20 drained, cooked won tons for 4 servings. As a light meal, add 48 drained, cooked won tons for 4 servings.

To serve plain won tons as a light meal for 4:
Put 48 drained, cooked won tons on a platter. Pour 1 tablespoon light soy sauce and 2 teaspoons sesame oil over them and serve hot. Or mix the soy sauce and sesame oil and use as a dip.

To serve panfried won tons as a light meal or appetizer:
After the won tons have been cooked in boiling water, drain and cool completely. Panfry them in a little oil to produce a brown crust on both sides. Serve with soy sauce and wine vinegar as a dip.

To serve fried won tons as an appetizer or light meal:
Deep fry uncooked won tons in 335° oil (2 cups) for 3 to 4 minutes. Drain on paper towels. Serve with wine vinegar and Hot Pepper Oil (page 208) as a dip or with Sweet-and-Sour Sauce (see recipe for Sweet-and-Sour Pork [page 116] for this sauce) as a dip.

Shao Mai
STEAMED MEAT DUMPLINGS

燒賣

1½ *cups finely chopped celery cabbage*
  2 *teaspoons salt*
  1 *pound finely ground pork (about 2 cups)*
  1 *tablespoon soy sauce*
  ½ *teaspoon sugar*
  1 *tablespoon cornstarch*
  2 *tablespoons peanut or corn oil*
  2 *tablespoons cold water*
 40 Shao Mai *Wrappers (page 283), each 3 inches in*
       diameter (ready-made wrappers can be used)

Place the chopped celery cabbage in a mixing bowl and sprinkle with 1 teaspoon salt. Mix well and pack down. Let stand for 10 minutes. Use a kitchen towel to squeeze the excess juice from the cabbage. Set aside.

Combine the pork with 1 teaspoon salt, soy sauce, sugar, cornstarch, peanut oil, and cold water. Mix the meat and seasoning in one direction until the meat holds together. Add the cabbage, and mix some more, stirring in the same direction. The filling is ready.

While making the *shao mai*, cover the wrappers with a damp cloth to prevent them from drying. To fill each *shao mai*, moisten the side of each wrapper with a little water and place about 1 tablespoon of filling in the center. Gather the sides of the wrapper around the filling, letting the wrapper form small pleats naturally. Squeeze the middle gently to make sure the wrapper sticks firmly against the filling and press down on a flat surface so that the *shao mai* flattens and can stand with the filling exposed at the top. Leave a narrow ruffled border of the wrapper unattached to the filling. Place the *shao mai* on a greased plate 1 inch smaller in diameter than your steamer.

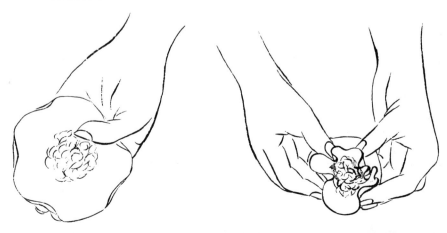

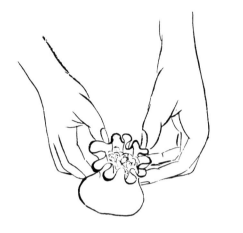

Cooking:
Sprinkle some water on each *shao mai*'s ruffles, which tend to dry up, and place the plate on the steamer rack. Cover the pot tightly and steam the *shao mai* over medium-high heat for 20 minutes. If a bamboo steamer is used; grease the rack and place the *shao mai* directly on the rack; steam for 15 minutes and serve directly from the steamer.

Yield: 6 servings as a light meal; 10 to 12 servings as an appetizer.

Variation: Beef may be used instead of pork; add 2 more table-spoons oil.

STEAMED *Har Gow* AND *Fun Gor*   蝦餃, 粉菓

Har gow and *fun gor* are Cantonese specialties. The cooked dough has a translucent appearance and delicate texture. However, the addition of boiling water to the dough should be a gradual process, accompanied by constant stirring. If the water is too hot, the dough will be too elastic, and if the water is too cold, the dough will crack.

Har Gow Filling

1 *pound raw shrimps, shelled, deveined, and finely*
      chopped
2 *tablespoons minced parboiled pork fat or fatty bacon*
1 *tablespoon finely chopped scallion (white part only)*
2 *tablespoons finely chopped water chestnuts*
1 *egg white*
1 *teaspoon cornstarch*
Dash of white pepper
1 *teaspoon salt*
1 *tablespoon light soy sauce*
1 *tablespoon peanut or corn oil*

Combine the above ingredients in a large bowl. Stir in one direction, mixing thoroughly. Refrigerate at least 1 hour.

Fun Gor Filling

½ *pound ground pork (about 1 cup)*
1 *teaspoon cornstarch*
½ *teaspoon sugar*
1 *tablespoon soy sauce*
2 *tablespoons peanut or corn oil*
2 *scallions, finely chopped*
½ *cup finely chopped bamboo shoots*
4 *dried mushrooms, soaked in warm water until soft,*
.   *stems removed, then finely chopped*
½ *teaspoon salt*
⅛ *teaspoon monosodium glutamate*
⅛ *teaspoon white pepper*
1 *teaspoon cornstarch combined with 1 tablespoon*
      water

Mix the pork thoroughly with the cornstarch, sugar, and soy sauce.
Stir-fry in 1 tablespoon peanut oil for 2 to 3 minutes. Remove and
set aside. Stir-fry the scallion in 1 tablespoon peanut oil for 1 minute, then stir in the bamboo shoots and mushrooms and cook and
mix together for another minute. Add the salt, monosodium glutamate, and pepper and mix well. Put back the cooked pork, mix,
and cook some more. Pour in the cornstarch and water mixture, stirring until the liquid thickens and coats the contents with a clear
glaze. Remove and allow the filling to cool.

Dough for Har Gow *and* Fun Gor *Wrapper*

1½ *cups sifted wheat starch*
½ *cup sifted tapioca flour*
1½ *cups (approximately) boiling water*
2 *tablespoons peanut or corn oil*

Resift together the wheat starch and tapioca flour into a large mixing bowl. Gradually add the boiling water, stirring at the same time, then add the peanut oil and let cool a little. Knead the dough until soft and smooth. Divide the dough into 2 halves. Keep one half covered in a bowl and place the other half on a lightly oiled surface. Knead, then roll into a sausagelike shape 1 inch in diameter. Cut crosswise into ½-inch-wide pieces. Cover with a dry cloth to prevent the dough from drying out.

Apply a little oil to both sides of a tortilla press. Put one piece of dough on the press, then press to make a thin sheet about 2½ inches in diameter. Do the same with all the pieces. The dough is now ready to be wrapped around the filling. (If you don't have a tortilla press, use a cleaver, brushing one side of it with a little oil, then flattening the small piece of dough between the blade and a flat surface by pressing on the cleaver evenly with the palm of your hand until the dough is very thin and about 2½ inches in diameter. A small oiled rolling pin may be used to roll out the dough instead of a tortilla press or cleaver.)

Yield: Makes 40 wrappers for either *har gow* or *fun gor*.

How to wrap har gow:
Take 1 piece of rolled dough and place 1 heaping teaspoon of shrimp filling in the center. Fold edges together, pleating one side, and press tightly so that the lower half of the shell acts as a pouch

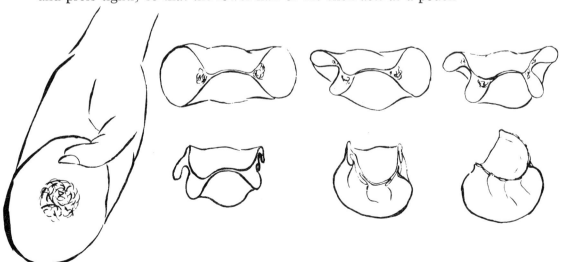

and the upper half of the shell is the cover. It will look like a miniature creel with a brim on the lid. Place the finished *har gow* on a lightly oiled flat plate. Repeat procedure until all the filling is used. Put the plate in a preheated steamer. Cover and steam for 5 minutes.

Yield: 40 *har gow.*

How to wrap fun gor:
Take 1 piece of rolled dough and place 1 heaping teaspoon of meat filling in the center. Fold edges together into a half-moon shape, pressing edges together tightly. Press down the *fun gor* slightly on a flat surface so that it stands firmly. Place the finished *fun gor* on a lightly oiled flat plate. Repeat procedure until all filling is used. Put the plate in the preheated steamer. Cover and steam for 5 minutes.

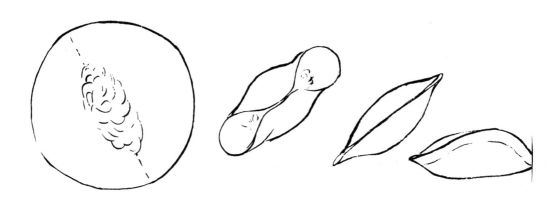

Yield: 40 *fun gor.*

Note: Both *har gow* and *fun gor* can be frozen before cooking.

Lo Po Kao
WHITE TURNIP CAKES

White turnip cake is a Cantonese *tien hsin* (*dim sim*). It is usually made around the New Year's holidays. It is similar to scrapple made from cornmeal mush, but it uses different materials. It may seem strange to anyone who tastes it for the first time.

2 *pounds Chinese white turnips*
2 *Chinese sausages*
⅓ *cup dried shrimps, soaked in ½ cup hot water*
   for ½ hour
4 *dried mushrooms, soaked in warm water for ½ hour*
2 *tablespoons Cantonese preserved vegetable, washed*
   well and finely chopped
1 *teaspoon salt*
¼ *teaspoon pepper*
¼ *teaspoon monosodium glutamate*
2 *tablespoons oil*
1 *tablespoon light soy sauce*
1 *pound fresh water-ground long-grain rice flour,*
   broken into fine meal

Peel the turnips and shred finely or grate them. You should have about 6 cups. Cover with water and bring to a boil. Simmer about 30 minutes or until very tender. Drain, reserving the juice. Finely chop the sausages, shrimps, and mushrooms. Add all the ingredients except the rice flour to the cooked and drained turnips and cook together for 5 minutes. Let cool.

Add 1 cup of the reserved turnip water, then slowly blend in the rice flour. Mix well, until the flour has been thoroughly blended in. Pour the mixture into 8 x 8 x 2-inch cake pan or 2 small loaf pans and steam for 1 hour. Allow the cake to cool and place in the refrigerator to chill overnight.

To serve, cut into ½-inch thick slices, 2 x 2 inches square. Panfry on both sides in a little oil until browned. Serve hot, with oyster sauce as a dip.

Yield: 8 servings as a light meal; 20 servings as an appetizer.

Note: Dried rice flour can be used, but use only 2 cups and add 1 cup more of turnip water. The steamed turnip cake can be frozen and fried before serving.

Variations: Szechuan preserved vegetable may be used instead of Cantonese preserved vegetables. Also, ¼ pound ground pork may be substituted for the Chinese sausages. Adjust seasonings.

DESSERTS (SWEET *TIEN HSIN*)

Chiu Niang
WINE RICE

酒釀

3 *cups glutinous rice* (*sweet rice*)
2 *teaspoons wine yeast*
1 *teaspoon flour*

Wash rice in cold water several times. Cover with cold water to 2 inches above the rice and soak for 4 hours. Wine yeast is sold in ball form, so you must mash it before using: Place between 2 sheets of waxed paper and mash with a rolling pin. Measure out 2 teaspoons and mix with flour. Set aside.

Line a steamer tier with a piece of cheesecloth. Spread rice evenly about ¼ inch deep. (With a small steamer, use 2 tiers.) Steam over high heat for 30 minutes.

Transfer the steamed rice to a large colander and rinse thoroughly, first with cold water, then with warm water (about 80°). Rinse a 2-quart earthenware casserole with warm water, then put the rice in it. Mix the wine yeast and flour with the rice. Gently pat the rice down evenly, making a 1-inch well in the center down to the bottom of the casserole. Cover.

Place the slightly warm container in an insulated bag or wrap in a blanket. Leave in a dark place for about 2 days. By this time a sweet liquid will have accumulated in the well and at the sides.

Transfer the wine rice to a glass container. Cover tightly and keep in the refrigerator, where it may be stored indefinitely. Be sure the juice covers the rice. Serve cold or hot.

Yield: 5 to 6 cups.

Ma T'uan
SESAME SEED BALLS

蔴糰

1 *pound glutinous rice flour*
1¼ *cups dark brown sugar*
1¼ *cups boiling water*
1 *cup Red Bean Paste* (*page* 300) (*canned paste can be used*)

¼ *cup white sesame seeds*
4 *cups peanut or corn oil*

Put the glutinous rice flour in a large mixing bowl. Dissolve the brown sugar in boiling water, then stir the sugar water into the flour until the dough is well-blended. Shape the dough into balls about the size of golf balls. Shape the Red Bean Paste also into balls, about the size of hazelnuts to use as fillings.

Take a ball of dough and press a hole into it, making a deep cup. Place a ball of filling in it and close the cup, making sure to completely cover the filling with dough. Press and seal the edges together well. Roll the filled balls between the palms of your hands to make them perfectly round, then roll in sesame seeds until the entire surface is covered. Gently press seeds into the surface. To make sesame seeds adhere, dampen the dough balls with a little water.

Heat the oil in a wok or deep fryer to about 325°. Add balls a few at time and let cook slightly. When the sesame seeds have turned light brown, apply some pressure on the balls with the back of a soup spoon against the side of the pan. They will increase slightly in size. Continuing to apply pressure to each ball, let it puff up until it becomes about 3 times its original size.

Yield: 20 balls.

Yen Wo T'ien T'ang
BIRD'S NESTS WITH ROCK SUGAR SOUP

燕 窩 甜 湯

2 *ounces bird's nests (about 6 whole ones)*
6 *crushed tablespoons rock sugar*
2 *cups water*

Soak the bird's nests in warm water for at least 4 hours. Rinse very well with water and pick out the down. Drain and place the bird's nests in a small saucepan and cover with 2 cups warm water and bring to a boil for 2 minutes. Rinse and drain the bird's nests and gently squeeze dry (you will have about 1½ cups).

Return the bird's nests to the saucepan. Add the water and bring to a boil. Simmer for about 5 minutes or until the bird's nests are very soft. Add rock sugar and dissolve. Serve hot.

Yield: 4 servings as a snack or dessert.

Variation: 2 ounces silver ears may be used as a substitute for the bird's nests. Add 3 cups warm water, slowly bring to a boil, and cook over low heat for 2 to 3 hours or until soft. Add rock sugar to taste.

Tou Sha

RED BEAN PASTE

豆 沙

1   *pound dried red beans*
1½   *cups sugar*
1½   *cups lard or peanut oil*

Check over the beans and discard the bad ones. Wash and soak the beans in water overnight. Drain. Add the beans and 6 cups cold water to a large pot, bring to a boil, then simmer for 1 to 2 hours or until the beans are very soft.

Use the blender to grind ⅓ of the cooked beans at a time with their liquid. Grind each batch for 5 minutes.

Pour the bean paste with the liquid into a cloth bag and tie the bag closed with a string. To press excess liquid out of the ground beans, put a heavy object on the tied bag to weight it down and let it drain in the sink for at least 4 hours. The bean paste will be quite dry by then.

Remove the bean paste from the bag and put it in a 3- to 4-quart stainless steel pot. Add the sugar and lard. Put an asbestos pad (flame tamer) on a burner. Using medium-low heat, cook for about 30 minutes or until the bean paste begins to get dryer (does not stick to one's finger when touched). Stir often to avoid lard splattering and burning the beans. Cool. The paste is now ready to be used as a filling for Red Bean Paste Steamed Buns (page 301), Eight Precious Rice Pudding (page 302), and Honey Bananas (page 307). Leftover bean paste can be stored in the refrigerator or freezer.

Yield: 6 cups.

Tou Sha Bao

豆沙飽

RED BEAN PASTE STEAMED BUNS

1 *recipe Yeast Dough* (*page 266*)
2 *cups Red Bean Paste* (*page 300*) (*canned paste can be used*)
Food coloring

How to make and steam the buns:
Follow the recipe for Roast Pork Steamed Buns (page 268), using a red bean paste filling instead of a roast pork filling. Put about 1 heaping tablespoon of red bean paste on the dough rounds and shape into buns as for roast pork buns. Roll the finished buns between the palms of your hands to make smooth balls. Let the filled balls rise for 45 minutes and steam for 15 minutes. Using the tip of a chopstick, stamp a food coloring dot on top of each bun.

Yield: 20 3-inch buns.

Hsing Jen Tou Fu

杏仁豆腐

ALMOND CURD

2 *packages unflavored gelatin*
½ *cup cold water*
1 *cup boiling water*
1 *cup milk*
1 *tablespoon almond extract*
½ *cup sugar*
1½ *cups water*

Sprinkle the gelatin over the cold water in a mixing bowl and let it soften for 5 minutes. Pour the boiling water into the softened gelatin. Stir until it has completely dissolved, then stir in milk and almond extract. Pour the mixture into a flat 8 x 8 x 2-inch cake pan or the like. The Almond Curd should be about ½ inch thick. Refrigerate for at least 3 to 4 hours or until firmly set.

Combine sugar with 1½ cups water and stir to dissolve completely. Chill the sugar water in the refrigerator.

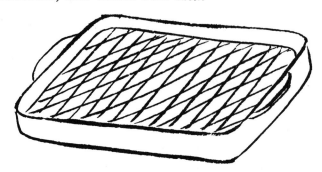

Using a small knife, make diagonal cuts ½ inch apart all the way through the Almond Curd. Repeat in the opposite direction to form diamond-shaped pieces. Lift them out with a spatula to a serving bowl. Pour the chilled sugar water over and serve cold.

Yield: 6 servings as a dessert.

Variations: Canned lychees, mandarin orange sections, or other fruits may be used as a garnish.

Pa Pao Fan

八寶飯

EIGHT PRECIOUS RICE PUDDING

20 *dried jujubes (red dates)*
 1 *cup glutinous rice (sweet rice)*
 1 *cup cold water*
 2 *teaspoons sugar*
 2 *tablespoons lard or corn oil*
 ½ *cup Red Bean Paste (page 300) (canned paste can be used)*

Sauce:
 1 *cup water*
 ½ *cup sugar*
 2 *teaspoons almond extract*
 2 *teaspoons cornstarch combined with 2 tablespoons water*

Preparation:
In a small saucepan soak the dried jujubes in hot water for 30 minutes. Wash several times and drain. Add ½ cup water and cook the jujubes over low heat for 30 minutes. The water will be almost gone and the jujubes will be soft enough to cut into halves and be pitted. Set aside.

Wash and soak the rice in the cold water in a 3- to 4-cup heatproof bowl for 30 minutes. Place the bowl in a pot containing water. The water level should be about 1½ inches below the bowl's rim. Cover the pot, bring to a boil, and steam for 30 minutes.

Mix the warm rice with sugar and lard. Spread a large piece of clear plastic wrap on the bottom of a shallow bowl (about 3 cups capacity). Take ⅔ of the cooked rice and line the sides and the bottom of the bowl on top of the plastic wrap. Spread the Red Bean Paste in a layer over the rice. Cover the bean paste with the remaining rice. The cooked glutinous rice acts as a pie crust. To decorate, invert the rice pudding onto a plate and make a design with the pitted dates. Carefully cover the pudding with the same plastic wrap and the bowl. Flip back. At this stage the dish can be set aside and kept in the refrigerator until ready to steam.

Cooking:
Bring water to a boil in a steamer. Place the pudding bowl on the rack and cover the pan tightly. Steam the pudding over moderate heat for 45 minutes.

A few minutes before the pudding is done, make the sauce by combining the water, sugar, and almond extract in a small saucepan. Stir the liquid and bring to a boil. Stir the cornstarch and water mixture and slowly add to the saucepan, stirring until the sauce thickens and boils again. Keep hot on burner.

Remove the pudding from the steamer and place a large plate over it. Invert onto plate. Peel off the clear plastic wrap. Pour the sauce over the pudding and cut into sections. Serve hot.

Yield: 8 servings as a dessert.

Variation: Pitted dates, candied cherries, or other candied fruit may be used instead of jujubes for decoration.

Ma La Kao

CANTONESE STEAMED CAKE

馬拉糕

    5 *eggs*
1¼ *cups (packed) light brown sugar*
    2 *cups sifted all-purpose flour*
    ½ *cup milk*
    1 *teaspoon vanilla extract*
    ½ *cup lard*
    2 *teaspoons baking powder*
    ½ *teaspoon baking soda*
    1 *tablespoon water*

Preparation:
Beat the eggs very well, add the brown sugar, and continue beating. Slowly and alternatingly add the flour, milk, and vanilla extract. Beat until well blended. Leave the cake mixture covered at room temperature for 1 hour.

Remove the bottom of an 8-inch spring-form cake pan. Shape a large piece of foil around the empty bottom and over the outside walls of the pan. Tie a string around the walls of the foil and pan to make sure the foil keeps its shape. (The aluminum foil bottom is better for steaming than the original thick cake pan bottom.)

Put lard in a cup and set on top of the pilot light of a range to melt it and keep it warm. Set up a steamer. Bring the steamer water to a boil.

Cooking:
Mix the baking powder and soda with water. Add to the cake mixture. Add the warm melted lard and mix well. Put the empty cake pan with the aluminum bottom on steamer rack. Pour in the cake mixture. The water should be at a rolling boil by now. Steam over high heat for 1 hour (make sure the steamer has enough water). Peel off the foil and cut cake into 2 x 3-inch diamond-shaped pieces. Always serve this cake hot. Leftover cake can be reheated by steaming.

Yield: 10 servings.

Ma T'i Kao
WATER CHESTNUT CAKE

馬 蹄 糕

  2 *cups water*
⅔ *cup rock or granulated sugar*
½ *cup water chestnut flour*
10 *fresh or canned water chestnuts, finely chopped*

Combine the water and sugar in a saucepan and bring to a boil. Keep at a slow boil.

Mix the water chestnut flour thoroughly with ½ cup water. Make sure the flour is in suspension. Slowly pour into the saucepan with the boiling sugar water, stirring until the contents thicken and become translucent. Mix in the chopped water chestnuts.

Pour the entire contents into a 6 x 3 x 2-inch mold and let cool at room temperature for about 3 to 4 hours. Cut into 1-inch-thick slices and chill in the refrigerator for 10 minutes. Serve cold. (It is best to serve this cake slightly chilled; when it is too cold, it tastes starchy.) The cake can also be served hot. Brush both sides of the slice with oil and broil on the top rack of the broiler for 5 minutes.

Yield: 20 pieces, each 1½ x 2 x 1 inch (10 servings as a dessert).

T'ang Ho T'ao
CANDIED PECANS

糖 核 桃

  6 *ounces shelled large pecans or walnuts (about 2 cups)*
¼ *cup sugar*
  1 *cup peanut or corn oil*

Put the pecans in a saucepan and add 1 quart water. Bring to a boil and cook for 5 minutes. Drain the pecans while they are still hot, put back into the pan, and add the sugar. Mix well.

The melted sugar should evenly coat the pecans. Transfer to a piece of waxed paper and spread out to dry for about 10 minutes.

Heat a wok over moderate heat and add the peanut oil. Fry the pecans 1 cup at a time for about 4 to 5 minutes or until the sugar has caramelized around each pecan. Stir constantly so that the pecans are evenly fried. Use a slotted spoon to transfer pecans to a large platter. Spread them apart into a single layer to cool, then transfer to paper towels to absorb the excess oil.

After cooling, the candied pecans can be stored in a jar or tin and will remain crisp and crunchy for months.

Variation: In China skinless walnuts are used instead of pecans and walnuts with skins.

Pa Szu P'in Kuo
SPUN APPLES

拔絲蘋果

¾ *cup flour*
 1 *egg, lightly beaten with ½ cup cold water*
 3 *medium-firm Delicious apples*
 2 *cups peanut or corn oil*
 1 *cup sugar*
¼ *cup water*
 1 *tablespoon black sesame seeds*

Preparation:
Place flour in a mixing bowl, then gradually add the egg and water mixture. Stir or beat until a smooth batter forms.

Peel the apples. Cut into 1-inch wedges, removing the cores. Put them in the batter.

Set aside near the cooking area a large serving plate and a large bowl filled with 1 quart cold water and a dozen ice cubes.

Cooking:
In a 2-quart saucepan heat the peanut oil to 350°. Take the coated apple pieces out of the batter one by one and fry in the oil until light brown, about 2 minutes. Fry 7 to 8 pieces at a time. Put on a tray to be refried again later and keep the oil hot. (This step can be done ahead of time, but reheat the oil.)

To a wok add 1 teaspoon of the peanut oil, the sugar, and water. Slowly bring to a boil, stirring only until the sugar is dissolved. Cook this mixture without stirring until it reaches the medium-hard crack stage and its color changes to light brown—i.e., when a drop of the syrup put into ice water forms a hard sugar mass instantly. Turn the heat down to its lowest point.

Reheat the apple pieces in the hot oil. Immediately lift them out of the oil, put them into the hot syrup, and sprinkle on the sesame seeds. Turn heat to medium and stir the wedges to coat them thoroughly with the syrup. Take them out one by one and drop them into the bowl of ice water. The syrup coating will harden instantly. Use a strainer to transfer the Spun Apples from the ice water to a serving plate. Serve immediately.

Yield: 8 to 10 servings as a dessert (24 Spun Apples).

Note: The ice water dipping can be done at the dining table. Bananas can be prepared in the same manner. In China we use peeled parboiled yucca instead of apples or bananas. Yucca can sometimes be purchased in Japanese food stores.

Hsiang Chiao Tou Sha
HONEY BANANAS

香蕉豆沙

In northern China and western China we have two bean paste-filled desserts that are quite similar in taste. The following recipe is a new version, adding banana to the bean paste.

    6 *just-ripe bananas*
    6 *tablespoons Red Bean Paste (page 300) (canned paste*
          can be used)
    1 *cup all-purpose flour*
    2 *tablespoons cornstarch*
    1 *cup water, approximately*
    2 *teaspoons baking powder*
    2 *cups peanut or corn oil*
  ¼ *cup sugar*

Preparation:
Peel the bananas. Split lengthwise and sandwich 1 tablespoon bean paste between each 2 banana halves. (If too much bean paste is placed between the banana halves, it will ooze out when frying.) Cut each banana into 1½-inch sections. Set on a plate.

Combine the flour and cornstarch together in a mixing bowl. Add the water and mix into a smooth batter. Mix and blend in the baking powder. The consistency should be slightly thick, just right for coating the bananas.

Cooking:
Heat a wok, add the peanut oil, and heat to 350°. Dip the banana sandwiches in the batter. Fry 7 to 8 pieces at a time until golden brown, about 2 minutes. Drain and serve hot, with sugar sprinkled on top.

Yield: 6 to 10 servings as a dessert.

Note: The fried bananas can be reheated in a preheated 400° oven for 10 minutes.

Ho T'ao Lao
WALNUT CREAM

核桃酪

This is a northern specialty. The jujube, or red date, is a small red-skinned datelike dried fruit. It is sweet and fragrant and has a high nutritive value. The Chinese like to serve jujubes hot. If jujubes are not available, use pitted dates instead. Just cut them into small pieces and add them to the blender with the walnuts.

2 tablespoons raw oval- or long-grain rice
½ cup dried jujubes (red dates)
3 cups water
½ cup shelled walnuts
¼ cup sugar

Preparation:
Wash the rice a few times and soak in cold water for at least 4 hours. Wash the jujubes in warm water several times and soak in 1 cup warm water for 4 hours or until soft. Use a small knife to remove the pits.

Drain the rice and put in a blender. Add the water. Blend for 2 minutes, then add the pitted jujubes and walnuts. Blend together for 5 minutes or until the jujubes and walnuts are pureed. Pour everything into a large saucepan, including the sugar. If the jujubes are not sweet enough, add more sugar.

Cooking:

While stirring, *slowly* bring the walnut cream to a boil over medium-low heat. The mixture will thicken to the consistency of a cream soup. It can be stored in the refrigerator for days. Just heat it up as needed and serve hot.

Yield: 6 to 8 servings as a dessert or snack.

Note: Pitted jujubes (sold in a box and already cooked), if available, can be used instead of the dried kind. If they are soft, they do not need soaking. Just cut them up and put them in the blender with the walnuts.

A Glossary of Chinese Ingredients Used in This Book

BEAN AND BEAN PRODUCTS

Fresh Young Soybeans

毛豆

Mao Tou

Fresh young soybeans are delicious to eat. They are in season in the early fall and are available in Chinese markets. They come in dark, fuzzy pods and are sold by weight. Young soybeans are like corn and should be eaten as soon as they are picked from the plant. They may be cooked with or without their pods.

Dried Soybeans

黄豆

Huang Tou

Dried soybeans are about the size of dried peas and are yellow in color. Packed in one-pound quantities in plastic bags, they are sold in many Oriental food shops and in health food stores.

Soybean Sprouts

黄豆芽

Huang Tou Ya

There are two kinds of beans that the Chinese germinate for bean sprouts: the mung bean and the soybean. Soybean sprouts are the more difficult ones to cook and are eaten mostly by people of Chinese origin in America. They are sold by weight in Chinese markets. The best bean sprouts are found in cooler weather. When bought fresh, they will keep in the refrigerator for two to three days. Mung bean sprouts are discussed on page 314.

Soy Sauce

Refer to "Condiments and Seasonings" (pages 325–329).

Salted Black Beans

Refer to "Condiments and Seasonings" (pages 325–329).

Brown Bean Sauce

Refer to "Condiments and Seasonings" (pages 325–329).

Ground Brown Bean Sauce

Refer to "Condiments and Seasonings" (pages 325–329).

Hoisin **Sauce**

Refer to "Condiments and Seasonings" (pages 325–329).

Soybean Milk 豆漿 *Tou Chiang*	Bean milk is extracted from soaked soybeans ground with water and is then strained through cloth. The straining removes the husk and most of the solid residue from the beans. The white liquid obtained is the bean milk, which contains most of the protein of the beans. Bean milk must be brought to a boil to get rid of the strong bean flavor. It is usually served hot as a beverage with breakfast. It should be stored in the same manner as regular milk.
Soybean Milk Skin 二竹 *Erh-Chu* 腐衣 *Fu-Yi*	When bean milk is boiled, a film forms on top of the liquid, very much as with regular milk. This film is lifted off of the boiling milk and dried. The skin of the bean milk is available in many shapes and sizes and is called by many names; each region and each manufacturer use a different name. The two kinds that are used in this book are *erh chu* and *fu-yi*. *Erh chu* is cut into rectangles 1½ x 4 inches and about ⅛ inch thick. The sheets come stacked and wrapped in paper, in half- or one-pound packages. *Fu-yi* is much thinner than *erh chu*. It is paper thin and almost transparent. It comes in large half-moon shaped sheets and is also wrapped in paper, in stacks of ten sheets. *Fu-yi* is very brittle and must be handled very gently. Since both *erh chu* and *fu-yi* come in a dried form, they need not be refrigerated. They should be used within about two months from the date of purchase, for they contain oil and can turn rancid.
Curdled Soybean Milk 豆腐花 *Tou Fu Hua*	When a coagulant is added to boiled soybean milk, it curdles. This curd is the most tender form of bean curd. It is eaten hot with soy sauce or cold with syrup as a snack.
Tender Soybean Curd 嫩豆腐 *Nen Tou Fu*	When some of the water is removed from the curdled bean milk, it becomes tender bean curd. It is cut into squares 4 x 4 inches, about 1½ inch thick.
Firm Soybean Curd 老豆腐 *Lao Tou Fu*	When a coagulant is added to boiled bean milk of a different concentration and some of the water is removed, the milk becomes firm bean curd. It is firmer than the tender bean curd and is cut into 3 x 3-inch squares, about ¾ inch thick. The size of the bean curd squares may vary, depending upon the manufacturers, who set their own standards. Bean curd spoils easily and so should be submerged in water in a container and placed in the coldest part of the refrigerator. If the water is changed daily, it can be kept unspoiled for at least a week if it was fresh when purchased.

Instant Soybean
Curd

即席豆腐
Chi Hsi Tou Fu

If fresh bean curd is not available, the Japanese produce
an instant bean curd mix, Instant Tou Fu, which is a good
substitute. It is made from dehydrated bean milk. Just
follow the directions on the package. The mix will not
fail as long as the bean milk powder is fresh. Packages of
Instant Tou Fu must always be kept in the refrigerator.

Pressed Soybean
Curd

豆腐乾
Tou Fu Kan

白豆腐乾
Pai Tou Fu Kan

五香豆腐乾
Seasoned or
*Wu Hsiang
Tou Fu Kan*

When even more water is pressed out of firm bean curd,
it becomes pressed bean curd. Its texture becomes much
firmer than that of regular bean curd and is almost like a
firm cheese. Pressed bean curd may be bought either plain
or seasoned. The plain curd is white and the seasoned
is cooked in soy sauce and star anise, giving it a brown
color. The two types are available in most Chinese grocery
stores and in some local Oriental food shops. They can
best be stored submerged in liquid. The white pressed
bean curd should be soaked in salt water made of 1 tablespoon salt to 4 cups water. The seasoned pressed bean
curd should be soaked in salt water and soy sauce. If kept
in the coldest part of the refrigerator, they will keep for
several weeks.

Fried Soybean
Curd

油豆腐
Yu Tou Fu

The name is self-explanatory. The bean curd is cut into
1½-inch cubes and deep fried in oil until a golden yellow
crust forms outside, while the inside of the bean curd remains soft. Fried soybean curd is sold by weight, usually
in half- or one-pound packages in plastic bags. Approximately twenty medium-fried bean curd cubes will weigh
one pound. The curd can be kept in the refrigerator without spoiling for two to three days and may also be frozen.

Fermented
Soybean Curd

腐乳(紅,白)
Fu-Ju

Fu-ju is fermented soybean curd, soaked in a solution of
salt, alcohol, and water. It comes in two colors, white and
red, with slightly different tastes to each. It has the texture of very soft cheese but is much saltier. *Fu-ju* can be
used to flavor vegetables and meats in cooking, or it can
be served right from the jar or can. When served as a
dish, a small amount is usually placed on a small dish and
eaten with congee. Once a can of *fu-ju* is opened, the
fu-ju should be transferred to a jar with a rustproof cap.
The process of fermentation does not stop; the longer the
fu-ju is kept, the softer it will be. But if it is kept in the
refrigerator, it will not spoil.

Mung Beans

綠豆
Lu Tou

Three very important food items are made from the mung
bean: bean sprouts, cellophane noodles, and mung bean
sheets.

Mung Bean Sprouts 綠豆芽 *Lu Tou Ya*	Mung bean sprouts are one of the most popular Chinese vegetables in the United States. They can be found in almost every large city supermarket. If very fresh and kept away from excess moisture, they can be kept in the refrigerator for two to three days.
Cellophane Noodles 粉絲 *Fen Szu* Mung Bean Sheets 粉皮 *Fen P'i*	When mung beans are soaked, ground, and strained, a translucent liquid is obtained. The liquid is then made into noodles and round sheets. Both the noodles and round sheets are transparent when warm and opaque when cool. This transparent quality is the reason the noodles are called cellophane noodles. They are sold in a dried form. The noodles are tied into bundles weighing two ounces, half a pound, and one pound. The mung bean sheets are sold in stacks of eight to ten sheets, packed in plastic bags.
Red Beans 紅豆 (赤豆) *Hung Tou* Red Bean Paste 紅豆沙 *Hung Tou Sha*	Red beans are used most often in sweet pastries in the form of paste. In the relatively few sweet dishes in Chinese cookery, red beans play an important role. The paste can be homemade or bought in cans. Red beans are sold by weight in plastic bags and may be found in many Oriental food stores.

SEEDS, NUTS, AND FRUITS

Sesame Seeds White Sesame Seeds 白芝蔴 *Pai Chih Ma* Black Sesame Seeds 黑芝蔴 *Hei Chih Ma*	Sesame seeds are black or white seeds that are slightly larger than poppy seeds. They are often used for their flavor. When toasted, they have a special fragrance. These seeds can be ground up to make a paste or to obtain oil. In southeastern China they are used mostly in sweet foods. Like the Italians, the Chinese also top their pastries with these seeds. Raw sesame seeds can be bought in Italian and Chinese groceries.
Sesame Paste	Refer to "Condiments and Seasonings" (pages 325–329).
Lotus Seeds 蓮心 *Lien Hsin*	Lotus seeds come from the seed pod of the lotus. They are used mostly in desserts or sweet soups. They are definitely a delicacy and are expensive, but the flavor and texture make the expense worthwhile. They come ready for use, sold by the pound, packed in plastic bags. They can be found in large Chinese grocery stores. It is best to use the seeds as soon as possible, since aging tends to affect their delicate texture.

Chestnuts

栗子
Li Tzu

Fresh chestnuts are at their best around Thanksgiving time. They have a tendency to mold easily if kept in a plastic bag, but a brown paper bag is porous enough to prevent them from spoiling. Dried chestnuts are available all year round and can be bought in Chinese and Italian markets. They should be soaked in cold water overnight before being cooked. It is important to cull the chestnuts so that any spoiled parts are removed. Inclusion of a few spoiled chestnuts can ruin all the effort that went into a delicious dish.

Gingko Nuts

白菓
Pai Kuo

The gingko is the edible pit of an inedible fruit. The gingko tree thrives in urban surroundings and is frequently used as a sidewalk shade tree. When the fruit is removed, the pit (or nut) is white and shaped like a tiny football, about the size of a jelly bean. The fresh meat of the nut is chartreuse and turns translucent when cooked. The nuts are never eaten raw. Gingko nuts are available canned, shelled, or loose in their shells and are sold by the pound.

Jujubes
(Red Dates)

紅棗
Hung Tsao

Jujubes come from the northern part of China. When fresh, they have a green color. They are crisp and sweet. They are generally available dried and have a crinkled skin and dark red appearance. Sizes vary from that of seedless grapes to that of large olives. They are best stored in the refrigerator or freezer and are sold in Chinese markets in plastic bags.

Longan or
Dragon Eyes

龍眼(桂圓)
Lung Yen

Dragon eyes are the same type of fruit as the lychee nut except that the shell is smoother and covered with a cinnamon-colored powder. They are slightly smaller than lychee nuts and have an entirely different taste. They come dried, canned, or pitted and are packed tightly into four-ounce packages. They are used for cooking in sweet soups or served as a fruit for dessert.

VEGETABLES

Fresh
Vegetables

The Chinese have developed the use of a great variety of leafy greens in their diet through centuries of experimentation. Some are cultivated, but others are indigenous vegetation that is foraged for throughout the countryside. Tender leaf buds of certain trees and bushes are considered prize delicacies, while others are merely seasonal vegetables. The Chinese have learned to use most edible indigenous vegetation, going as far as to reach under water to find edible leaves and roots, both nutritious and delicious. The list below deals with only a fraction of the vegetables used in Chinese cooking. Although available all year round, each vegetable is generally most flavorful at certain stages of its growth. For instance, the *bok chou* family of vegetables is best when picked after the "black frost," the first frost of the year. The leafy greens can be stored in the refrigerator doubly wrapped (first in a brown paper bag, then sealed with a plastic one) for as long as three weeks if the vegetable is fresh and free from excess moisture. Some of these vegetables are available in supermarkets; others are only sold in Chinese markets.

Bok Choy
白菜
Pai Ts'ai

Bok choy is eaten at different stages of growth. The *bok choy* sold in Chinese markets is full grown, with white stems, dark green leaves, and sometimes a sprig of yellow blossom in the center.

Mustard Greens
芥菜
Chieh Ts'ai

Both the stem and the leaves of the mustard green have the color of a greening apple. The mature plant has a very loosely wrapped head, and each individual stem is wide and has a full, ruffled leaf.

Chinese Celery Cabbage (Long Head)
天津白菜
Tientsin Pai Ts'ai

Long-headed Chinese celery cabbage originally came from Tientsin. It is noted for its pale yellow color and tightly wrapped elongated head. Two thirds of the plant is stem, while the leaves are comparatively small. It may be stored for a long time in the refrigerator.

Chinese Celery Cabbage (Short Head)
山東白菜
Shantung Pai Ts'ai

This Chinese celery cabbage is very similar to the long-headed variety, except that its leaves are curlier and it has a shorter and fatter head. The head is also tightly wrapped. It is named after the province of Shantung.

Chrysanthemum Greens
茼蒿菜
Tung Hao Ts'ai

Edible chrysanthemums, though cultivated, grow like weeds. They should be eaten before they begin to bloom. This vegetable is harvested by picking off the top several inches of the stem where the leaves and the stems are still tender. They are sold by the bunch and can be grown at home in almost any type of soil.

Amaranth
莧菜
Hsien Ts'ai

Amaranth comes either with a green or red stem, with dark green leaves. Seedlings can be eaten, but as the plant grows, tender stems and leaves can be cropped off for consumption in the late spring to early summer. It is sold by the bunch.

Bean Sprouts Refer to "Bean and Bean Products" (pages 311–314).

Soybean Sprouts Refer to "Bean and Bean Products" (pages 311–314).

Mung Bean Sprouts Refer to "Bean and Bean Products" (pages 311–314).

Chinese White Turnips

白蘿蔔
Pai Lo Po

Many varieties of turnips are suitable for Chinese cooking. The best flavor comes from large white ones, about eight inches long and two to three inches in diameter. Sizes vary with the growing conditions. This type of turnip can be cooked until tender without becoming mealy.

Butternut Squash and Buttercup Squash

南瓜
Nan Kua

The butternut squash has a taste similar to that of the Chinese pumpkin. It is readily available in the fall. The buttercup squash is starchier and sweeter than the butternut squash. It is not used with the same popularity as the butternut squash, but the flavor is far superior to that of the pie pumpkin, so it is worth the effort to search for this squash. The squash is available at some farm stands. It is dark green, with a knob on top like a brioche, and is about the size of a medium head of cabbage.

Winter Melon

冬瓜
Tung Kua

Winter melon is actually a vegetable of the squash family. It has a hard dark green peel that is coated with a frost-like white powder. This melon is sold in wedges by weight. It will keep in the refrigerator for a long time if loosely covered with waxed paper. Since it is loosely wrapped, the outer layer may become dry. This dried-out part should be removed along with the peel before cooking. A tightly sealed plastic bag tends to promote quick rotting of the melon.

Water Chestnuts

馬蹄 (荸薺)
Ma T'i

Water chestnuts are actually not part of the chestnut family. They are the starchy stalks of a water plant whose leaves grow above water. They are available fresh, canned, and powdered. The fresh water chestnut is so superior in texture and flavor that it can not be compared with the canned. Fresh water chestnuts are difficult to peel, a time-consuming process, but are well worth the effort. They can be candied like apples. The street vendors in China used to string these candied water chestnuts on a thin bamboo skewer, which made them look like large bright red beads. Canned water chestnuts retain only the texture of the fresh ones, not the flavor. Powdered water chestnuts are discussed under Water Chestnut Flour in "Grains, Flours, and Grain Products" (pages 329–332). Canned water chestnuts are available in most supermarkets, but the powdered and fresh ones can be obtained only in Chinese markets and in specialty shops. The fresh ones do not spoil so readily and can be kept in the refrigerator for about three weeks. Once peeled, they keep well in the freezer.

Chinese Leeks

韮菜
Chin Ts'ai

The Chinese leek is a perennial plant allied to the onion. Its dark green grasslike leaves are used for flavoring and sometimes as a vegetable. Chinese leeks only come fresh and are sold by the bunch in Chinese vegetable stores. They have a strong aroma and spoil easily. They should be stored in the refrigerator, double bagged (placed first in a paper bag, then in a plastic one). Depending upon the freshness of the leeks, they can keep up to a week.

Mushrooms

Although all mushrooms are fungi, for the purposes of Chinese cooking they are differentiated into those that grow in dirt (mushrooms) and those that grow on trees (fungi). Fresh mushrooms and fungi are sold locally, but after they have been dried, they are sold all over the world. Several varieties of both mushrooms and fungi can be found in the Chinatowns of large cities. The dried mushrooms come in several grades. They can keep indefinitely if kept dry or in the freezer.

Dried, or Black, Mushrooms

香菌

Hsiang Chun

This most popular type of mushroom is used in many dishes as a complementary vegetable for its flavor. Soaking in water for thirty minutes will bring the mushrooms back to their original shapes.

Winter Mushrooms

冬菇

Tung Ku

This is a thicker variety of black mushroom that, after soaking, is more tender than the dried, or black, mushroom. They are also more expensive and have a better flavor and aroma. These mushrooms need at least one to two hours to redevelop.

Straw Mushrooms

草菇

Ts'ao Ku

Straw mushrooms have a completely different texture and flavor. Their caps are pointed, as opposed to the disklike shape of the dried, or black, or winter mushroom. They come canned or dried.

Fresh, or White, Mushrooms

鮮菇

Hsien Ku

This term is used in recipes when referring to the fresh mushrooms available in all supermarkets. They may be used instead of the black mushrooms, but they have an entirely different flavor, and their taste will not be a substitute in a given recipe.

Tree Ears (Cloud Ears, or Black Fungus)

木耳 (雲耳)

Mu Er or Yün Er

Tree ears are also called cloud ears. When in a dried state, they have the nondescript appearance of dark chips. They vary in color from dark brown to gray to black. When redeveloped and if they are of good quality, they have the shape of the petals of double petunias. To redevelop, simply soak them in boiling water; when they are cool enough, remove and discard the hard woody substance at the stem, if any, and rinse them several times in water. The flavor and taste, though mild, can be compared to nothing in American cookery, so it is best to taste them.

Silver Ears (White Fungus)

白木耳

Pai Mu Er

These are similar to cloud ears but are more expensive. They are considered a tonic for maintaining one's health. The flavor is different from that of cloud ears. Silver ears are often added to vegetarian dishes and soups. They are also used in sweet dessert soups.

Winter Bamboo
Shoots

冬筍
Tung Sun

Spring Bamboo
Shoots

毛筍
Mao Sun

Summer
Bamboo Shoots

竹筍
Chu Sun

Bamboo stalks grow shoots during different seasons. In the winter, when the shoots first begin to grow, they are collected by digging under ground. That is why these shoots are called winter bamboo shoots. They are relatively small in size and are the best tasting of all bamboo shoots. They have a smooth beige-colored shell, and when peeled, they are about the size of medium pine cones. The spring shoots grow straight up from the ground. They are the largest of all the shoots and sometimes may reach several feet in height and three to four inches in diameter. The shells are dark brown, fuzzy, and have a sheen. Hence the spring shoots are called hair bamboo shoots. In the summer there are two kinds of bamboo shoots. One comes from a smaller species of bamboo that grow shoots the size of thin asparagus. These are called bamboo bamboo shoots. The other shoots that grow in the summertime are actually shoots from the roots. They grow horizontally underground. These look flat, as opposed to the cone-shaped ones, and so are called flat bamboo shoots. Shoots grown during one season differ subtly in texture and flavor from those grown in other seasons. Shoots are best eaten fresh; once preserved, they lose much of their flavor. The texture remains, however, and the crispy consistency can still be enjoyed. The spring and winter shoots are canned unseasoned, packed in water. Once the can is opened, the shoots may be kept submerged in their own liquid or in cold water in a covered jar in the refrigerator for several days. If the water in the jar is changed every four to five days, the bamboo shoots can be kept for several weeks. As with asparagus, the tip of the bamboo shoot is most tender, growing tougher as you go downward. Cans of bamboo shoots contain both tender and tough parts. Through proper cutting, both parts can be put to good use without waste: The tender parts can be cut into chunks by using the roll cut method, and the tougher parts can be diced into small cubes or julienne strips.

Braised Bamboo
Shoots

油燜筍
Yu Men Sun

Canned braised bamboo shoots are seasoned and can be eaten right out of the can without further preparation.

Flat-Tip
Bamboo Shoots

扁尖筍
Pien Chien Sun

The flat bamboo shoots that also grow in the summer are preserved mainly with salt, then dried. Only the tender tips are used; thus they are called flat-tip bamboo shoots. They should be rinsed in cold water and soaked in hot water before cooking with other foods. These shoots have a definite flavor and give a good taste, especially to soups. In China the flat-tip bamboo shoots are packed in loosely woven bamboo baskets lined with bamboo leaves. But in America a basketful is too large a quantity to be sold to one person. Thus it is divided into small portions and packed in plastic bags to be sold by weight. It can be stored in the refrigerator in a plastic bag or in a non-metallic container for at least one year.

Preserved
Vegetables

鹹菜

Hsien Ts'ai

Salting, drying, and drying after salting are the early methods that the Chinese used to preserve food. In all the different regions of China the vegetables of the cabbage and turnip family are preserved. Each region uses its own indigenous variety and employs its own methods of preservation. Although it is common to preserve vegetables, there are certain provinces where the local vegetables are renowned for their individual flavors. Some vegetables are named after the places they are produced. These specially preserved vegetables are shipped all over China for use in cooking. They are made from either only the stems or both the stems and leaves. The vegetables contain large amounts of salt, and only small amounts of the vegetable are used to complement a dish. An entire can or jar cannot be used up at one time. Store the remaining vegetable in a jar with a rustproof cover. It will keep for a long time in the refrigerator.

The Japanese pack preserved vegetables in plastic bags and prepare them with liberal amounts of monosodium glutamate. If these preserved vegetables are found to have a strong taste, simply wash and squeese them dry to get as much liquid out as possible and to remove some of the monosodium glutamate before cooking. The salt content of the Japanese vegetables is not as high as that of the Chinese ones, so the Japanese vegetables spoil more readily and should be used up within a few days after the bag has been opened.

Cantonese
Preserved
Vegetable

廣東冲菜

*Canton
Ch'ung Ts'ai*

This vegetable is Cantonese in origin. It is made with *bok choy*. It is cut into small bits and preserved with salt, and usually comes in a small can.

Szechuan
Preserved
Vegetable

四川榨菜

*Szechuan
Cha Ts'ai*

This vegetable is a specialty of the Szechuan province. It is made from a special variety of the mustard green that has many knobby stems. Only these stems are used. It is preserved in salt along with minced, hot chili pepper. It comes either chopped or in chunks and packed into jars or cans. If it tastes too peppery, wash out some of the hot chili flavor before cooking. This vegetable is available in Oriental food shops and Chinese markets.

Tientsin Preserved Vegetable 天津冬菜 *Tientsin Tung Ts'ai*	This vegetable is a famous product of the city of Tientsin. It is made with Chinese celery cabbage (*Tientsin pai ts'ai*). Both leaves and stem are used. It is cut into small bits and preserved with salt, garlic, and other spices. The color of this vegetable is light brown, and it is packed very tightly in earthenware or glass jars. It can be found in Chinese markets.

Sour Mustard Greens

酸菜
Suan Ts'ai

The Cantonese pickle mustard greens by parboiling the whole plant, stems and leaves uncut, and putting it into brine. It is left to ferment until it has just begun to sour. It is then ready to be eaten. Sour mustard greens are sold packed in jars or in open vats, soaking in the original brine. They can be found in some Oriental food shops and in Chinese markets. If this vegetable is found to be too sour, it can be rinsed in cold water before cooking.

Red-in-Snow

雪裡紅
Hsüeh Li Hung

People of Chekiang and Kiangsu preserve delicious pickled vegetables literally translated as "red-in-snow," which is salted and fermented. Red-in-snow is like the top of a turnip. Both the leaves and stem are preserved. It is grown in the United States and can be bought fresh in Chinese markets. Only the tender part of this vegetable, the heart, is eaten fresh. To make the preserved vegetable, it must be salted several days before it is ready to be eaten. Red-in-snow comes in 7-ounce cans and is cut into 2- to 3-inch sections. The best brand is Ma-ling, produced in Shanghai.

Seaweeds

Seaweeds are cooked with food, mixed in salad, or made into desserts to give interesting flavors and textures. They are sold dried and should be kept away from moisture in tightly capped glass jars. They do not need refrigeration. They are available in large Chinese grocery shops and are sold in small quantities, packed in plastic bags.

Green Seaweed

苔條
T'ai T'iao

This mosslike seaweed is green in color. It comes dried, in wads, or in matted chips. When fried in oil, it has a toasted fragrance and a slight iodine taste. It is used to flavor foods.

Hair Seaweed

髮菜
Fa Ts'ai

Hair seaweed derives its name from its appearance: It is dark purple or almost black and looks like intertwined strands of hair. It has very little flavor but gives an interesting texture to dishes.

Agar-Agar

洋菜
Yang Ts'ai

Agar-agar is a gelatinous substance obtained from seaweeds. It comes in powder form, in long solid rectangular sections, or in fine strips. The powdered and solid forms are used to make gelatin desserts. The fine strips are used for salads. Only cold water should be used to soften the agar-agar, for it will melt in hot water.

Lotus Roots

藕

Ou

Lotus roots are tubers of the lotus plant. They grow in sections, each ranging from four to eight inches long and two to three inches in diameter. They are best between July and February. The rest of the year they can be obtained either dried or canned. The fresh roots can be kept in the refrigerator for about three weeks. Dried lotus roots should be soaked in hot water for twenty minutes before cooking. They are used both as a vegetable and as a dessert.

Tiger Lily Buds (Golden Needles)

金針

Chin Chen

Tiger lily buds come from a special type of lily. They are dried and used as a complementary vegetable. Soak them in boiling water for about ten minutes and then remove the hard stems. They are often used in combination with tree ears. The water used for soaking is generally discarded.

SEAFOOD, MEATS, AND EGGS

Abalone

鮑魚

Pao Yü

Abalone is a shellfish that lives attached to rocks in the Pacific Ocean. It is available fresh, dried, and canned. The most common form used in the United States is the canned. Abalone is canned in saltwater and may be eaten right out of the can. This delicate-tasting shellfish only requires heating through. Overcooking tends to turn it tough and rubbery.

Sharks' Fins

魚翅

Yü Chih

Sharks' fins are sold in various stages of preparation. The easiest ones to prepare are the precooked canned ones. The dried fins need to be soaked ahead of time. For directions on redeveloping, see the recipe for Shark's Fin Soup (page 232).

Fish Maw

魚肚

Yü Tu

Fish maw is actually the air bladder of a large fish. It is dried and has to be deep fried before being used in a dish. After it is fried, it has a puffy, spongy, but crispy texture and is always cooked in a rich meat stock. Fish maw can be purchased already fried in Chinese food stores.

Sea Cucumber

海參

Hai Sheng

Sea cucumber is a boneless animal that lives at the bottom of the ocean. It is considered a delicacy and is frequently served at banquets. It comes dried and needs to be soaked in water. It is sold in Chinese food stores.

Dried Scallops

干貝

Kan Pei

Scallops are bivalved mollusks. The only edible parts of a scallop are its adductor muscle and its roe. Dried scallops are expensive, but a few ounces will go a long way. To redevelop the muscles, soak them in warm water, then soften by steaming.

Dried Shrimps

蝦米

Hsia Mi

Dried shrimps are a variety of small shrimp prepared by salting, shelling, and lastly drying. To redevelop, soak them in hot water. Store at room temperature in a covered glass jar or in a well-sealed plastic bag for a few months. It will keep indefinitely if stored in a covered glass jar in the refrigerator.

Jellyfish

海蜇皮

Hai Che P'i

Jellyfish come in round sheets about ⅛ inch thick. They also come already cut into thin strips. They are salted and partially dried before being shipped to this country. To redevelop, soak the jellyfish in cold water for at least four hours, changing the water several times to remove all the salt.

Preserved Fish

鹹魚

Tsien Yü

As with many other foods, fish may be preserved by either canning, drying, salting, or drying after salting. The variety of preserved fish used in Chinese cooking is extensive. Crustacea, mollusks, and jellyfish are also preserved besides the usual kinds of scaled fishes. The flavor of these preserved fish is very different and much stronger than when fresh. Those who are accustomed to the flavor are very fond of them. Usually the fish are very salty and are eaten in small quantities, as a "rice-sending" dish, or are eaten with congee. They may be obtained in Chinese grocery stores and some Oriental food shops. All the dried varieties can be kept indefinitely in plastic bags at room temperature. The canned salted fish are usually packed in oil and are better kept in the refrigerator, submerged in the oil. Should there not be enough original oil, cooking oil can be added in order to submerge the fish.

Dried Flat Fish Fillet

扁魚

Pien Yü

This is a dried unsalted fish fillet. It is made from small flat fish, similar to butter fish. This dried fish can be kept in a sealed bag indefinitely in the freezer.

Squid

尤魚

Yu Yü

Squid is a ten-armed cephalopod that squirts an ink-like fluid for protection. It comes fresh, frozen, and dried. Only the body and the firm tentacles are eaten. Dried squid must be presoaked before cooking. Fresh ones are most often stir-fried.

Cuttle Fish

墨魚

Mu Yü

Cuttlefish is much like squid. It comes fresh-frozen and is available in Chinese markets and Italian fish markets. It is much larger than squid and the meat is thicker. It is most often cooked with pork in soy sauce, like a stew.

Smithfield Ham

火腿

Huo T'ui

Smithfield ham has a flavor very much like that of Chinese Kinhwa and Yunnan ham. For the purposes of Chinese cooking, the ham is cut into three- or four-inch sections across the grain, then either steamed or cooked in simmering water. The ham is also available in smaller sections in Chinese markets. In delicatessens it is sold ready to eat by the slice. For storage, wrap each section tightly and keep it in the freezer, or submerge it in oil in a jar in the refrigerator. Uncooked whole Smithfield hams need to be washed thoroughly, making sure that all pepper particles are removed.

Preserved Pork
Belly

臘肉
La Jou

Pork belly is much like pressed duck but is sweeter in taste.

Chinese
Sausages
(Pork and Pork
Liver)

臘腸
La Ch'ang

肝腸
Kan Ch'ang

Two kinds of sausages are made by the Chinese meat processor. One is made with pork and the other with pork liver. They are sold by the pound and threaded in pairs on strings. They may be stored in the refrigerator for several weeks and for a longer time in the freezer. The pork liver sausage is sweeter than the pork sausage.

Pressed Duck

臘鴨
La Ya

Pressed duck is duck preserved with salt while it is being flattened. It is then dried in the open air and stored in oil during shipping to the United States. If it is too salty, the duck can be soaked in water before cooking, but soaking is generally unnecessary.

Bird's Nests

燕窩
Yen Wo

Bird's nests are collected in the South Pacific Islands. The nests are made by swiftlets from seaweed and are built on cave walls. A nest is like the petals of a white lotus and is sold in this original form in Chinese food stores. For directions on cleaning and redevelopment, see the recipe for Bird's Nests with Rock Sugar Soup (page 299).

Salted Duck
Eggs

鹹蛋
Hsien Tan

Salted eggs are duck eggs preserved in brine. The salt penetrates the shells and makes the eggs salty. Salted eggs must be cooked before they can be eaten.

Thousand-Year
Eggs

皮蛋
P'i Tan

Thousand-year eggs are preserved in an alkaline mud mixture. The chemical penetrates the eggshell, turning both the white and yolk a dark brownish-green color. The egg is eaten uncooked. Before cracking the egg shell, all the mud must be removed, then the egg thoroughly cleaned. Once it is cleaned, it is cut lengthwise into wedges and put on a plate to be served with soy sauce. It is sometimes garnished with gingerroot strips. The preservative coating of the eggs dries up easily in dry weather and in the refrigerator. The eggs should thus be kept in tightly sealed plastic bags.

Quail Eggs

鵪鶉蛋

An Chu'un Tan

Quail eggs come only in cans and are already hard-boiled. They are available in Chinese markets and in delicacy shops.

CONDIMENTS AND SEASONINGS

Soy Sauce

醬油

Chiang Yu

Dark Soy Sauce

老抽(深)

Lao Ch'ou

Light Soy Sauce

生抽(淺)

Sheng Ch'ou

Soy sauce is the most important seasoning liquid in Chinese cooking and is often used in place of salt. It comes in various-size containers and in many brands. Some makers produce two kinds of soy sauce, dark and light. Both light and dark soy sauces are good for cooking. The light one is preferred for dipping. Some people combine the sauces to suit their taste. It is a good idea to try different brands until a suitable sauce is found. Always use the same brand so that an accurate degree of saltiness is obtained for every dish prepared. Soy sauce is commonly found in many supermarkets that have a Chinese food section. If the soy sauce is in a can, it should be transferred to a glass bottle once the can has been opened. It can be kept at room temperature indefinitely.

Salted Black Beans

豆豉

Tou Shih

Black beans preserved in salt are used to flavor bland foods, such as steamed fish or the white meat of chicken. They come in small plastic bags, in jars, or in cans. The beans are sold in Chinese markets. They can be stored in a jar in the refrigerator indefinitely.

Brown Bean Sauce

原晒豉

Yüan Shai Shih

Ground Brown Bean Sauce

豉原磨

Shih Yüan Mo

Brown bean sauce is made from fermented soybeans and wheat flour mixed with salt and water. The beans in the sauce may be either ground up or left whole. To this basic bean sauce spices and other seasonings are added, forming many varieties. Seasonings and spices are added to the bean sauce in different proportions in different regions of China: In Szechuan large amounts of hot pepper and crushed Szechuan peppercorns are added; in the northern provinces, garlic and scallions; in Chekiang and Kiangsu, moderate amounts of sugar; in Canton, large amounts of sugar, garlic, and spices. There are no set rules as to the amount of seasoning or spice added to the bean sauce; it is a question of personal taste. Many types of bean sauce can be made, each having a slightly different flavor, but they are all made from the same basic bean sauce. Many people prefer to use a plain sauce because one has control of the taste. Seasoning and spices may be added according to the wishes of the cook. Bean sauces are packed in many different types and sizes of cans and jars. If the sauce is from a can, it should be transferred to a dry, rustproof container and kept in the refrigerator. It will not spoil for a long time. Bean sauce can be found in many Oriental food stores.

Hoisin Sauce

海鮮醬

Hai Hsien Chiang

Hoisin sauce is ground bean sauce to which sugar, garlic, and other flavorings have been added. It is the most popular commercially prepared bean sauce. It is used for cooking or very often as a dip for seafood and Peking Duck. It is packed in cans; once the can is opened, the sauce should be stored in the same manner as brown bean sauce.

Fish Sauce

魚露

Yü Lou

Fish sauce is the juice extracted from layers of fish alternated with layers of salt. When pressed, these layers of fish drip out juice. Since the fish is preserved with a large amount of salt, the liquid is very salty and has a strong fish flavor. The liquid is slightly aged and has an excellent taste. Fish sauce is used for dips. It can also be cooked in foods and soups. Fish sauce is sold in small bottles in Chinese grocery stores. Once the bottle is opened, it should be kept in the refrigerator. Since it is very salty, the sauce can keep for a long time.

Oyster Sauce

蠔油

Hao Yu

Oyster sauce is thicker than fish sauce and is made from ground oysters. Although the taste is different from fish sauce, it is used in the same manner. This sauce should be stored in the same way as the fish sauce.

Sesame Oil

麻油

Ma Yu

Chinese sesame oil has a strong, nutlike, aromatic fragrance. In the northern region of China it is used as a cooking oil, but generally it is used to flavor soups and hot or cold dishes. Adding a few drops of sesame oil to a dish that is ready to be served gives it a good flavor. The sesame oil with a paler color that comes from the Middle East is made from raw sesame seeds. It has a completely different flavor and is unsuitable for Chinese cooking. Sesame oil is available in most Oriental food shops. It should be stored in the refrigerator to prevent it from turning rancid.

Sesame Paste

芝蔴醬

Chih Ma Chiang

In America sesame paste is not easily available, but peanut butter mixed with sesame oil is sometimes used as a substitute. In northern China sesame paste is used to make dressings and for cooking, for both its flavor and rich texture.

Gingerroot

薑

Chiang

Young Gingerroot

Gingerroot is a plant that grows tubers underground. As it grows, it spreads by sprouting small lobes up to the size of a small potato, depending on the stage of growth and conditions. It will grow as many lobes as the season will allow. There are usually three, four, or five lobes in a chain. When young, each lobe has a sprouting point that is pinkish or purplish in color. The remainder of the lobe is pale yellow with a tender skin.

子薑
Tzu Chiang

Mature
Gingerroot

老薑
La Chiang

If it is found to be too peppery, the gingerroot can be blanched before cooking after being cut into thin slices. When the gingerroot is left in the ground to mature, its peel becomes a beige color. The inside color varies from light yellow to pale yellowish green as it is exposed to daylight. It has a sharp aroma and is used to flavor salads, vegetables, meats, and fish. It is generally not used in cooking clear, light, and delicately flavored soups. Only a small amount is necessary in seasoning. A chunk weighing about two ounces can last a long time if properly stored in the refrigerator. Droplets of water will rot the gingerroot. When it is left uncovered, it will shrivel until it is too hard to use. The best way to store fresh gingerroot is in double bags (a heavy brown bag covered with a plastic bag) in the vegetable compartment of the refrigerator. Gingerroot will keep for over a month.

Coriander
Leaves

香菜(芫茜)
Hsiang Ts'ai

A Chinese cook would use coriander leaves as a Western cook would use parsley. Coriander is actually an herb of the parsley family. It is sold by the bunch.

Hot Chili
Peppers

辣椒
La Chiao

There are many varieties of pepper and the degree of spiciness differs. When a recipe calls for hot pepper, use any kind of pepper that has a hot flavor, or use the kind that best suits the desired taste.

Hot Chili
Pepper Oil

辣油
La Yu

Hot pepper oil is often added to noodles or meat-filled dumplings to give an extra-spicy taste. This hot pepper oil is made by simply frying any one of the pungent peppers in oil until the capsaicin is extracted from the peppers. The oil turns red and its taste becomes pungent. The pepper pods are drained off and may be used in other dishes. The seasoned oil is stored in a bottle and is ready for use whenever desired.

Rice Vinegar

朱醋
Mi Ts'u

Black rice vinegar is a mild vinegar with a flavor of its own. It is most often used as a dip or condiment. It originally came from the city of Chenkiang in the province of Kiangsu. It comes packed in glass bottles and is available in Chinese groceries. The vinegar may be stored at room temperature.

Rock Sugar

冰糖
Ping T'ang

Rock sugar is crystallized sugar, much like rock candy, but it is made from raw sugar, giving the crystals a slight brown tinge. It has a better flavor than rock candy and gives a dish a rich color as well as a glossy appearance. To measure rock sugar, simply crush and measure with measuring spoons.

Monosodium Glutamate 味精 *Wei-Ching*	The Chinese call monosodium glutamate *wei-ching*, literally translated as "the essence of taste." It is a chemical in the form of white granules, very much like shiny table salt. In Japan monosodium glutamate is present in almost every kind of prepared food. It is a substance that enhances the taste of food. A good cook never automatically adds monosodium glutamate to every dish prepared. Using good-quality and fresh ingredients and the right combination with proper preparation eliminates the need for monosodium glutamate. Occasionally, however, certain dishes need the enhancing effect of it, such as those made with frozen meats or vegetables. One should never use monosodium glutamate in large quantities; a pinch to ¼ teaspoon is sufficient, depending upon the size of the dish.
Spices	Many seasonings generally thought of in connection with the baking and preparation of sweet dishes in Western cooking are used to season meats and vegetables in Chinese cooking. Only those that are used in the recipes in this book are discussed below. They are available in Chinese groceries and in some Oriental food shops and are sold by the ounce in plastic bags. Spices should be stored in glass jars at room temperature. They will keep up to one year.
Chinese Cinnamon Bark 桂皮 *Kuei P'i*	Cinnamon bark is used in Chinese cooking in both the powdered as well as the stick form. Chinese bark is thinner than American cinnamon sticks, and is available in Chinese markets.
Dried Tangerine Peel 陳皮 *Ch'en P'i*	Tangerine peel is peel that has been sun-dried and packaged. Nothing else has been done to it, so it would be very easy to prepare at home.
Star Anise 八角 *Pa Chiao*	This anise comes in the shape of an eight-pointed star and differs slightly in flavor from aniseed. Often it is used to flavor beef as one would use bay leaf.
Szechuan Peppercorns 花椒 *Hua Chiao*	This peppercorn has a different flavor from the ordinary black peppercorn in that it is not peppery but gives a numbing sensation to the tongue. It also has a distinct aroma after roasting in a dry frying pan. This peppercorn has dark red husks that are open. The seeds are not enclosed in the hulls and are a darker red, almost black. After roasting, crush the spice with a rolling pin and keep it in a tightly capped jar.

Fennel Seeds

小茴香

Hsiao Hui
Hsiang

Fennel seeds are a little larger than sesame seeds and are olive-gray in color. They are usually used in marinades.

Five-Spice Powder

五香粉

Wu Hsiang Fen

Five-spice powder is a combination of many seasonings, much as curry powder is made of a combination of spices. It is used for seasoning poultry, meat, and fish. The powder can be a combination of star anise, fennel seeds, cloves, cinnamon bark, Szechuan peppercorns, licorice, gingerroot, and nutmeg. Different brands use different combinations of spices, and depending upon the manufacturer, they may vary in aroma and taste.

Cassia Blossoms

桂花

K'uei Hua

The cassia blossom is a tiny yellow four-petaled flower that grows in clusters on the branch of the cassia tree. The tree blooms in late September. In New Orleans this tree is used as an ornamental hedge and is called sweet olive. The blossoms are collected and preserved in salt and sugar. They are used for flavoring sweet dishes and sweet soups.

GRAINS, FLOURS, AND GRAIN PRODUCTS

Fermented Rice

As with the soybean, many products are made with rice. One method is fermentation. It produces the same kind of action as when yeast is mixed with dough.

Red Fermented Rice

紅米

Hung Mi

Red fermented rice is dried after fermentation. It is used to season and to add color and flavor to meat and poultry. This rice gives a rich flavor to dishes. It is available in Chinese grocery stores, packed in plastic bags and sold in small amounts.

Wine Rice

酒釀

Chiu Niang

Wine Yeast

酒藥

Chiu-Yao

Wine rice is another form of fermented rice and comes soaked in liquid. It can be made at home with special wine yeast (*chiu-yao*), which is available in Chinese markets and herb shops. Wine yeast comes in walnut-size balls and has a fermenting effect. Ready-made wine rice comes in glass jars and is sold in some of the larger Chinese groceries. Wine rice must be stored in the refrigerator.

Wine Paste

酒糟

Chiu Tsao

Wine paste is the residue left from the production of rice wine. It is used to preserve and season fish and some vegetables. The Japanese also pack wine paste under the name *sako kosa*. It is available in Chinese groceries and Japanese food shops, packed in sealed plastic bags. It needs refrigeration.

Rice Wine

黃 酒

Huang Chiu

Shaohsing rice wine is the best Chinese rice wine. It can be purchased in some wine stores. If it is not obtainable, use dry sherry instead.

Flour Products

The starch from different plants is ground into flour and can then be made into many delicious foods. The flours have no definite flavor. When made into dough and cooked, they all have different consistencies and outstanding characteristics. With the exception of water chestnut flour, which comes in smaller packages, all these flours are packed in brightly printed paper wrappers covered with cellophane, in one-pound units. They are available in Chinese grocery stores and in some Oriental food shops. They may be stored as one would store ordinary wheat flour, and if kept in the freezer, will keep indefinitely.

Wheat Starch

澄 麵

Ch'eng Fen

When the protein part of wheat flour is removed to make gluten, the remaining part is called wheat starch.

Tapioca

西米粉

Hsi Mi Fen

Tapioca starch comes from casava root starch. The root starch is ground into flour and made into granules of different sizes. The big granules are called fish eyes and smaller ones pearls. Both wheat and tapioca starches are used for making shells to wrap shrimp or meat fillings. The shells made from these two starches have a crisp texture.

Water Chestnut Flour

馬蹄粉

Ma T'i Fen

Water chestnut flour is used to make batters and to thicken sauces. It gives a shiny glaze to cooked food. This flour is also used for making cakes. Only small amounts are used to thicken a sauce. Therefore half- or quarter-pound packages are available. Only the larger Chinese grocery stores carry this special flour.

Rice Flour

粘米粉

Chan Mi Fen

Rice flour is ground from long-grain rice. It is used for making cakes and shells to wrap either sweet or salty fillings.

Glutinous, or Sweet Rice, Flour

糯米粉

No Mi Fen

Sweet rice flour is ground from glutinous rice. It is used in the same way as plain rice flour, though they are not interchangeable. Sweet rice flour has a softer texture than plain rice flour. Japanese sweet rice flour is less glutinous than that of the Chinese.

Water-Ground Rice Flour

水磨粉

Shui Mo Fen

Rice ground with water is another method of making rice flour. The long-grain or the glutinous rice kernels are soaked in water and ground while wet. Afterward the excess water is squeezed out. This method produces a finer texture than the dry-ground flours. Because of easy spoilage, they are sold only during cooler weather in lumps by weight. They are used in the same manner as the dry rice flours. Less water is used when mixing the dough. These flours must be kept in the coldest part of the refrigerator and only for two to three days or they may be frozen for longer periods. The water-ground flours are sold in Chinese bean cake shops.

Wheat Gluten

麵筋

Mien Ching

Deep-Fried
Gluten

油麵筋

Yu Mien Ching

Wheat gluten is made by washing the starch out of wheat flour. One of the best ways of preparing this good vegetable protein is to deep fry it. When it is fried to a golden brown, it puffs up into a ball. Usually the balls are about 1½ inches in diameter. They are packed in plastic bags and sold in Chinese food stores. They may be kept in the refrigerator for three to four days or frozen.

Mock Abalone

素鮑魚

Su Pao Yü

Dried Wheat
Gluten and
Fresh Wheat
Gluten

烤麩

K'ao Fu

Wheat gluten also comes dried, canned, or fresh. The canned gluten is generally called mock abalone and vegetable steak. It is seasoned and can be eaten directly from the can. The dried gluten is packed in plastic bags. It needs to be soaked before cooking. Fresh gluten comes frozen from Taiwan. It is available in Chinese markets and is sold by weight. It has to be deep fried before being cooked in a dish.

Rice Cakes

寧波年糕

*Ningpo Nien
Kao*

Rice cakes are a specialty of the seaport city of Ningpo. They are commonly called Ningpo rice cakes and are made from a mixture of water-ground flours of long- and oval-grain rices. They may be bought in Chinese markets in plastic bags containing stacks of eight to ten rectangles, 5 x 1½ x ½ inch. Since they do not contain any salt, the rice cakes cannot be stored for long perods. They can be kept in the coldest part of the refrigerator for up to two months by slicing and submerging them in cold water, then changing the water weekly. They also come in dried slices. Just soak them in cold water until soft.

Rice Noodles

米粉

Mi Fen

Rice noodles are made from rice flour. They come in two thicknesses: One is the size of cellophane noodles and the other is even finer. These noodles do not need to be parboiled. They need only to be soaked in water before cooking with other foods. Rice noodles can be stir-fried or dropped into soups. If boiled, they will turn into paste. They are available in dry wads wrapped in paper in one-pound packages. Each package is divided into four wads, easily accessible serving portions. They are sold in Chinese groceries. There are several brands that are generally equally good.

Egg Noodles

蛋 麵

Tan Mien

Egg noodles are sold fresh in Chinese groceries. They may be found in the refrigerated cases in one-pound plastic bags. The thicknesses vary, depending upon the manufacturer. Fresh egg noodles can be kept in the freezer. If frozen, the noodles should be dropped into boiling water immediately after removal from the freezer. Just drop them into the boiling water and stir until they have completely thawed. Boil to the desired tenderness.

Won Ton
Wrappers

餛 飩皮

Won Ton P'i

The thickness of won ton wrappers depends on the manufacturer. They vary anywhere from 75 to 150 wrappers per pound. Won ton wrappers are sold in one-pound packages, wrapped in waxed paper.

Canton Spring
Roll Wrappers
(Egg Roll
Wrappers)

廣東春捲皮

*Kuang Tung
Ch'un Chüan
P'i*

Regular egg roll wrappers are like won ton wrappers except for the addition of egg and coloring. There are no standard sizes, but they are usually squares, 7 x 7 inches. They come wrapped in waxed paper in one-pound packages.

Shanghai Spring
Roll Wrappers
(Egg Roll
Wrappers)

上海春捲皮

*Shang Hai Ch'un
Chüan P'i*

Shanghai spring roll wrappers are either square or round, and resemble doilies about 7 inches in diameter. They are packed in stacks of ten to twenty pieces in plastic bags. All these three kinds of wrappers dry easily. When dry, they are very hard to handle and make wrapping almost impossible. As soon as they are brought home from the shop, the wrappers should be put into tightly sealed plastic bags and stored in the refrigerator or in the freezer. The wrappers freeze very well. If they should become dried, wrap the wrappers in a damp cloth for a few hours before using. Won ton, Canton spring roll, and Shanghai spring roll wrappers are available in many Oriental food shops.

Index

Egg Yolks, 48–49, 94–95
Green Beans and Water Chestnuts,
    184–185, 188–189
Lamb with Scallions, 98–99, 138–139
Liver with Onions, 96–97, 112–113
Lobster with Black Bean Sauce, 142-
    143, 176–177
Pork with Bean Milk Skin, 98–99, 120–
    121
Pork with Broccoli, 96–97, 102–103
Rice Cake, 244–245, 260
Scallops, 142–143, 172–173
Shrimp, 142–143, 164
Shrimp with Rice Noodles and
    Vegetables, 244–245, 262
Spinach, 184–185, 188
Stir Frying. *See* Chinese cooking, methods
    of
Steaming. *See* Chinese cooking, methods
    of
Sweet-and-Sour Cabbage, 184–185, 191
Sweet-and-Sour Pork, 96–97, 116–118
Sweet-and-Sour Sauce, 140–141, 159
Szechuan Style
  Bean Curd
    Fried, with Hot Bean Sauce, 184–
        185, 192
    Home Town, 186–187, 207
  Beef
    Ants on the Tree, 98–99, 134
    Dried Spicy, 98–99, 134–135
    Spicy, with Rice Noodles, 98–99,
        136–137
  Cabbage
    Pickled, 184–185, 203
    Sweet-and-Sour, 184–185, 191
  Chicken
    Fish-Flavored, 48–49, 73–75
    Odd-Flavored, 46–47, 55–56
    with Peanuts, 46–47, 72–73
    Peng Peng, 46–47, 54–55
    Smoked, 48–49, 77–78
  Duckling
    Crispy, 48–49, 83–84
  Eggplant, 186–187, 206
    Stuffed, 186–187, 205
  Eggs
    Fish-Flavored Party, 48–49, 93–94
  Fish
    Carp with Hot Bean Sauce, 140–
        141, 147–148
  Green Beans
    Fried, with Minced Meat, 186–187,
        204
  Meatball with Spinach Soup, 216–217,
      223–224
  Peppercorns
    Hot Pepper Oil, 186–187, 208–209
    Roasted, 186–187, 208
  Pork

Kidney with Spicy Sauce, 98–99,
    124–125
Pearl Balls, 98–99, 123–124
Spicy, with Bean Curd, 98–99, 121–
    122
with Szechuan Preserved Vegetable
    Soup, 218–219, 234–235
Twice-Cooked, 98–99, 122–123
  Rice
    Patties, 244–245, 254–255
    Sizzling Soup, 218–219, 235–236
  Salad
    Noodle, 244–245, 264
  Shrimp
    Seafood Sizzling Rice, 142–143,
        170–171
    in Shells, 142–143, 167–168

Tai Shan Style Shrimp
  Stir-Fried Dried, with Cellophane
      Noodles, 184–185, 202
Tea, 41–43
  brewing, 43
  kinds of, 42–43
  unique aspects of drinking, 41–42
Tea Eggs, 48–49, 90
Ten Varieties Hot Pot, 216–217, 229–230
Tomatoes
  Glazed Beef with, 98–99, 130–131
Tripe
  Hot-and-Sour Soup, 218–219, 240–241
Tsinan Style Shrimp
  Diced, with Croutons, 142–143, 169–
      170
  Dried, with Cellophane Noodle Soup,
      218–219, 239–240
Turnips. *See* White Turnips, Chinese

Utensils, 10–19
  See also Chinese cooking, utensils

Vegetables, 184–215
  Boneless Duck with, 48–49, 79–80
  Buns Steamed with Meat and, 246–
      247, 270–271
  Filling for Meat Dumplings, 277
  Rice Congee, 244–245, 259
  Shredded Pork with Preserved, 96–97,
      110–111
  Shrimp Balls with, 140–141, 162
  Squid with Preserved, 142–143, 175
  Stir-Fried Rice Noodles with Shrimp
      and, 244–245, 262
  Thin Steak with, 98–99, 133
  Vegetarian Soup, 216–217, 222–223
  Wheat Gluten with, 184–185, 194–195
  See also names of vegetables
Vegetarian Vegetable Soup, 216–217,
    222–223
Vinegar and Soy Sauce, 265